# THE MYTH OF
# AMERICAN ECLIPSE

# The Myth of American Eclipse

## The New Global Age

Alfred Balk

Transaction Publishers
New Brunswick (U.S.A.) and London (U.K.)

*26645*

Copyright © 1990 by Alfred Balk

**Library of Congress Catalog Number:** 90-10918
ISBN: 0-88738-369-6 (cloth); 0-88738-858-2 (Paper)
Printed in the United States of America


**Library of Congress Cataloging-in-Publication Data**
Balk, Alfred.
  The myth of American eclipse : the new global age / Alfred Balk.
    p. cm.
ISBN 0-88738-369-6 — ISBN 0-88738-858-2 (pbk.)
  1. United States—Economic conditions—1981- 2. United States—
Economic policy—1981- 3. Competition. International.
4. Industrial productivity—United States. I.Title
HC106.8.B35    1990
338.973—dc20                             90-10918
                                                    CIP

*There will be no day of days...when a new world order comes into being. Step by step and here and there it will arrive, and, even as it comes into being it will develop fresh perspectives, discover unsuspected problems, and go on to new adventure.*

— H. G. Wells

*For Phyllis*

# Contents

# *Foreword*

More than fifteen years ago Al Balk, with Iowa business leader C. Maxwell Stanley as one of his partners, helped revive *Atlas* magazine (since renamed *World Press Review*) to provide American citizens access to international perspectives on global issues. Subsequently the Stanley Foundation became *WPR*'s publisher. Many times over the years, I used the magazine in teaching at the University of Denver's Center for Teaching International Relations. It remains one of the finest resources available for learning about the world.

Max Stanley died in 1984, which resulted in a circumstance that led to this book. Al Balk substituted for him in an address to the Great Lakes Regional Council of Social Studies. After his presentation, on globalization, he was surrounded by teachers asking where they could find more information on the subject. Unfortunately there was no single, easily understood source.

Some months later Al Balk visited the American Forum for Global Education and told me of his plans to help fill that vacuum and inform the general public. He had just left the editorship of *World Press Review* to try to make sense, in a concise book, out of the myriad of global issues that bombard us daily. Al had impressive credentials in writing and editing on public affairs and unique international contacts. He and his wife were willing to risk their joint savings to see the project through. I promised to do everything I could to assist.

The result of more than two years of research and writing is *The Myth of American Eclipse: The New Global Age.* While no single book can be expected to illuminate all the disparate global phenomena, this one goes a long way toward overcoming the declinist malaise prevalent in America during the late 1980s and presents cogent insights into America's role in the "post-cold-war" world. Some insights challenge long-held, deeply ingrained, traditional American beliefs, and not every reader will agree with them. But it is a tribute to Al Balk's analysis that, after he completed the bulk of the manuscript, when dramatic changes swept Eastern Europe, Central America, and Southern Africa no major text revisions were required. Any analysis that weathers such cataclysms so well merits attention.

We need a national dialogue about the U.S. role in a world that has changed dramatically since the cold war. This book is an important starting point. If it can help set dimensions for this dialogue it will have made a timely contribution.

The book, in a special edition, is a major new addition to the American Forum's publication program as well as a hardcover release by Transaction Books. In the past our publications have concentrated entirely upon formal education. It is our hope that this will be the first in an American Forum series, for educators and public alike, on the global dimensions of our daily lives.

Our participation was made possible by financial assistance from the Stanley Foundation for printing and production. In part this is a tribute to the late Max Stanley, who not only supported Al Balk during the building of *World Press Review* but, with his late wife, Elizabeth (Betty), contributed to many other international education projects and programs. Their foundation, which conducts programs in international education and world affairs, constitutes a tremendous force for good. Global and international educators owe them a deep debt and much gratitude.

Andrew F. Smith, President
The American Forum for Global Education
New York, New York

# *Introduction*

This book is the product of a unique experience: For over a decade, as editor of the magazine *World Press Review,* I was privileged to live in two worlds: that of an American served by the American press (now, in deference to TV-radio, more fashionably and inclusively called "the media"), and that of an American also immersed in the press around the world. During this period I traveled widely abroad, monitored worldwide media opinion, and discoursed with opinion-leaders outside our borders. It quickly became apparent that there are two different worlds—the one Americans think we live in, and a very different one perceived by everyone else.

The question of our international status illustrates. For several years the prevailing mood in America appears to have been that the United States is in eclipse, the "American Century" is over, and our future is behind us. This was a major reason for the unexpected 1987 success of *The Rise and Fall of the Great Powers* by Yale historian Paul Kennedy. Dense, scholarly, and analytical, it hardly seemed a candidate for bestsellerdom. But its implicit pessimism about our international status and direction obviously touched a nerve. So did an avalanche of similarly negative media reports, political oratory, and other books, some bearing alarmist titles such as *Can America Compete?, Trading Places: How We Allowed Japan to Take the Lead,* and *Yen! Japan's New Financial Empire and Its Threat to America.*

The nerve Kennedy touched was a quivering one that produces a sensation that might be called "declinitis." Until early 1989 it seemed omnipresent among American thought-leaders. This surprised me, among others. In my experience at *World Press Review,* I had found the consensus of mainstream thinkers abroad to be that, though our status unquestionably was changing, it was not to the degree that we were a sunset power. Rather, in a suddenly altered international environment that increasingly challenged and left us insecure, we remained the world's

1

preeminent political, economic, and cultural force, with a prospect for remaining so for years to come.

Nor was that opinion about our status restricted to foreigners. Managers in American business, economics, and science/technology, I found, were operating with different attitudes, on different premises, with vastly different expectations from those of the declinists. So, quietly, were many public officials.

An experience with an investment executive whose firm occupied the offices adjacent to our magazine's illustrates. Throughout the late 1970s' and early 1980s' gloom among American intellectuals and media savants, we would lunch periodically. Inevitably he would ask, "What are the journalistic experts saying about economic prospects?" I would summarize their bearishness, including that of several liberal West European editors. He would puff his pipe.

"I'm surprised to hear that," he would say. "We're having a good year, with a few bumps and adjustments here and there. We've pulled back some, but we've made some good deals buying and revamping and selling companies. They're prospering, and we expect to make a lot more." Meanwhile, at home and abroad, American business—and our economy—though severely buffeted, kept expanding.

Looking back, I marveled at the dichotomies of mood. We do indeed have pluralistic elites of diverse views. But beyond a point, that pluralism becomes submerged in a kind of public orthodoxy. Those who conform to it occupy center stage. Those who dissent from it tend to be silent or scorned or both. Their caveats become overwhelmed, their perspectives ignored.

Except abroad, that seemed to be the lot of the non-declinists until early 1989. Then a counterattack began. Mainstream media had chronicled diverse Soviet humiliations and the winding down of the cold war, and *Business Week, Fortune,* and other economic periodicals had analyzed and quantified American competitiveness and business successes. But it remained for Samuel P. Huntington, director of Harvard's Center for International Affairs, to fire the first major intellectual salvo making a cohesive, overall anti-declinist case, in a treatise in the winter issue of *Foreign Affairs.* It was titled "The U.S.—Decline or Renewal?"

The *Wall Street Journal* followed, with a late January-February series on comparative national power that concluded in one headline, "For All Its Difficulties, U.S. Stands to Retain Its Global Leadership." The first breakthrough in a general-audience intellectual publication followed in October: an *Atlantic Monthly* cover feature titled "The Coming Global Boom." It also was noteworthy for mea culpas in an editors' column that acknowledged both a concentration on declinist coverage and that "there is something to be said on the other side."

Indeed there is. One need not accept such against-the-mainstream premises to find them worthy of hearing, if only to keep abreast of the latest heresy—which might, history shows, contain at least a seed of a later new orthodoxy. This book tries to encapsulate that heresy. Based largely on my experience of seeing the world and the United States "as others see us," it draws on non-U.S. reporting, analysis, and perceptions to explain why, in a historical and global context, the assumptions of U.S. decline have been overstated—why despite short-term appearances to the contrary, we are not a sunset power (at least not yet).

In essence, what has happened is that we and the world are experiencing a triple revolution. One revolution is globalization: an internationalization of economics, politics, science/technology, culture, and communications that is fundamentally altering human affairs. A second revolution is reindustrialization: a post-Industrial upheaval that futurist Alvin Toffler calls "the third wave," built on high technology and the internationalization of economic activity. A third revolution is the ascent of a scientific, technocratic, megascale culture of incessant, ever-accelerating change and stress for which we are institutionally and temperamentally unprepared. All three revolutions alter the context in which both absolute and comparative power should be measured. Disruptive as they are, in the long term all work more in favor of the United States than of any other single nation.

America's problem, then, is not that it is in genuine long-term international decline—at least it need not be. It is that more than ever we are the world's leader, amid changing conditions, while remaining collectively blind to that reality and a de facto threat to our leadership. That threat is essentially internal. To paraphrase Shakespeare: The fault, dear Brutus, is not in our stars—nor the Soviets, nor the Japanese, nor any other recent object of national phobia—but in ourselves.

# 1

# *Ascent and Decline: Image and Reality*

Americans are seen abroad as an insecure lot. We affect a posture of confidence, even bravado. The boastful booster, usually a Texan, is part of our image. Yet to the bemusement and occasional despair of less privileged peoples, we seem constantly to feel threatened.

So it has been for most of the past two decades. The Russians were coming, the Russians were coming. Then the OPEC oil sheiks. Now the Japanese, the impending 1992 European "single market," you name it. We seem persuaded that internationally we are in decline, if not eclipse—that "the American Century" is over and our future lies behind us.

Yet if one travels extensively abroad or genuinely listens to the dialogue outside our borders, the opposite seems true. Symbols of American power and influence are almost everywhere. The problem is not finding but escaping them. The world never has seemed more Americanized. The most pervasive concerns elsewhere are not our absence nor the likelihood of it, but our overwhelming presence and its cultural, economic, and political consequences.

Justifiable insecurity is one thing; unjustified or needless insecurity based on misperception is another. Which is at work here?

Let us examine the question, and let us begin with our perceptions of decline. These may seem like a recent phenomenon; they are not. They are what horticulturalists call a hardy perennial. Indeed, an American of mature years, upon contemplation, might be hard put to recall how often or precisely when he or she first heard talk of decline.

The Soviets' *Sputnik* space satellite coup of 1957 might have been the first occasion. Or, years earlier, the Soviets' blockade of Berlin when, rather than smartly dispatching the Marines to evict them, we mounted a heroic airlift to supply the partitioned city. Or possibly the demarcation was the news that the Soviets had detonated a nuclear bomb. But it was only later that concern over decline seemed to become widely manifest: during Vietnam, the 1960s assassination wave, the 1970s oil embargoes, or indignities such as the Iranian hostage crisis, Afghanistan, and the terrorist deaths of U.S. Marines in Lebanon.

By no stretch can such events be deemed ornaments of our history. But if taken in context, singly or together they need not necessarily denote nor portend permanent "decline." In fact, the case can be made that only leading, or at least strikingly stable, powers can sustain such blows and recover. In life or geopolitics leadership is not, in the modern vernacular, a rose garden.

Ah, the skeptics may say, but to everything there is a season. Historically the great powers all have had their autumns. Take the sobering examples of Great Britain, France, Spain, and other once-imperial hegemonists chronicled by Paul Kennedy in *The Rise and Fall of the Great Powers*. Or, from still earlier eras, Rome, Venice, the Ottomans, Austro-Hungary, and the like. Look at them. How all-powerful and intimidating they once were, and for so long. How humbled they now are. Why not us, too?

This is a fair question. A fair answer is that of course America's reign as world leader eventually must end. But a related question is, How relevant is it to equate the previous powers' fates with the United States' position now? There is no question about the denouement of eclipsed past empires. Those books have been closed. But our international future remains very much open.

Consider several realities of history. By its slow-drip timetable, conclusive evidence of decline must be cumulative over decades. Can we say it is in our case? Over how many decades is there conclusive evidence? This is our first caveat.

Then there is the term "decline" itself. It is comparative. The first question it invites is, "Decline compared to what?" Therein lies the next caveat.

Declinists customarily point to a grandiose baseline for power comparisons: not our international status over the past century, or even fifty years, but the early postwar years. It was then that we seemed unsurpassed as a superpower and our ears rang with Henry Luce's proclamation of "the American century." But can that be a definitive comparison? Logic suggests that this deceives.

The immediate postwar period was an atypical blip in history. World War II was the largest, most destructive conflagration ever. It laid waste all the other leading industrial nations. Thus at its end, by serendipity we towered over the world like a colossus.

As the "arsenal of democracy," using depression-idled capacity and a work force augmented by women and blacks, we nearly tripled our gross national product (GNP) in six years. When peace descended, we possessed more than half the shattered world's industrial capacity. Among the great powers, says historian Kennedy, we were the only one that "became richer—in fact, much richer—rather than poorer because of the war."

That snapshot in history is not a rational baseline for long-term comparisons. It might be if one logically could presume that a war-shattered world and colonialism, with its enforced underdevelopment, might have been perpetuated. They could not have been. Nor did we intend them to be. Our enduring pride was postwar statesmanship, unlike Europe's after World War I, that promoted global stability, freedom, and prosperity.

We were marvelously rewarded. Both we and the world attained prosperity on a scale never before seen: In 1953-73 global manufacturing output tripled. In 1960-80 gross world-product growth averaged double the historical norm—some 5 per cent annually. Our own growth set records, doubling our median family income in a quarter-century.

This was unprecedented—an economic Camelot. Yet like its namesake, destined to be a brief "shining moment"—historically atypical and probably unique. It was the "flip" side of the devastation and suffering of World War II.

But that has become part of history's attic. The war ended nearly a half-century ago. A new century is but ten years away. How long can we remain in the thrall of this Camelot?

The same caveat applies to U.S. geopolitical power. It, too, constituted a war-related Camelot, bestowing as "artificially high" a status—in Kennedy's term—as Great Britain's after the Napoleonic wars.

We do not, however, think of it as "artificial." Rather it has been transmogrified into our norm. If we recognize and accept it as atypical and by no defensible logic attainable for the long term, then descending from this "artificial high" need not bespeak decline. It could mean a return to long-term trends.

Such trends do not place us in eclipse. Again, look at history. Before World War II there were five great powers: Great Britain, France, Germany, Japan, and the United States, with the Soviet Union and China at the margins. Now there are two superpowers. Of the two, we are indisputably the leader. Other prewar powers march in second or third ranks. This is decline?

We occupy the pinnacle of world leadership. Consider our economic power: We are the Mount Everest of nations, at a rarefied altitude shared by none, and still thrusting upward. Our wealth (GNP) is some twenty times its total at war's end—about $5 trillion, compared to $220 billion (in constant dollars).

This makes us the world's richest nation, with wealth (GNP) comparable to that of all of Western Europe, and double that of Japan or the Soviet Union. For a century, including this decade, our growth has forged steadily upward with only minor deviations. That is decline?

Beyond our borders our record is envied. In the "real world"—the planet of the possible, reflecting cyclical changes and the constraints of the human condition—we merit this envy.

The respected *Financial Times* of London points out:

- We produce solid economic growth: "U.S. growth has never fallen in the last four or five years below 2 to 3 per cent per annum and has averaged nearly 3½ per cent...."
- We maintain a stunning job-creation record: "Unemployment [is] below 7 per cent, compared with 11 per cent in the European Community...."
- We lead in research: "The U.S....spends far more on research and development than any other Western country—almost $120 billion in 1986...and has an unrivaled record of imaginative breakthroughs at the frontiers of science...."
- We excel in high-technology competitiveness: "U.S. companies account for two-thirds of the world's commercial aircraft;...half of all computer sales; and in semiconductors are still the world leader."

Our economic bloodstream frequently is portrayed as anemic. But Samuel P. Huntington, director of the Center for International Affairs at Harvard, provides this evidence to the contrary:

- We have maintained a consistent global market share: The U.S. ratio of gross world product has remained at 20 to 25 per cent since the late 1960s, and "certainly has not declined more rapidly in the past two decades than it did during the previous two decades." In 1970-87 our share varied between 22 and 25 per cent.

- Our share of developed-world exports is little-changed: Our ratio of exports among the seven "economic summit" countries was about the same in 1987 as in 1970—23 versus 24 per cent.
- Our high-technology export share has remained consistent: Our ratio of world exports of technology-intensive products has varied only about two percentage points between 1965 and 1984—27.5 versus 25.2.
- We have accelerated economic growth, not declined: During the 1980s, our economic performance "improved markedly" compared to that of other leading nations: from number fifteen in economic growth among nineteen industrialized market economies in 1965-80 to number three in 1980-86.
- In the 1980s we surpassed Japan in the rate of economic growth: In 1980-86 our growth spurted to 110.7 per cent of 1965-80, while Japan's fell to 58.7. In 1983-87 we grew at about the same rate as Japan, and in three of those five years we led it.

"The argument can be made," he concludes, "that the GNP pattern that has emerged in the past two decades is in some sense historically normal pattern, roughly approximating the distribution that existed before World War II.

For the foreseeable future, aside from accelerated growth in some developing nations, this comparative pattern is forecast as unlikely to change. One Pentagon study, for example, put our share of fifteen major countries gross national product at 31.6 per cent in 1980 and projects it for 2010 at 29.2 per cent—twice the projected GNPs of China, Japan, or the Soviet Union.*

This is our trumpeted-from-the-ramparts decline?

Judged against the imperial nations discussed in Kennedy's *The Rise and Fall of the Great Powers,* of course we have declined. We do not possess the relative—or, as Professor Susan Strange of the London School of Economics and Political Science calls it, "relational"—hegemonic power of the giants of history. That is, "the power of A to get B to do something it would not otherwise do."

We did possess that power in Camelot. But except with tiny nations in our own sphere of influence, did we ever consistently at any other time? Now times have changed for everyone. Apart from severely restricted near-border spheres, neither superpower has, nor feels free

*The totals (in 1986 dollars): United States, $7.86 trillion; China, $3.89 trillion; Japan, $3.71 trillion; Soviet Union, $2.87 trillion.

to exercise, that power now. In a pluralistic, interdependent age, no nation can.

In this new, postimperial era we must calibrate our position by a different measure: what Professor Strange calls "structural power." That is, "the power to choose and to shape the structures of the global political economy within which other states, their political institutions, their economic enterprises, and (not least) their professional people have to operate."

Such structural power, she postulates, consists of four interrelated frameworks "like the four sides of a pyramid." Each is supported by the other three. The four are the ability to exercise control over the following: others' security from violence; the system of production; the structure of finance and credit, through which purchasing power is obtained "without having either to work or to trade for it"; and the acquisition, communication, and storage of knowledge and information.

By these criteria, she says, there is little question about our combined structural power. "Neither Europe nor Japan can equal the Americans' performance across all four structures. Since each of them interacts with the other three, and the Europeans and Japanese are so far behind militarily, it seems likely that America will enjoy the power to act as a hegemon for some time to come."

In a variation, Huntington sees America's influence as resting on a tripod unmatched by any other nation:

1) "Peculiarly multidimensional" strength. Our chief global rival, the Soviet Union, is "a one-dimensional superpower," with influence based almost entirely on military might. Our main economic challenger, Japan, derives its power from manufacturing performance and control of financial resources. In contrast we rank "extraordinarily high" not only in these realms but in almost all other major sources of power.* Thus reverses in one area are compensated by strengths in others—an advantage that no nation can challenge for the foreseeable future.

2) Influence based on our "structural position" in world politics. This position stems from five advantages, all of which he sees as

---

*These include population size, education, natural resources, economic development, social cohesion, political stability, military strength, ideological appeal, diplomatic alliances, and technological achievement.

creating "a demand for the American presence overseas" that draws us naturally to leadership. These are: our geographical distance from "most major areas of world conflict," a history "relatively free of overseas imperialism," an anti-statist philosophy that is "less likely to be threatening to other peoples," a "diversified network of alliances," and "identification with universal international institutions." Again, no other nation approaches us in these attributes.

3) No likely alternative hegemonic power in the next century. In the media and in back-fence conversation, Japan frequently is mentioned as a candidate to succeed us. On close examination that won't wash. Huntington summarizes why. Japan, he notes, "has neither the size, natural resources, military strength, diplomatic affiliates, nor, most important, the ideological appeal to be a twentieth-century superpower."

Japan is seen abroad as the quintessential "me" nation, standing clearly and unabashedly for its own self-interest. Yet "an idea with appeal beyond its borders" is a prerequisite to superpower status. In recent years, only the United States and Soviet Union have possessed this. The Soviets' message now is defunct.

Helmut Schmidt, former chancellor of West Germany, puts it this way. In weight of raw power, he says, there are three capitals: Washington, Moscow, and Beijing. In the economic realm there are three: the United States, Western Europe, and Japan. Only the United States qualifies in both categories.

Even Japanese authorities concur. "American society," says Hiroshi Takuchi, chief economist of Japan's Long-Term Credit Bank, "is very strong, [with] the scale and resources that [Japan] simply never will possess." His colleague, Keio university economist Fuji Kamiya, calls it *sokojikara*—or latent power—"to be a world leader for many years."

West German journalist Josef Joffe puts it another way. "Oh, Lord," he said in mock entreaty at a conference on declinism, "if I have to live in a declining country, please let it be America."

# 2

# *A New World*

All this is not to suggest that nothing about our status has changed. On the contrary. The whole political, economic, and cultural milieu in which America functions has been altered—more and faster than in any comparable period.

We are caught in a triple revolution. Its three components are globalization, reindustrialization, and a scientific, technocratic, megascale culture of ever-accelerating change. Together, they are sweeping politics, economics, science, communications, and culture into a new era: a Post-Modern, or Global, Age.

To understand why our changed circumstances do not constitute eclipse, we must comprehend the nature of this age. Its implications are breathtaking. When fully evolved it will be as different as was the era into which most of us were born—the Modern, or Nation-State, Age—from the epoch that preceded it, the Middle Ages.

Only vestiges of that pre-Industrial period now remain, mainly in quaint castles and cathedrals that dot Europe. They bespeak the immense disparities between before and after. Agriculture then was the chief economic activity. Privilege resided in royalty and the church. The European continent was a mosaic of religious enclaves, baronial fiefs, and seaside or land-locked city-states. North America and sub-Saharan Africa, though inhabited, remained "undiscovered." Except for arduous overland and, later, seaborne commerce and conquest, China, the Islamic empire, and other major cultures were isolated.

That epoch ended in a series of historical flashes in the fifteenth century. In close succession, historian Arthur M. Schlesinger, Jr., observed, "Columbus made his discovery and Gutenberg made his invention..., [and] Erasmus, Machiavelli, Sir Thomas More, and Copernicus [were nurtured]." That single astonishing century, Schlesinger notes, "marked the end of the isolation of cultures, the beginning of the long epoch of European penetration of the non-European world."

A series of comparable bolts has made the twentieth century a counterpart of the fifteenth. Again, almost simultaneously an eruption of new knowledge, irresistible forces, and altered relationships has created a new age. That age, we now can see, is destined to culminate in such wondrous developments as manned interplanetary exploration, and, eventually, colonization of space. Over time this epochal leap of human mastery clearly is within reach. Thus the new Post-Modern, or Global, Age is a precursor to, and first phase of, the Space Age.

Immersed in workaday diversions, we tend to ignore that and its inexorable implications. This is not surprising. None of the intellectual pioneers of the fifteenth century, nor their most prescient peers, could have known the consequences of the tides that they unleashed. They only knew that discovery of the New World, the knowledge and instruments and sensibilities that made it possible, and the liberation of information dissemination from single-copy, handwritten reproduction opened unimagined frontiers.

Similarly, we can sense some implications of the explosive change of recent years. Again, take space. Approximately three decades of exploration, extending to the outer reaches of the solar system, have demonstrated the inevitability of quantum leaps. They also demonstrate the impossibility of single nations achieving them.

For we now know that giant strides into space are beyond the resources of any one nation. Also that, except for national pride, they yield no peculiarly national benefit. On the contrary. They have transcendental post-national implications. Thus post-national arrangements to implement such steps are inevitable.

So it is in many other fields. The nature of the new age ordains this. It is defined by fifteen elemental forces. To comprehend what is happening to us and what this might mean, these forces must be understood. They are:

1) Hyperchange.

Change has achieved a magnitude that creates what Alvin Toffler described as "future shock." Nothing seems permanent. The half-lives of institutions, procedures, and values keep shrinking.

In the twilight of the nineteenth century, American historian Henry Adams foresaw this phenomenon. Pondering the dramatic progress since 1800, he concluded, "The world did not double or treble its movement....The tension and vibration and volume and so-called progression of society were fully a thousand times greater in 1900." This he ascribed to a science-driven law of acceleration. It would, he predicted, cause "the sharpest change of direction, taken at the highest rate of speed, ever effected by the human mind." Adams' vision has become reality.

As Toffler has written, if all the change in human history were measured according to lifetimes, there has been more during our own than in all the lifetimes preceding it. Atomic science, space flight, computers, transistors, robots, biotechnology, superconductivity—the list of contemporary discoveries seems almost infinite. Nor is any end in sight. Nine-tenths of all the scientists and engineers who ever lived people the world's laboratories—and double their numbers are preparing in classrooms. As a result, the sum of scientific knowledge doubles every thirteen to fifteen years.

As change begets change, it creates change "squared," requiring virtuosic individual and collective adaptability.

2) Megascale.

The second elemental change is in scale. Since World War II the size and complexity of institutions and their impact on human affairs have expanded exponentially. "Mega," "hyper," "super," "quantum"—all suddenly have become commonplace. We have entered a new age of megascale.

A few years ago "billion"—1,000 million—was perceived as awesome. No more. Now "trillion"—1,000 billion—has preempted that status. Our 1988-89 federal budget was $1.1 trillion. Every day New York bank clearing houses process computerized payments exceeding $1 trillion. Other trillionaire categories abound.

Megascale envelops us. Human population—1.7 billion at the beginning of this century—more than doubled by 1987, to over 5 billion. By the next century, just ten years from now, it will have risen another billion—tripling in a single lifetime.

Megascale population creates—necessitates—megascale institutions. One is gigantic multinational corporations. About ten thousand firms of various nations now operate in six or more countries. But like their smaller corporate ancestors, even these immense conglomerates are transitory. The trend now is to coalitions of giants, known as "cross-border joint ventures" or "global strategic partnerships." Such arrangements involve almost every major corporation and innumerable smaller firms. By the early 1990s, it is projected, some three hundred will employ one-fifth of the world's work force and account for more than three-fourths of its gross product.

"Competition," says Carlo de Benedetti of Italy's Olivetti, "no longer is just between individual companies, it is between mobile and expanding alliances of companies."

Scale—megascale—matters. It permeates every aspect of life. The more the changes, the more the unforeseen impacts and permutations. Once institutions and clusters of them swell to large enough size, for example, they not only keep growing but subdivide—in Toffler's term, "demassify"—into satellites, subcultures, and reoriented organizational structures. Changes in scale then proceed on two levels: an upper, or macroscale, framework, and an inner, more heterogeneous, flexible web. This now is occurring in every field, from demographics to politics.

Bigness, then, is not just "more." Beyond a threshold, it is "different."

3) The Global Village.

Perhaps the most significant manifestation of megascale is globalization. As mammoth institutions grow larger, only a global arena can accommodate them. Once they attain this megascale, a new range of circumstances and relationships is created.

Two decades ago Canadian media theorist Marshall McLuhan postulated one implication: a "global village." He referred to a world in which instant communication makes all peoples equidistant. That now is a reality. The planet, says historian William H. McNeill, author of *The Rise of the West,* "has become a city...[that] does not end at its municipal boundaries but extends as far as the ganglia of modern communications can reach."

More than two hundred offspring of the communications satellite *Early Bird,* orbited in 1965, are the nerve centers of this ganglia. These are complemented by new undersea and underground multiple-circuit fiber-optic tubes. Along with microchips and computerization, they have revolutionized business, diplomacy, science, and journalism.

Computer networks are global. Some two billion international telephone calls are placed annually—nearly twenty-three thousand an hour. Television and the cinema are international. A billion people—some one-fifth of humanity—simultaneously viewed the first moonwalk in 1969. More than a decade later 1.5 billion in 152 nations shared in the *Live Aid* concert. At least a billion view each Olympics.

Outside the United States, one-third of all TV programming is imported. At just one huge annual bazaar in Cannes, France, some fifteen hundred TV organizations buy and sell rights to over thirty thousand TV programs.* Cable News Network exemplifies another phenomenon. At least one-third of the world's countries receive its programs. Other American and British newscasts, with language subtitles, also are seen regularly abroad.**

There is a global *lingua franca,* English, spoken by about 1.4 billion people, or nearly one of every three humans. It is the language of science, diplomacy, commerce, law, and transportation—standard in international Morse Code, four-fifths of all computer data, half of all telephone conversations, and half of the world's newspapers.

"English is now so dominant," says the magazine *Language Monthly,* "that some French and German medical publishers have to publish their specialist books in English. If they did not do so, their authors would not sell in sufficient numbers to be profitable."

4) The Global Marketplace.

Business, too, has become globalized. A postwar shift from a colonial-based international business pattern, built on regional production, marketing, and raw-materials transfer to world corporations marked an epochal shift—"easily of comparable sweep" to that of the Industrial Revolution, according to U.S. Chamber of Commerce economist Judd Polk.

Now world corporations have moved a step further. They view overseas factories and markets not as adjuncts to home operations but, with them, as a single economic unit. They are, says Theodore Levitt, former editor of the *Harvard Business Review,* global corporations that "sell standardized products in the same way everywhere."

Manufactured, or "hard," goods are only part of the profile. With data and money electronically transferable, and a bank, investment house, or stock exchange always open, the sun never sets on "invisible trade"—borrowing, lending, or currency and securities trading. By the mid-1980s, such capital movements exceeded the dollar volume of goods and ser-

---

*Predictably, the United States, Great Britain, and France are leading suppliers, but Mexico, Brazil, and China also rank high. Brazil sells to about a hundred nations, including prime-time soap operas—"telenovels"—dubbed even into Chinese.

**"It's hard to walk around Paris these days without being asked what you thought of Dan Rather last night—or this morning," columnist Richard Reeves observed during one French sojourn.

vices trade some thirtyfold. Global financial flows, in management expert Peter F. Drucker's phrase, have become "the flywheel of the world economy."

When New York City recovered from its 1970s financial crisis, it was not alone due to domestic factors but to an upsurge of foreign corporate, tourist, and real estate investment. When recessions and the global debt crises failed to slow the Dow Jones index's mid-1980s run-up to 2500, foreign funds were the explanation. Similarly, the "Black Monday" quake that obliterated one-fifth of our stock market's value originated at earlier-opening exchanges abroad, where panic and computerized program-trading spread shock throughout a global electronic network.

Money-center banks' growth, Wall Street's partial recovery, and escalating price tags on real estate, corporations, and artistic and entertainment properties now all must be evaluated with a "G-factor"—global economic conditions—in mind. For nations' and businesses' economic affairs, says Drucker, it now is "the world economy that leads."

5) The Global Factory.

Manufacturing also has become globalized. This is part of what sociologist Daniel Bell calls the Third Transition, in which work increasingly has become "detached from place." With jet aircraft, containerized cargo vessels, and high-speed computerization, transcontinental shipment is fast, inexpensive—and routine.

Virtually no product of substantial size or complexity is made entirely in one country. The auto business illustrates. Some two dozen major car- and truck-makers have made three hundred joint design and production agreements—fifty involving General Motors. Cars with American nameplates may consist of parts from four continents. Some are completely assembled elsewhere and imported almost directly to dealer showrooms—the Mercury Tracer, for example, from Mexico, or the Ford Festiva, from South Korea.

For smaller products the trend is even more pronounced. More than one-third of personal computers shipped to the United States in 1986, for instance, many with American brand names, were assembled overseas. Now, according to one estimate, "contract assembly" covers nearly 40 per cent of all U.S. electronics production—with 90 per cent of it overseas.

Bell Telephones? They are made in Singapore and Taiwan. Spalding NBA basketballs? South Korea. Rawlings baseballs? Haiti. Rockport shoes? Portugal and Taiwan.

When the Brookings Institution analyzed this trend it used the term "the Global Factory." "The internationalization of industry," it concluded, "has become a lasting feature of the world economic system."

6) Military might has become unusable.

In a supremely ironic change, military power has become so destructive that it is unusable. The superpowers' nuclear arsenals illustrate. Together they include some fifty-thousand nuclear bombs, missiles, and shells. Just one nuclear artillery shell such as both we and they possess equals the destructive power of the Hiroshima bomb. One *Minuteman II* nuclear missile equals eighty-four Hiroshimas.

We both possess three-branch nuclear arsenals. If the main one— land-based strategic missiles—is incapacitated, submarine- and bomber-launched weapons (including radar-evading "cruise" missiles) remain. In the West these are supplemented by British and French missile-carrying submarines, themselves capable of leveling most major Soviet targets. The total overkill on either side could, in Winston Churchill's phrase, "make the rubble bounce." This is mutually assured destruction— appropriately, in acronym, MAD.

Not even the proposed strategic defense initiative (SDI) ("Star Wars") can alter it. Even were SDI's multi-trillion-dollar "hardware" of lasers, armed satellites, and high-speed computers perfectable (and affordable), the required "software" to enable computer location, tracking, and un-failing destruction of thousands of warheads—real and decoy—is beyond foreseeable reach. Only a few nuclear missiles need penetrate to make this space-based Maginot Line a macabre reminder of its World War II forerunner.*

A policy to initiate war of such ghoulish nature is unthinkable. Any triumph of surviving it would be hollow. No conquerer could cope with its aftermath. Indeed, the climatic consequences of a nuclear exchange could deaden the planet.

Even non-nuclear ventures now are counterproductive. The United States discovered this in Vietnam; the Soviets, in Afghanistan. Great-power arms races and military polemics persist. All-out great-power wars are obsolete.

---

*Beyond nuclear missiles there also are chemical and bacteriological weapons— described by one authority as "the poor nations' atomic bomb." Both superpowers as well as developing nations possess ominously swelling stockpiles.

7) Arms have become prohibitively expensive.

The operational unusability of armaments does not render them ir-relevant. On the contrary, territory and wealth still require defense, and an armed, pluralistic world needs policing. But modern arms' cost is becoming prohibitive.

As Yale's Kennedy observed in *The Rise and Fall of the Great Powers,* "one of the few constancies in history is that the scale of commitment on military spending always has risen." With high technology the rise has become exponential. For example:

- $.5 billion for one B-2 "Stealth" bomber —$1.4 billion for one Trident submarine
- $11.5 million for one twin-engine attack helicopter
- $2.8 million for one Leopard marine battle tank
- $13,500 for one anti-tank missile

Bombers, calculates one British defense expert, cost two hundred times more than in World War II. Fighters, at least a hundred times. Aircraft carriers, twenty times. Tanks, fifteen times.

For the same sums spent in the 1950s, the Pentagon now receives three hundred jet fighters instead of five thousand—and one hundred, not six hundred, tanks. At current progressions, according to one estimate, by the year 2020—just three decades away—today's entire Air Force budget would buy one plane!

"Only the largest powers or states," says Richard Rosecrance, inter-national politics specialist at UCLA and author of *The Rise of the Trading State,* "can afford this expense over a long period, and even the super-powers cannot if it means that they will ultimately be economically out-paced."

8) Trade and technology are the new talismen of power.

Clearly, more than ever military power is only one component of the strategic equation—and more and more, if out of proportion, a poten-tially negative one. In a global age, other means of advancement are necessary—what Rosecrance calls "a strategy of economic development based on trade" rather than military intervention.

Japan and West Germany illustrate its potential. Stripped of prewar land and resources—Germany of its eastern "half," Japan of mainland Asia and island possessions—both have risen from war's devastation to alpine heights. Neither employed military power. In fact, Germany allocates some 2 per cent of GNP to the military; Japan, perhaps 1.5 per cent. In contrast, the U.S. and Soviet ratios are about 7 per cent each.*

While the superpowers have competed to outarm each other, both of their main former adversaries have leapfrogged through trade. This occurred in a period when trade broke records. (It quadrupled in 1950-73—double the growth in the half-century "golden age of world trade" that preceded World War I.)** Amid globalization trade can only continue expanding: soon, according to some authorities, at nearly double the pace of world production. Industrial and technological prowess will be the keys to sharing in that growth.

9) Politics has become a pawn of economics, science, and technology.

The global trade explosion has done more than displace territorial conquest as a ladder upward. It has laid the foundations of an integrated international economy. This, says Jean-Louis Servan-Schreiber, whose brother Jean-Jacques wrote the 1960s classic *The American Challenge,* has become a "post-political era." Economics now dominates politics.

Science and technology in turn drive economics. Advances in communications, transportation, computerization, and materials science have revolutionized industry. Product life cycles are evanescent. Productivity—in agriculture, manufacturing, and services—continually spirals. "We are," as French president Francois Mitterrand told a conference of Nobel laureates, "seeing a transfer of power...to science."

10) The world has become exponentially richer and better fed.

The four decades following World War II marked the planet's greatest economic strides. In 1953-73, world manufacturing output tripled. In 1960-80, gross world product rose some 5 per cent annually—as previously noted, double the historical norm, and the highest ever for any two decades. In that same period, worldwide personal incomes rose 3.2 per cent a year. All this, notwithstanding megascale population increases.

Indeed, in aggregate the economic growth of the deprived South

---

*U.S. military spending totaled $293 billion in 1987; the Soviet Union's, $260 billion. Together we spend about $1.5 billion a day.

**In 1970, one-eighth of global output was traded; ten years later, one-fourth.

approximated that of the North. Rutherford M. Poats, chairman of the Development Assistance Committee of the Organization for Economic Cooperation and Development (OECD), summarizes the quarter-century through 1984:

- For all developing countries ("the poor"), average annual per-capita gross-product growth was 3.4 per cent.
- Since 1960, despite widespread recession, developing countries have increased goods and services output sixfold.
- Other indices also improved dramatically. In 1960-83, for instance, average life expectancy for all developing countries rose from forty-four to fifty-nine years; adult literacy, from 37 to 59 per cent; and primary-school enrollment, from 60 to 86 per cent of eligible children (excluding China, "where it was virtually universal").

Nearly two centuries ago British clergyman-economist Thomas Malthus warned that population growth tends to outrun the means of subsistence. This no longer applies to food, whose output is rising twice as fast as population.

"If all the food produced in the world were divided equally among all the people in it," says George Zeidenstein, president of the Rockefeller-supported Population Council, "each person's share would have increased since 1950—by as much as a quarter....Thus global food production has grown geometrically, as Malthus said it could not."

India and China, which together contain nearly half of the world's population, report stunning agricultural gains: The 1980s saw India begin exporting grain. China, with agricultural output up 50 per cent since 1978, is expected to export food by the year 2000. Even destitute Bangladesh has become technically food self-sufficient—not dependent upon imports—though at intolerably low levels.

Droughts and other disasters intervene. But worldwide, the food problem has shifted from underproduction to maldistribution. Among the richer nations, subsidized farm surpluses, not shortages, persist. (The United States spends $20 billion a year on agricultural subsidies and stores a third of its annual grain output; the European Community (EC) subsidies exceed $16 billion, with one-fifth of the output stored. The Soviet Union is the world's only large grain importer.)

This global shift is the result of agriculture's Third Revolution: plant genetics. The first revolution (mechanization) and second (fertilizers and pesticides) mainly affected developed nations, which contain a minority of the world's arable land and population. "The plant genetics revolution," State Department analyst Dennis. T. Avery points out, "is affecting 90 per cent of the land and 4.5 billion people."

Plant genetics enables farmers to sow in now-barren areas, increase grain yields by orders of magnitude, enhance plants' disease resistance, and, through tree-cloning, eventually relieve firewood shortages and denuding of dry regions. So powerful is this new science's promise that, one authority predicts, "an overproduction crisis of major proportions" impends.

11) World economic power has been dispersed.

We tend to perceive the global economy in split-level postwar terms. That is, the three worlds posited by Franz Fanon: the industrialized non-Communist nations, the Communist bloc, and the non-Communist, less developed countries. But instead of Fanon's three worlds, there now are at least five. They are:

- The four advanced centers of high industrialization— Western Europe, North America, Japan, and Eastern Europe.
- Some twenty newly industrializing countries in Latin America, Southern Europe, and East Asia. Over two decades they have averaged 8.4 per cent growth and doubled their share of global output to 10 per cent.
- The Middle East's capital-surplus, oil-exporting countries. Since the early 1970s they have imported four million workers and aggressively developed and diversified their economies.
- The populous nations of nonindustrialized Asia. There "miracles" of agriculture and modernization have enabled raising per-capita income by 50 per cent in two decades while population increased by 700 million.
- Eighteen sub-Saharan African countries whose per-capita income declined in the 1970s.

"Complexity," says A.W. Clausen, former president of the World Bank, "is what we have in the world economy today: a whole complicated ganglia of interdependent relationships, and a very dynamic environment in which they are all interacting."

"Confucian capitalism" epitomizes this dynamism. Japan, its leader, requires no introduction. Its other main disciples, Asia's four "little tigers," may. Together the four—South Korea, Taiwan, Hong Kong, and Singapore—produce exports totaling four-fifths of Japan's. All have been instrumental in shaking the economic firmament. Among their achievements:

- South Korea. In 1960 it compared with Ghana and the Sudan in gross output. Since then its forty million people have increased their GNP by an average 8 per cent a year, life expectancy by eight months annually, and literacy to nearly 100 per cent. South Korea has Pacific Asia's largest middle class outside Japan. For 1986 *Fortune* ranked two of its nine conglomerates (Hyundai and Samsung) among the world's top fifty industrial corporations.
- Taiwan. Little more than three decades ago it also compared economically to Ghana and the Sudan. Now its twenty million residents have a life expectancy at European and U.S. levels, virtual 100 per cent literacy, productive farming, and a formidable export-oriented industrial base.
- Hong Kong. Scheduled to revert from British to Chinese jurisdiction in 1997, it has thrived as a regional financial capital, tourist magnet, and free-trade and light-manufacturing center.
- Singapore. Evolving from colonial status to independent prosperity, it has displaced Rotterdam as the world's largest port, ranks number three in refining and shipbuilding, and is a growing power in electronics manufacturing, regional finance, and services.

All five "Confucian achievers" benefited greatly from special ties to us or other powers. But their economic virtuosity is undisputed. "There is," points out economist Robert Heilbroner, "no commodity that has not been made in these countries, from television sets and integrated circuits to steel and automobiles and none that cannot be made." He adds, "If the story of Taiwan and South Korea can sooner or later be duplicated in Turkey and Egypt, Nigeria and Indonesia, Argentina and India—and why should it not be?—the present industrial core of capitalism would face a challenge of unprecedented magnitude."

12) More economic challengers await.

This challenge described by Heilbroner now is upon us. One reason is the unprecedented postwar industrial, markets, and trade expansion. Another is a worldwide education explosion.

In just one generation (1960-82), notes former Johnson White House adviser W. W. Rostow, now a professor of political economy at the University of Texas at Austin, the proportion of young adults in higher education in what the World Bank classifies as "lower-middle-income countries" more than tripled. More than one of every ten young adults in those countries now are in college, and the ratio continues upward.

Modest as this may seem to more privileged venues, it produces dramatic fallout. Slight, soft-spoken Tunisian journalist-businessman Bechir Ben Yahmed offers one example among many I know. The founder of *Jeune Afrique* and other Paris-based African publications, he was among only a small minority of high-school graduates when Tunisia became independent. This won him immediate appointment to the national Cabinet, a major role in policymaking, and an enviable career launching pad.

"Education became our highest priority," he says. "We allotted less than 10 per cent of our budget to military spending and 35 per cent every year for the past twenty-five years to education. At independence we had about 450 doctors for five million people. Less than three decades later we have 3,000 doctors. Even the poorest children now go to school. In the Moslem nations girls previously did not go to school. Now they do."

Rostow notes another significant aspect of developing-country education: "a radical shift towards science and engineering." India, which could claim only about 190,000 scientists/engineers in 1960, had 2.4 million in 1984—"a critical mass," he says, "only exceeded in the United States and the Soviet Union." In Mexico, from 1957 to 1973, the annual rate of increase in natural-science graduates accelerated fivefold.

These figures, says Rostow, signal "a surge in technological absorptive capacity." In the next five decades he expects this to produce new "technological virtuosity" for countries with at least 56 per cent of world population. "We are," he says, "talking about a great historical transformation."

13)    Advanced economies are being "reindustrialized."

With science and technology endlessly gestating new products and processes and the world now an integrated factory and marketplace, commerce and industry are restratifying. Industrialized nations with affluent, educated populations are becoming high-technology, services-employment centers atop an elastic worldwide pyramid. Each innovation produces ripples that push earlier products and processes down a global development line. Thus advanced economies are incessantly creating, consolidating, and restructuring whole industries, turning ripples into waves that become tides that wash over economic shorelines and structures everywhere.

This is part of an evolution described by Bell, Toffler, Drucker, and others. Every major stage of human economic activity carries within it the seeds of the next. As the next evolves, it overwhelms and supersedes earlier ones, decreasing existing institutional employment needs and absorbing and redeploying the surplus. Thus Toffler's First Wave (mechanization of agriculture) was succeeded by the Second (industrialization), which now is being transformed by the Third (high-technology, knowledge-based services). This succession is inexorable.

In the United States, for instance, in 1950 manufacturing occupied one-third of the nonfarm work force; in 1986, less than one-fifth. Over the next twenty years blue-collar manufacturing employment will fall perhaps another 40 per cent. A quarter-century from now, says Peter Drucker, manufacturing in developed countries like the United States and Japan will employ about the same ratio of workers as farming does now.

Science and technology will continue to create new jobs—and alter economies. This will expand services employment worldwide, especially in advanced economies. These, it is now known, are inherently services-intensive—a by-product of industrialization.

A World Bank development profile traces this progression. In industrialization's first stage, it notes, transportation, distribution, communications, finance, insurance, and the like all "have to expand to facilitate industrial growth." Urbanization—another by-product of industrialization—further commands new services: police, sanitation, municipal administration, and the like. Then a takeoff occurs. Manufacturing expands. Cleaning, information processing, advertising, and other services are "contracted out." This spawns new services firms.

Increased affluence supports still more—real estate, finance, retail sales, entertainment. Longer life expectancy requires yet more. (Senior citizens use disproportionate shares of services, from health care to travel and financial.) And so the snowball rolls—at accelerating speed in a mass-market, high-technology society, while First-, Second-, and Third-Wave phases constantly interact worldwide.

14) The "Pacific Tilt."

"Pacific tilt" is more than jargon. "Every day," *The Australian* of Sydney has noted, "four out of five of the world's big jetliners are to be found in flight not between New York and [London], nor serving the historic cities of Europe, but somewhere above the endless waters of the Pacific."

In 1977 American trade across the Pacific surpassed that across the Atlantic. The differential now exceeds one-fourth and continues to widen.

The Pacific Basin encompasses half the world's population and wealth, including one-fifth of world oil reserves. Since 1960 the aggregate product of Asia-Pacific countries, excluding the United States, has more than doubled, to 16.4 per cent of world output. By the year 2000 it is expected to exceed Western Europe's and equal ours. According to one forecast, the entire Pacific Rim, including the United States, then will produce half of the world's goods and services.

For such reasons, says *The Australian,* "Increasing numbers of far-sighted people see [the Asia-Pacific region] playing the same central role in the twenty-first century as the Mediterranean in the Elizabethan Age or the Atlantic throughout the Industrial Revolution."

This is not to intimate that Europe is passe. On the contrary. It remains a vital economic and strategic fulcrum. The European Community's population—an aggregate 320 million—exceeds that of the United States or the Soviet Union. It remains our largest export market, surpassing our largest single customer (in dollar value), Canada. Its gross product and output of autos, steel, and other manufactured items exceed ours. Its educational and scientific establishments command international respect.

West Germany alone accounts for 18 per cent of world trade—just 2 per cent behind us and ahead of Japan. France and Italy in particular have restructured impressively. The French phone system—long a cosmic joke—is a state-of-the-art symbol of the nation's high-technology achievements. Italy's economic rejuvenation is comparably impressive. Fiat has become a world leader in automation, and Carlo de Benedetti of Olivetti one of Europe's executive stars.

The European Community itself is a major reason for continental optimism. Evolved from the postwar Coal and Steel Community, it has surmounted historic rivalries to inch toward confederation. The next phase, in 1992, is to be a borderless economy in which goods and services are to move as freely as in the United States. This, it is estimated, will add 4.5 per cent to the region's economic growth, creating 1.8 million new jobs. If the two Germanies are reunited and Eastern Europe integrated into the EC, even more exciting long-run potential exists.

15) National power is flowing to multinational institutions.

For various reasons, political institutions everywhere are faltering. One is the simple acceleration of change, which threatens all institutions' ability to adapt. Another is what Daniel Bell calls a "mismatch of scale." That is, "The nation-state is becoming too small for the big problems of life and too big for the small problems."

A propos the big problems, international mechanisms remain too underdeveloped to cope with capital flows, commodity imbalances, job movements, and demographic tidal waves expected in the next twenty years. Concerning the small, gravitation of power to a national center inhibits responsiveness to local needs, and local populations' abilities to control resources and decisions. These disparities must be reconciled.

A reordering has begun. The European Community is one example. En route to 1992, its twelve members already have established an open travel and immigration zone, many common laws, a regional parliament and courts, and subsidies and other economic stabilizers. In the other direction, our federal government has returned a number of functions to state jurisdictions. Both the Soviets' *perestroika* and China's putative post-Mao reforms involve similar devolutions.

Internationally, an evolving global structure is dimly visible. The United Nations, with its underpublicized field agencies, occupies the center. The World Bank—with some five thousand staff members—and the International Monetary Fund are prominent cross-beams. Other activity-specific apparatus are proliferating.

The OECD, comprised of two dozen leading industrial democracies, including the U.S., is one example.* International postal flow, weights and measures, medical-pharmaceutical specifications, and the monetary system long have been internationally managed. More recently, transnational air, ocean, and land transportation became regulated, then radio-TV, phone, and data transmission channels.

---

*Its members maintain a staff in Paris, exchange national economic data, sponsor analyses and reports, and coordinate policy changes. Most conspicuously, perhaps, their leaders, the Group of Seven—the United States, Great Britain, Canada, France, West Germany, Italy, and Japan—hold annual economic summits.

With space activity came international allocation of communications satellite "parking orbits" and a whole new field of space law.* Other international law or treaties cover rules of war, nuclear weapons testing, air and water pollution, and criminal activity and extradition. According to one survey, the United States alone is party to five dozen two-party and three dozen multilateral treaties referable for interpretation by the World Court.

The Court—formally, the International Court of Justice—is itself a significant development. Part of the UN system, in forty years it has delivered over one hundred major decisions in "contentious cases."** Its prospects achieved a quantum advance in early 1989 when the Soviet Union recognized Court jurisdiction under five human rights treaties and the superpowers pledged adherence to Court decisions under seven treaties on issues not affecting national sovereignty.

On the regional level below the high-profile European Community, the Organization of African Unity, though criticized as ineffectual, has prevented post-Independence African wars over inherited colonial-era borders. In the Mideast, the Gulf Cooperation Council is seen as a nascent Persian Gulf-area European Economic Community.*** Similarly, an Association of Southeast Asian Nations (ASEAN) and the Organization of American States (OAS) are credited with at least modest achievements regarded as harbingers of more substantial ones.

---

*Provisions govern registration of objects launched, liability for accidents, rescue and return of objects to Earth, exploration or use of the moon and other bodies, and the use of Space for manufacturing.

**These include disputes over territory, the waters of rivers, ocean-floor resources, and fishing grounds; government responsibilities to foreign enterprises within its jurisdiction; ships exploded by mines in international waters; and diplomats taken hostage.

***Composed of major southern Gulf countries minus Iran, it operates an Arabsat satellite and other programs to facilitate opening borders and reduce trade and travel barriers, such as common radio-television productions.

# 3

# *The Globalizing of America*

How do these elemental forces affect us? They permeate every aspect of life. This is one root of our national malaise. We sense that everything is changing—a new game with new rules for domestic and public policy. But we are baffled by the changes, and see them as sweeping and disruptive and frequently adverse to our interests.

Take the recent evolution of the United States. We know it no longer is the simple society painted by Norman Rockwell. But we have yet to comprehend the extent of the transformation.

We live in a new America—a globalized, reindustrialized, high-technology, multicolor mass society inextricably entwined with the rest of an equally kaleidoscopic world. Comfortable stereotypes no longer serve.

Begin with economics.

"We still see ourselves as an island surrounded on the east and west by great oceans and to the north and south by friendly neighbors," says American University economist Howard M. Wachtel. "But the economic reality is different." That reality includes:

- Almost one-fifth of our industrial output is exported.
- Two of every five acres of farmland are used for export.
- About one-third of our corporate profits flow either from exports or investments abroad.
- One-fifth of our corporate assets are outside the United States.
- One-fourth of our business loans come from foreign sources.
- Some five million American jobs depend on trade.
- About fifteen hundred U.S. banks belong to syndicates with loans of about $550 billion to nations whose ability to repay, as Wachtel delicately puts it, is "periodically in doubt."

As the President's Commission on Industrial Competitiveness noted

in 1985, "Quite simply no longer is there a truly domestic economy."
Nor is·our national financial structure "truly domestic."

As most Americans are aware, foreign investment in the United States
has boomed—to $1.5 trillion. Once quintessentially American institu-
tions indeed have become foreign owned.

In publishing, for example, when you subscribe to *Scientific American,
Ms., Woman's Day, Seventeen,* or *TV Guide,* or select books from Double-
day & Co., Harper & Row, Macmillan, Viking Press, and E.P. Dutton,
you are buying from foreign entities.

In food, when you pick Burger King, or Green Giant, Pillsbury,
A & P, Grand Union, and many other labels, they are foreign owned.

Similarly, in department stores and clothing, when shopping at Bloom-
ingdale's, Macy's, Saks Fifth Avenue, and Brooks Brothers.

And in entertainment and the arts, when enjoying releases from 20th
Century Fox, Columbia Pictures, CBS or RCA Records, and MTM
Enterprises (former producing unit for Mary Tyler Moore).

The list goes on, from Magnavox, Firestone, Farberware, and Betty
Crocker baking products to the Holiday Inn chain, hotels such as Manhattan's famed Algonquin, and firearms from the makers of "the gun that
won the West," Smith & Wesson.

In Los Angeles, at least a third of the downtown office buildings are
foreign owned. In Manhattan, so also are the Tiffany, Exxon, ABC, and
other landmark buildings, including a share of Rockefeller Center. In
Hawaii the Japanese alone own virtually all of famed Waikiki Beach's
hotels, plus shopping centers, resorts, and hundreds of other select
properties.

But the Japanese are not alone. Canadians rank high, especially in
New York City. One Toronto firm, Olympia & York, is said to own 8
per cent of Manhattan's office space, including the $1.5 billion Battery
Park City and World Financial Center. Canadians also own more than
half of Denver's new downtown commercial buildings and nearly a third
of Minneapolis' core-city offices. The British, Germans, Dutch, French,
and Arabs also have prominent American portfolios.*

In industry, about five hundred Japanese firms now manufacture or
assemble products in the United States. Some are huge joint ventures,

---

*In Washington, D.C., the British own some 45 per cent of downtown properties.
"Another 5 per cent," a British commercial agent and property expert jokes, "and they
would own the White House."

such as a General Motors-Toyota plant in Fremont, Calif., and the world's most advanced sheet-rolling plant, a partnership of the Inland and Nippon Steel companies, in northern Indiana. Most are wholly owned enterprises.*

Like that of other countries, American industry also has joined the move offshore. This, as well as foreign competition, has triggered anguished alarms about "the export of American jobs." But the philosophy of "the global factory" prevails: Production elsewhere may be cheaper, closer to outside markets, and therefore too enticing to reject. Some of the resultant industrial clusters are immense.

The *maquiladores* program in Mexico illustrates. Under it parts can be imported by Mexico duty free, assembled, and shipped as finished products subject only to U.S. duty on the value added by assembly. More than twelve hundred such plants, employing at least 300,000 Mexicans, now are strung along the U.S.-Mexican border. Over five hundred are clustered in Tijuana, transforming it from a shabby "sin city" to a thriving industrial and commercial center larger than San Francisco, Seattle, or Portland.

Most *maquiladores* are American owned, two dozen by GM alone. Wages are as little as $3 a day—less than our own minimum hourly wage. For competitiveness reasons, a GM spokesman insists, "The choice is not [between] the U.S. or Mexico...but Mexico or some other cost-effective location."

More than sixty American companies have foreign data-processing bases. These range from Barbados—where American Airlines records are keypunched for return satellite transmission—to Ireland, India, China, and Singapore. U.S. banking, accounting, insurance, periodical, and other data-intensive enterprises also ceaselessly prowl potential new low-cost "backoffice" sites abroad. Ireland, one of the most aggressive recruiters, has landed branches of 350 U.S. firms with such incentives as training grants, near-zero tax rates, and duty-free access to the European Community. Average returns on investment there approach 30 per cent.

After World War II European cars, hi-fi's, and other products briefly were novelties. Now they are integral to our lives. Russell Baker, in one

---

*By the year 2000, Japan's Ministry of International Trade and Industry (MITI) projects a nearly tenfold increase in Japanese manufacturing in the United States, creating 840,000 jobs. Honda, among other firms, expects to supply both the American market and others—including Japan—from U.S. plants.

of his more whimsical moods, conceded a personal dependence on foreign products. "This," he began one column, "is being written on a computer made in the U.S.A. at a desk made in Denmark. When completed it will be reproduced on paper made in the U.S.A. by a printing device made in Japan. The person writing it is wearing shoes made in Ireland, a sweater made in England, assorted cotton goods made in the U.S.A., and dental inlays of material mined in South Africa....[He] is appalled at the thought of how thoroughly his life may have been invaded by alien goods."

Baker is not alone. Both business and the good life are defined by access to a cornucopia of products and services. This is true not only at the consumer but the production level. Many of our steel, machine tools, and other components of production now routinely are imported. Even the American food industry has conformed. While a global grain glut has decimated farm exports, U.S. food imports have nearly doubled since 1980. We now are the world's second-largest food importer, at $24 billion worth annually.*

Increasingly the Pentagon, too, shops for and licenses technology abroad. Microchip, machine tool, and other essential supplies regularly must be acquired overseas. Japan, West Germany, Great Britain, and Israel, among others, all have been recruited for Star Wars research. Indeed, the Pentagon led a lobbying effort to end a Tokyo ban on use of Japanese technology in American weapons. The embargo finally was lifted.

"Co-production," says Marvin Cetron of Forecasting International, "is the latest [military] buzzword. To sell a squadron of fighters, the Pentagon is all too ready to hand part of the production job even to second- or third-tier countries such as Brazil, Spain, or Indonesia."

In technology, says Robert Reich, professor of political economy at Harvard, the ruling concept now is "techno-globalism." Scientific and technological independence, or "techno-nationalism," he says, is history. Techno-globalism now is our "central, albeit tacit, organizing principle for developing new technologies." Indeed, both "the notion of 'American' technology" and the idea of "uniquely American" corporate identities have become meaningless.

---

*Burger King alone imports six million pounds of beef a year from Costa Rica. Mexican growers, with American financing, provide about half our vegetables. Tropicana, Minute Maid, and other juice brands use fifty-fifty blends of Brazilian and American oranges.

"What's an 'American' firm?" asks Reich. "Suppose that a large and growing minority of the firm's shareholders are foreign, and 40 per cent of its employees live and work abroad? Does this firm qualify? (It's IBM.) Or consider an American-owned-and-managed firm that has factories and research laboratories around the globe....The questions grow even more tangled."

We think of ourselves—and have been thought of abroad—as preponderantly a nation of whites. But more than is generally realized, our ethnic complexion, too, is changing. The 1970s brought the largest immigration wave since the 1920s—some four million legal arrivals. In the 1980s this became a flood of some six million more "legals"—second only to the ten-year record 8.8 million of this century's first decade. This is the equivalent, in just two decades, of virtually another entire New England plus Oregon and Hawaii. Most of these new "huddled masses" were Asians and Hispanics.

Racially and ethnically, there is a new America. By about the year 2000, one of every three Americans will be nonwhite.* Already, Hispanics comprise some one-fifth of the Southwest and Pacific states' population. Nearly half of Florida's Dade County (Miami) and at least a fourth of New York, Los Angeles, and Houston is Hispanic. In half of our states, public enrollments are at least one-fourth nonwhite. All of our top two dozen largest city school systems have minority majorities. Without Asian and Hispanic employees, hospital support staffs, restaurant-kitchen work, domestic-help, fruit-harvesting, and other services would wheeze to a halt.

The fastest-growing racial group, accounting for about half of all recent legal immigration, is Asian.** By the mid-twenty-first century— looking forward, as close as 1930 is, looking backward—it will equal our Hispanic population. Arab and Iranian expatriates also are a swelling presence. This includes some 300,000 Palestinians—an estimated 50,000 in Michigan alone.

When will this great shift be translated into a nonwhite or Hispanic president? Who can say? But clearly, the 1988 Jesse Jackson phenomenon marked a political beginning, not an end.

Nearly a half-million foreign students are enrolled on American

---

*A decade later non-Hispanic whites will be a minority in California, metropolitan Miami, San Antonio, and elsewhere.

**In 1970-80 it more than doubled, to 3.5 million. By the year 2000 it will be equivalent to our black population of 1920.

campuses annually. A stroll through Harvard Yard, MIT, Caltech, or other elite universities is like a visit to the United Nations. Asians in particular stand out. This, too, represents a snowball of internationalization that will continue to roll. By the mid-1990s, a committee of the American Council on Education projects, one of every ten students in American higher education will be foreign.*

Like Europe in the nineteenth century, says French author Jean-Jacques Servan-Schreiber of *The American Challenge* fame, "America is becoming a university of the world."

What are the implications of these changes? To many Americans they are one more evidence of lost power—part of an inexorable demarcation from a halcyon era of national sovereignty and self-sufficiency, when we were the arbiters of our fate and masters of our future. But no more. Now, do not these changes demonstrate how we suddenly are mere pawns, at the mercy of foreign dictates and alien invaders?

Not really. As in other realms, except for our postwar Camelot, most such perceptions of past status are romanticized. Domestically, our history is one of major foreign economic presence and constant demographic assimilation and instability, especially in great cities and regions in transition. We tend to forget the foreign capital influxes and violence, economic and ideological conflicts, and developmental travails of the past. We also remain susceptible to much myth and exaggeration surrounding our globalization.

"America," we are told, "is being bought. Foreigners have gained control over our banking and financial systems, and possibly the U.S. Treasury. We're now dependent on them." Suppose they "pull the plug"?

June Collier of Montgomery, Ala., typifies this school. The president of an auto parts supplier called National Industries, she founded Citizens Against Foreign Control of America (CAFCA) as a kind of organizational Paul Revere. "When foreigners 'invest' in something," she declares, "they're buying control of your future." She advocates requiring every company on our soil to fly the flag of the country that owns it. "When the people can really see how much is owned by foreigners," she says, "they'll rise up and toss them out!"

What are the facts about this invasion?

The volume of foreign investment in the United States is indeed large,

*South and East Asia provide a third of current enrollees, and the Middle East approximately another third. No European country ranks in the top ten.

and growing. But to understand what this means, first one must consider the quantity of the acquisitions, or the dollars involved, in relationship to our economy as a whole. Second, the difference between passive assets, such as bonds or securities, and fixed physical assets, such as land or business and industrial enterprises.

Begin with the ominous specter of total dollar value of foreign investment here. In 1988, it was estimated at more than $1.5 trillion. This is a formidable figure—but in our mega-size economy, no more than 5 to 6 per cent of all American assets, estimated at $30 trillion.

Of the $1.5 trillion, about 80 per cent was in government and private securities—passive cross-border investment of a type common throughout the world. Among key private sector subcategories, foreign shares in our economy in 1986 were:

- Some 4 per cent ownership of American manufacturing;
- Some 1 per cent ownership of U.S. real estate and farmland;
- Some 5 per cent of total U.S. corporate earnings;
- Employment of some 4 per cent of the American work force.

What of the impact on U.S. industry? Foreign investments, an analysis by the Congressional Research Service notes, "have grown over the years, but their share of total U.S. economic activity remains small."

Infiltration of key industrial sectors? A *Fortune* compilation reveals no sectoral penetration remotely approaching the critical mass required for control, or even potential destabilization.* Neither the macro-size U.S. economy nor its immense and complicated sectors and companies are as susceptible to foreign penetration or manipulation as readily presumed. Smaller countries than we have adapted with alacrity to larger ratios of foreign money. In Western Europe, 15 per cent of jobholders work for foreign-owned companies—nearly four times our ratio. In West Germany alone, foreign-owned companies account for over 20 per cent of industrial production; in Canada, 50 per cent.

---

*The top ten sectors, with their foreign investment totals: manufacturing ($60.8 billion), petroleum ($28.1 billion), wholesale trade ($27.5 billion), real estate ($18.6 billion), banking ($11.5 billion), insurance ($11 billion), retail trade ($6.7 billion), finance ($4.7 billion), mining ($4 billion), other ($10 billion).

In foreign-owned firms' employment by industry group, petroleum and mining led, with nearly 20 per cent; manufacturing had 8 per cent; banking, 5.3 per cent.

"No one," says Anthony M. Solomon, former president of the Federal Reserve Bank of New York, who heads S.G. Warburg (U.S.A.), "seriously argues that foreign ownership has caused a "loss of control' in Belgium, West Germany, or Britain."

Nor, as alarmists contend, are "all bars down" and "all doors open." Foreigners are prohibited from owning U.S. television stations or airlines. The Federal Reserve must approve foreign investment in financial institutions. The president can disallow foreign acquisitions on national security grounds. All these provisions have been invoked, and will be again.

But what about the Japanese? Hasn't their invasion swelled to such magnitude that our economy might be "Japanized"? Hardly. An improvised trivia game illustrates:

Q. How many of the top ten foreign-owned firms in the United States in 1987 were Japanese?

A. One. According to a *Forbes* listing of the top one hundred, it was Mitsui & Co., which deals in feed additives and plastics.

Q. Where did it rank?

A. Eighth.*

Q. How many Japanese firms are in the next ten?

A. None.**

Q. Of the four top nationality groups in control of direct-foreign-owned assets in the United States, where do the Japanese rank?

A. Third—behind Great Britain and the Netherlands.***

---

*The top ten: Seagram Co. (Canada); Royal Dutch/Shell Group (Netherlands/U.K.); British Petroleum (U.K.); B.A.T. Industries Plc (U.K./Canada); Tengelmann Group (Germany); Unilever NV (Netherlands); Nestle (Switzerland); Mitsui & Co. (Japan); Petroleos de Venezuela SA (Venezuela); Regie Nationale des Usines Renault (France).

**The second ten: Philips NV (Netherlands); Hoechst AG (Germany); Campeau (Canada); Bayer AG (Germany); Volkswagenwerk AG (Germany); Group Bruxelles Lambert (Belgium); Hanson Trust Plc (U.K.); BASF Group (Germany); Anglo American of South Africa (South Africa/Bermuda/U.K.); and Bell Canada Enterprises (Canada).

***The British lead in overall U.S. direct investment (ownership of 10 per cent or more of a firm's assets, with $100 billion (1989 estimate by J.P. Morgan & Co.)— about double that of the Japanese, who rank close to the longtime number two Dutch. From 1984 to 1988, the British added $50 billion to their U.S. holdings, almost two-fifths more than Japan's $33 billion increase.

Because of their momentum and second rank among world economies, the Japanese are destined to lead in foreign-owned assets here. But they are not the buccaneers of popular image. Conditioned by a history of insularity and insecurity, they are extraordinarily sensitive about overreaching, either in finance or trade. They also are exceedingly selective in foreign ventures. Hence, their steps have been more measured and their footprints smaller here than generally surmised.

Theoretically, foreign buying of U.S. bank assets could make us vulnerable to outside financial subversion. In practice, hardly. By Congressional Research Service estimate, only about 4 per cent of U.S. bank assets are foreign owned. The Federal Reserve retains veto power over transfers to non-American ownership. We are not immune to recessions, depressions, or bank frauds and failures. But U.S. banking regulations, despite flaws, are more stringently enforced than those for almost any other industry, and both U.S. and world banking weathered crucial early international debt-crisis stages with remarkable resilience.

Even our sudden descent into mega-debt, though a domestic hazard, need not expose us to exploitation. Only about 10 per cent of our federal debt is foreign held. This and our size, economic vigor, and importance to creditors' own welfare provide built-in defenses. "The debt issue has been blown out of proportion, at least as a short-term constraint on American independence," *Financial Times* of London expert Anatole Kaletsky told me. "Nobody has the power to 'pull the plug' on America. Others need you more than you need them."

Actually, the alarms of economic xenophobes notwithstanding, our flood of foreign money arguably has proved beneficial. First, as essential "bridge" funding to help us maintain economic growth. Second, as a vote of confidence in our future—to which investors are inextricably tied. Shortly after taking office, Federal Reserve Chairman Alan Greenspan testified as much to Congress.

"I am very little concerned about the issue of foreign investment in the United States," he said. "Integration of world economies is a desirable trend. We will find that foreign investment in the United States will be a plus."

The case also has been made by Alexander Trowbridge, president of the National Association of Manufacturers. "Foreign investment," he says, "brings new jobs and new manufacturing and service capacity to our economy. Secondly, it helps us pay our trade and federal budget deficits. And thirdly, if we restrict unduly the foreign investment flow, we invite retaliation against American investment overseas, which is a very important asset that earns funds that come back to not only buy American exports but to help us in our balance of payments." Foreign investors, he adds, "have to obey the same laws American companies do" and "compete in our market."

Beyond all this, we should note, too, that simultaneous with the influx of foreign investors we continually have expanded our own economic empires abroad. By a huge margin we are the world's number one international investor in plants outside home borders.

Our empire of foreign direct investment through 1987 officially exceeded $309 billion—40 per cent of the world total—compared to $262 billion by foreigners in the United States.* Actually, a 1989 analysis by the Association for International Investment calculated based on Federal Reserve data, our assets probably exceed $785 billion, compared to $466 billion of foreign investment here. Due to quaint government accounting of our acquisitions at original cost—perhaps one-third of present market value—U.S. assets abroad almost always are egregiously understated.

Further, in the 1980s we continued to lead all others in the rate of foreign direct investment, with nearly a one-third increase through 1987.** In 1989, in Europe alone, Americans spent $15 billion on acquiring companies—nine times the total of the Japanese.

The pattern was set immediately after World War II, when our corporations opened more than six thousand foreign branches in just fifteen years. By the 1970s, IBM's overseas World Trade Corp. was generating nearly one-third of its revenue. Exxon was allocating over half of its investment, and almost two-thirds of its work force, to foreign activities. The Big Three auto-makers and other U.S. giants similarly moved abroad.

By the 1980s, one analysis noted, our industry had "transcended

---

*This is quadruple Japan's, which ranked fifth, behind Great Britain, West Germany, and the Netherlands.

**Calculated in SDRs (standard drawing rights) terms. Of our 1987 total, 18 per cent was invested in Canada, 15 per cent in Great Britain, 8 per cent in West Germany, 17 per cent in other European Community nations, 18 per cent in other developed countries, and 24 per cent in developing nations.

geography." Gillette, Woolworth's, Pfizer, Mobil, Citibank, and other large American enterprises were earning more than half of their profits overseas. Ford, ITT, Chrysler, Kodak, and Procter & Gamble deployed more than a third of their work forces abroad.*

This expansion has continued. In 1988 nearly 17 per cent of American corporate assets were abroad. Among individual corporations, GM's overseas manufacturing complexes, if a separate company, would be our twenty-second- largest firm. At Ford, nearly 60 per cent of production, and the majority of profits, now originate outside the United States. IBM, our largest non-petroleum industrial enterprise, reaps over half of its revenues from overseas. It is France's sixth-largest taxpayer and Britain's fifth-largest exporter. Citicorp has more than twenty-six thousand retail bankers in forty nations.

"The United States does not have an automatic call on our resources," says Cyrill Stewart, chief financial officer of the Colgate-Palmolive Co., whose foreign sales of soap, toothpaste, and other toiletries surpass those in the United States. "There is no mindset that puts this country first."

---

*Ford alone has 10,500 dealers in two hundred countries. In 1988 in Western Europe, where it employs 110,000 people and ranks number four in sales, it sold 11.5 per cent of the 12.5 million autos and 11.2 per cent of the 1.8 million trucks, and announced plans to expand into Eastern Europe and, through its Mazda affiliate, to sell more aggressively in Japan.

# 4

# *Economic Retreat—or Renewal?*

"All right," believers in decline then may say. "Suppose we are persuaded to accept all that. What about the new 'U.S. disease'? Aren't our living standards in retreat? Isn't our manufacturing capacity being decimated? Aren't we running out of jobs, except for low quality and low pay? And haven't we become uncompetitive? Tell me these are not signs of decline."

One might concur could these allegations be substantiated. But again, image and reality differ. The evidence suggests that a British commentator is correct: There is a "U.S. disease"—hypochondria.

The triple revolution of globalization, reindustrialization, and scientific/technological/cultural hyperchange is recasting our economic infrastructure. That is disruptive, but not necessarily tantamount to decline. Consider five propositions often advanced by declinists. All are largely myth.

## Myth #1
### Our Living Standards Are Falling

Return to our postwar Camelot. That is the seat of this myth. As previously noted, in just a quarter-century (1947-73), our GNP exploded upward and median family income approximately doubled. Historically, that is fantastic. The postwar recovery boom, national and international, raised all our boats as never before.

The boom ended in 1973 with a double shock: a Mideast War in which Egypt and Syria invaded Israeli-occupied land, and OPEC attempted to double crude-oil prices, to $6 a barrel. Giant Western oil companies, accustomed to dictating, refused. When the "hot war" cooled and oil sales resumed, they were on OPEC's terms—up to $30 a barrel. Import dependent for one-third of our oil, with expectations of permanently cheap energy, we instantly paid the price—an end to the great postwar industrial surge.

For more than a decade, real (inflation-adjusted) incomes in America stagnated. Our nadir was 1980-82, the deepest recession since the 1930s. Now we have returned to our long-term economic growth rate.

This is a comedown from Camelot. But living standards are not falling. In 1987-88, real income per person rose by $1,500, to a record $12,287 a year. Median family incomes and living standards for the middle class ($20-50,000 income) also have climbed.* Yet average American families feel caught in a vise. Why?

One reason is changed living-cost distribution. In Camelot housing was readily affordable for most. But cartelized wages and building codes, an amenities revolution, and other factors have ended that. Health-care, college, and other expenses also have surged.

Another shift is the new amenities base fostered by married women's working for pay (now over half).** Dependent on two incomes by necessity or preference, families push expectations and acceptable amenities minimums upward. Hence, the phenomena of an increasingly unachievable ante for "the game," of "working poor," and of "downwardly mobile" young.

On the whole these squeezes, including our widespread poverty, are less the fault of overall economic performance than of life style shifts and social policy. We generate sufficient national wealth, but misallocate—squander—it.

We are a high-consumption society. We equate spending with the good life. Many of us have lifted expectations and acquisitiveness to exceptional heights. Similarly, adverse poverty trends are partly attributable to an immigration flood of the poor—legal and illegal. This, like high military spending, tax and revenue distribution, and contracting social programs, reflects conscious national policies.

This is not to minimize new hardships. Technology-intensive, consumption-based norms make American life a high-overhead rat race—expensive, complex, and vastly different from, say, that in a less

---

*Median family income (inflation adjusted) was $28,880 in 1970, $28,996 in 1980, and $30,853 in 1987. Families in the middle ($20-50,000) class shrank. from 33.3 to 26.7 per cent over that period—but those over $50,000 increased, from 15.4 to 22.9 per cent. Families at $10-20,000 remained at some 19 per cent; and poor, about 12 per cent.

**Some twenty-nine million mothers aged 25-44—nearly a third more than in 1980—work for pay, with the fastest increase among those with toddlers under age 3. Women now attend college in record numbers, earning degrees at about the same rate as men. Married or single, motherhood or not, female graduates expect to pursue careers.

consumption-oriented Western Europe. For the middle class, getting ahead is a challenge; for the underclass, virtually impossible. But in large degree our most persistent problem is self-imposed—a set of untenable long-run social policies and economic choices.

## Myth #2
### We Are Being Deindustrialized

We repeatedly are admonished that we are "deindustrializing"— "retreating" from our core enterprises such as auto, steel, textiles, and electronics to services industries with mainly marginal pay and advancement. One book, *Manufacturing Matters: The Myth of the Post-Industrial Economy,* was built on the premise that we risk accepting such a shift.

But we are not deindustrializing. We are reindustrializing. As a ratio of gross national product—some 24 per cent—manufacturing has not changed for over three decades. The shift has been in the percentage of our work force engaged in production. Like that for farming, it consistently has fallen—and will continue to fall. Yet this has not decimated overall job potential in manufacturing. Through 1984 our total number of manufacturing jobs rose. Then it dipped—to some 8 per cent below its peak.

Our method of "saving" manufacturing industries has been automation and restructuring. Steel, autos, textiles, and other industries all have been streamlined: In 1987, for example, Ford made 10 per cent more cars than nine years earlier—with 47 per cent fewer production workers. Such pruning reached a peak in the mid-1980s when GM, in one restructuring, announced a cutback of 29,000 workers.*

Technology is driving all large industries toward computerized, automated, "flexible" manufacturing. With this, in the next two decades with no increase in industrial employment, our output is projected to double.

The pages of industrial history have turned. We do indeed live in a knowledge, or information, economy: what Alvin Toffler calls the Third Wave of technological development, following the First, affecting agriculture, and the Second, industry. The Third is built on computerization, automation, and other knowledge applications of electronics.

This means we must surmount a fixation on autos, steel, and other

---

* In mining, since World War II employment has fallen by 300,000 while production has risen by half. In textiles, yardage has remained constant despite cutting 550,000 jobs.

established smokestack industries as either an economic base or performance bellwether.* Electronics now is our largest industry, with some 2.5 million workers. Our computer industry alone exceeds autos or steel in employment. Based on 1988 stock value IBM—not GM or U.S. Steel (now USX Corp.)—is our richest nonpetroleum corporation.**

This is not the only primary change. Another is that increasingly it is not gigantic but small firms that create the most jobs. According to one study, from 1976 to 1984, while large manufacturers lost 300,000 jobs, firms with fewer than five hundred workers created 1.2 million. Another survey showed that companies with twenty or fewer employees generated nine-tenths of our net employment gains since 1981.

We are living out a scenario postulated by economist Joseph Schumpeter, that "creative destruction" is the engine of progress. Inexorably, we are gestating new industries that supersede others. *Forbes* magazine, in analyzing the fates of the top one hundred U.S. corporations over the past seventy years, charted this trend.

In most of those seven decades we achieved striking, sometimes stunning, economic growth. Yet only a handful of giants from America's 1917 roster survived as large independent companies.*** "Nothing," *Forbes* concluded, "is permanent...but change."

## Myth #3
### We Are Running Out of Jobs

But what about jobs? What has "creative destruction" done to employment? As most Americans know, the impact has been immense. But it has not resulted in fewer jobs.

Reports of layoffs and plant closings are not contrived: thirteen million jobs disappeared in 1980-86. But concurrently we created even more: twenty-five million—for a net gain of twelve million. This followed a net increase of 38.5 million in the previous fifteen years. In 1986 both

---

*Actually, though in earlier days the auto or steel industries were smokestack-era bellwethers, in aggregate they never employed more than 1.5 per cent of our work force.

**In the early 1980s it employed nearly 400,000 persons worldwide.

***Among the deceased were Baldwin Locomotive, Studebaker, steel and coal giants, and other smokestack powers of their day.

Approximately as *Forbes'* report went to press, in a fitting footnote, RCA also vanished, engorged by General Electric. Over the previous six years GE had pared its work force by 100,000, sold its consumer small-appliance business, and gravitated toward high technology and services, which now provide 70 per cent of its profits.

total U.S. employment (114 million) and the percentage of the working-age population with jobs (62 per cent) set records.

No other industrial nation has approached this pace. "The Europeans," says Janet L. Norwood, commissioner of the Bureau of Labor Statistics, "consider this a miracle." This is no exaggeration. One reads and hears such sentiments throughout Western Europe.

We are not running out of jobs. Technology has an infinite capacity to create more. But this is obscured. Drama, conflict, pathos—plant closings, farm bankruptcies, job dislocations—are the coin of media and political discourse.

Yet the promise of new discoveries and whole new high-technology industries is equally stunning. The impact of just one discovery, the transistor, illustrates. Developed by Bell Labs in 1947, it spawned a worldwide, $32 billion, still-expanding semiconductor industry.

Though its economic fallout has been global, we are the prime beneficiaries. In one Department of Labor study of seventeen high-growth U.S. manufacturing industries, five are "principal users" and three "significant users" of semiconductors. This did not happen overnight, nor with headlines or TV specials tracing the drama. (Nor, incidentally, did Bell Labs, with its patent licensing, reap even a substantial share of the fruits of its discovery. Nor was hand-wringing over piracy or giveaways then in fashion—this was basic science.)

Consider also superconductivity. The first successful flexible, current-carrying ceramic-wire "superconductor" was fabricated by the Argonne National Laboratory and Bell Labs in 1987. Argonne's director compared it to the laser or transistor in capacity to "spawn a whole industry or series of industries."* Except in the business and science/technology presses, the story quickly faded.

All about us, scientific progress is accelerating. Materials science, for example, is advancing so fast that one can identify a need and then create a material to meet it. Some chemists never set foot in a wet lab of beakers and test tubes. They conduct their experiments at computers.

Using computers, chemists and polymer scientists formulate new "super-plastics" that are superseding steel in buildings, oil rigs, aircraft,

---

*Among the potential by-products: cheaper power transmission, off-peak energy generation and storage, nuclear or solar power plants far from populated areas, mini-computers, and fast-levitating trains.

and autos. Thus by the year 2000 we may have super-plastic cars that
weigh only one thousand pounds and can stay in service over twenty years.
A National Academy of Sciences study predicts other breakthroughs:

- In telecommunications, speech processing by computer to enable
automated voice dialing or translation, and optical communications
channels that will greatly reduce the cost of transmitting information.
- In biotechnology, new vaccines, therapeutics, diagnostics,
delivery systems, transplants, and gene therapy, also affecting animal
agriculture.
- For crops, advances in soil inoculants, plant testing, genetical-
ly engineered seeds, and biocontrol agents for insects and weeds.

Technology, which consistently generates more jobs than it destroys,
is only part of the equation. By the late 1990s, due to lower birthrates,
we and other industrial societies will face severe labor shortages.* Its
beginnings already are apparent, in fewer and often lower-qualified candidates for entry-level jobs than in recent memory—a shift, as the Bureau
of Labor Statistics' New York regional director put it, "from Baby Boom
to Baby Bust."

## Myth #4
### We Are Creating a Low-Pay, Low-Quality Job Market

Most of our new jobs, as has been freely headlined, were in services.
"Ah, yes," declinists may say, "and therein is part of our problem." Services: the "s" word—so easily pronounced with a hiss. "Here, indeed,
lies the downward road."

There are two flaws in this response. One is that, as we have seen,
services growth is a concomitant of mature industrial economies. All
are heading in the same direction. Just as manufacturing supersedes
agricultural employment in importance, so the services sector ultimately supersedes both. The second problem is a misconception about services' growth. It does not, as some critics warn, portend workplace
doom—a "Taco Bell economy" in which we serve one another fast food
or punch checkout cash registers.

---

* In 1979-86, the number of Americans aged sixteen to twenty-four dropped from
thirty-seven to thirty-four million—and, despite the influx of women into the work place,
total workers entering our labor market now are the lowest in forty years.

It is true that more than half of the new jobs created in 1970-80 were in low-skill, low-pay categories. Many also were part-time or temporary, especially in services.* But beware of stopping there. In isolation such facts mislead.

First, as to skills and pay: A high-technology economy changes the entire job market. Skills, not simple strength, dexterity, or assembly-line endurance, command the priorities. Increasingly, in both manufac-turing and services, jobs go to the specifically trained—who may be paid well. More than ever, upward mobility depends on this and a willingness to move.

Second, as to part-time and temporary jobs: We have a two-gender job market. Many women, especially young mothers, prefer part-time jobs. Most full-time students have little choice. Employers, in quest of maximum flexibility and minimum benefits obligations, are pleased to comply. Ergo, inevitable growth in that realm.

High-skill, high-pay jobs are not scarce. On the contrary. In 1970-80, over one-fourth of the new jobs were the more prestigious professional and manager/administrative.** Indeed, a National Academy of Engineer-ing (NAE) study showed, much of the services sector's growth over the past decade occurred in the better-paid professional categories.

Services are not only what we readily assume: fast-food, cleaning, and cashier jobs. They also encompass education, health, financial, business, communications, transportation, lodging, and professional fields—legal, engineering, accounting, and the like. In short, almost everything but manufacturing, mining, and farming. Many, in fact, are performed inside firms in the latter fields but, in tabulations, are misclassified.

Services should not, the NAE study emphasizes, be a dirty word, either from an individual or national perspective. They offer a variety of op-portunities without the monotony, danger, and other detriments of jobs they replace. More than goods-producing industries, they inhibit reces-sion. They consistently have shown a positive trade balance and, despite lags in productivity growth, generally respond to technological

---

*Along with self-employed and illegal immigrant "contingent" workers, part-time/tem-poraries now exceed one-fourth of our work force.

**Three—executives/administrators/managers, technicians and support employees, and professional workers—proliferated faster than sales and administrative support and clerical workers.

innovation—in some cases spectacularly—when the investment is deemed worthwhile.*

We have a vast head start in services competitiveness—including productivity levels in most fields that exceed Japan's. "We should not," the study concludes, "fear an economy dominated by services."

What we should fear is failing to understand the long-term implications of our economic evolution. For it is not a Taco Bell, but a four-level economy, with a shrunken blue-collar middle segment, that is evolving. Sociologist Daniel Bell describes these tiers as: upper middle class: professional/managerial workers (25 per cent); middle class: technical/administrative support (35 per cent); service class (25 per cent); underclass: menial labor, odd jobs, unemployed (15 per cent).

At the high end of this structure, says Congress' Office of Technology Assessment (OTA), "technical and professional workers, many of them in computer-related occupations, can expect high earnings and ample opportunity to move upward." Our problem, as we shall discuss, is a counterpart group the OTA sees as "stuck at the bottom." Its racial and geographical characteristics: In largest proportion, says Bell, "black and non-Cuban Hispanic. The concentrations in the several states and the central cities...will provide an explosive mixture."

## Myth #5
### We Have Become Uncompetitive

We long have been the archetypical unchallenged industrial Nation of Big Shoulders. But a 1970s flood of Asian imports, plant closings, layoffs, and a swelling trade gap obliterated that image. "Competitiveness" became a buzzword—one, many of us believed, with negative connotations. We had, many became convinced, become uncompetitive.

What did this mean? We never stopped to define it.** To most Americans, it meant high productivity*** that translated into low or competitive prices.

---

*Over three decades through 1980, while manufacturing employment fell by 8.3 per cent during recessions, services grew more than 2 per cent. Because wages in services are translated into goods purchases, they help reduce the length and depth of recessions in manufacturing. They also provide a major market for capital products.

**To the President's Commission on Industrial Competitiveness, it meant "the degree to which a nation can, under free and fair market conditions, produce goods and services that meet the test of international markets while simultaneously maintaining or expanding the real incomes of its citizens."

***Defined by economists as "output value divided by total hours worked."

The prevailing impression was that our productivity lagged. But the President's Commission on Industrial Competitiveness, headed by Hewlett-Packard chief John M. Young, in 1985 said not. Many nations, it acknowledged, have "consistently outstripped" the United States in raising productivity. But in absolute terms in 1973-83 we remained "the most productive of the world's major economies"—and in 1983-84 we recorded new gains. Since then our productivity has continued upward. In 1989 *Fortune* estimated it at $33,000 in gross national product per worker—by far the world's largest—compared to $24,000 in 1960.

Even two customary icons of the growth field, Japan and West Germany, suffer by comparison. In a 1987 analysis published by the Federal Reserve Bank of Boston, Japan's 1984 manufacturing productivity was only 93 per cent of ours; Germany's, 90 per cent. In 1986 U.S. productivity growth in manufacturing outpaced that of nine other major industrial nations.* Because our economy has operated at full speed since the 1950s while others accelerated later, *Fortune* explained in its 1989 assessment, recent years' comparisons "made U.S. productivity appear worse than it was."

This does not mean that productivity cannot or must not be improved. It does mean that, rhetoric to the contrary, we are not the productivity klutzes of popular image. Indeed, in manufacturing productivity, we are thoroughbreds.

What about our massive trade gap? Doesn't this signify un-competitiveness? Yes and no. Again, our economic capacity and our policies for managing it must be differentiated. We unquestionably spend far more on imports than our experts earn—by over $100 billion a year. This is our official trade deficit. But it is not a measure of what we sell abroad.

First, of course, we sell conventional exports. Over the past two decades, as global trade has grown, so have our exports. They remain a stable share—some 17 per cent—of all world exports. But second, remember our companies' vast complex of foreign subsidiaries and affiliates. We also sell through them. Yet their sales do not count as U.S. exports. In the same period their share of world sales, compared to those of others' overseas companies, shot upward by about a third.

---

*A rate of 3.5 per cent per hour for us, compared, for example, to 1.8 per cent in Japan and 1.9 per cent in France and West Germany. But since all nine major industrial nations share in technological advances and product innovations, productivity for all is expected to keep converging.

Indeed, in 1985 our foreign affiliates' sales ($835 billion) exceeded the value of all exports from our shores by over three to one. Had these "overseas-based exports" been counted as U.S. trade, that year's deficit ($148.5 billion) would have been a surplus ($151.4 billion)! This is uncompetitiveness?

The mirror image is exports from our soil by foreign-owned plants. Since these originate here, they are U.S. "exports." In 1987 they accounted for nearly one-tenth of our manufactured-export sales. This is more than all the goods we sold to a main trading partner, West Germany.

But what about the publicized declining ratios of output and trade in individual industries such as autos? These mean that such industries are shrinking, correct? Las Vegas should offer such choices. When the whole is expanding, a decline in shares can mean absolute gains.

Take the auto industry. In 1960 we produced 52 per cent of the world's cars; in 1980, 23 per cent. But in that period the industry mushroomed. Thus, our auto business, instead of shriveling, actually expanded—by 300,000 cars.* This is regression? Not in sales.

Then there is high-technology trade. Again, we are regaled about decline: From 1962 to 1978, our export share among all industrialized countries fell by one-fourth (from 30 to 22 per cent). But again, the whole expanded and so did our absolute totals—so greatly that the U.S. high-technology trade balance rose eightfold.

In analyses by the OTA, we remain overwhelmingly this sector's world leader, with pluses far surpassing minuses. The London School's Prof. Susan Strange notes:

- "Of the largest corporations producing computers, the top six are American, as are twelve of the top twenty....They produce 62.3 per cent of total world production and have over 50 per cent of world [sales]...,
- "[In] integrated circuits, Texas Instruments and IBM are the leading world producers, even ahead of the Japanese.
- "In telecommunications...AT&T and ITT are the top two...in sales...
- "[In aircraft], six of the top nine companies, including the two largest, are American....

---

*When the world market was 12.8 million units, we produced 6.65 million. When it rose to 30 million, our sales also rose, to 6.9 million.

- "[In pharmaceuticals], the corporations with the biggest research budgets...and three of the largest five companies are American."

This tumultuous field is one industrial tide of the future. But because it is so unsettled, status reports are deceptive. After a robust birth, for instance, our microchip industry lost $2 billion and twenty-five thousand jobs in nearly three years. This meant its death knell, right?

Wrong. Births, mergers, shifts to advanced chips, and a research consortium, Sematech, spurred a renaissance. Now we have a new-wave chip industry organized—but not stabilized (no industry can be)—along more global lines. In a 1988 compilation by *Fortune*, four of the world's top seven chipmakers—and seven of the largest fifteen—remained American, a status that, in such an unstable field, could not last, but amid competitiveness jeremiads were surprising nonetheless.*

For all our industrial sector's faults, our greatest competitiveness problem arguably has not been the fault of industry, but government. The Reagan administration's super-Keynesian policies, for example, created the high dollar that suddenly inflated the prices of all our exports by half. This tied the hands of American management and workers. Our overseas markets shrank. Imports and foreign investment cascaded in. Our trade deficit escalated.

The problem was public policy, not industrial, uncompetitiveness. After the administration began reigning in deficits and persuaded our economic partners to help lower the dollar, our products almost instantly regained competitiveness. Our trade deficit began to shrink. With many firms newly downsized, automated, and globalized, a hum returned to American industry—and to our economy.

This hum will rise—though never again to Camelot levels—as the dollar, to reflect new global economic equilibriums, slips lower and as American business becomes more export minded. These are two keys to reducing our trade deficit. Another, farm exports, alas now is passe amid global plenty.

Other equally important ones lie in the trade-balance segment rarely discussed: imports. Here, too, the picture is complex. One reason is

---

*This has not eliminated boom-bust cycles. Like many young industries, it changes so fast that many company and product half-lives are short. It also made the error of overspecializing in supplying of personal-computer manufacturers, rather than the diversifying as Europeans and Japanese have done. That, too, is changing.

a new factor in trade-gap analysis: imports from ourselves. U.S. corporations' foreign affiliates and subsidiaries that sell abroad sell to us. By 1985 they accounted for 60 per cent of our trade deficit.*

Then there is the impact of two arcane categories: capital goods and oil. Autos, videocassette recorders, and other high-visibility consumer products get the publicity. But capital goods—robots, machine tools, and other production components—and industrial supplies accounted for over half of our 1980s trade deficits. And by 1989 oil was the fastest-rising contribution to our negative balance, accounting for about one-third.

Realistically, we can do little to change the imports to ourselves, capital goods/industrial supplies, or other non-oil imports. But we can, and must, reduce oil imports.

The most obvious way is by conservation. We could abet that, and help reduce our federal deficit, with a stiffer gasoline tax. But we are obsessed with cheap gasoline. With our Gatsby sensibility of the 1980s, we also prefer not to confront the deficit.

Our cheap-oil fixation bemuses our foreign friends. Especially many of the most gifted cartoonists abroad. Daily, one confessed, he faces West, rather than East, in gratitude for such unending eccentricities. This one is irrational, of course. For in truth our oil-import dependency is not cheap at all.

Like an anguished opera heroine, we have ritualized a beating of breasts in lament over uncompetitiveness, an economic squeeze, and loss of national independence. Then, at the moment of truth, in the splendid traditions of the most fickle divas, we resist renouncing the profligacy that at once makes us less competitive, prosperous, and vulnerable to blackmail by the villain.

The villain, in burnoose, whom we all remember from an earlier act, waits patiently in the wings, rubbing his hands with glee, as our oil-dependency mounts. When it reaches 50 per cent in the early 1990s, once again a morality lesson will be played out: The comely heroine, by her prodigality, will have brought new suffering upon herself.

---

*This included nearly half of our $22 billion trading deficit with Canada. Two of Taiwan's four leading exporters—RCA (GE) and AT&T—are American, both producing heavily for the U.S. market. IBM, with eighteen thousand employees in Japan, long has ranked as that country's number-one exporter of computers, also largely to us. Indeed, one-fifth of our multinationals' imports into the United States are entirely intracompany trade, from affiliates.

# 5

# *Future Has-Beens?*

What, then, can we conclude about our economic structure and international power position? Measured against the atypical blip of our postwar Camelot or chances for imperial-age hegemony, both have slipped. But this is the Global Age. Modern-Age imperial criteria no longer define the power-status-progress game. The triple revolution has ordained that.

Fortunately for us the new game and new rules are far from adverse to our interests. Indeed, they portend not merely promising, but exciting, prospects. For, notwithstanding our perceptions of decline, we stand on the threshold of a potentially golden era. As former secretary of state George Shultz put it, "We have a winning hand. We just have to play it."

That hand now includes:

- The world's largest and richest economy;
- Leadership of the most prosperous alliance of nations;
- Internationally ascendant ideals of individual and marketplace freedom;
- A currency that dominates, and will remain prominent in, the world economy;
- The language in which the world communicates;
- Ranking mastery of modern living, working, governing, and thinking on a macroscale;
- The most powerful national influence culturally on the planet.

Anyone who doubts these points need only examine global politics and economics from other nations' perspective. Or travel in a variety of countries, eavesdrop on their media, and discourse with their opinion-leaders. Or sample global cultural phenomena—from popular music, films, and TV to the omnipresent Coca-Cola, McDonald's, or teenage life-styles and fashion fads. If this does not reveal an overwhelming American presence—for better or worse (often both)—you need a perception check.

Japanese billboards may line Manhattan's Times Square and Los Angeles' freeways, and hotels abroad may be crammed with West European, Asian, and other canny businessmen. But no other influence approaches the Americanization of the world. Chicago *Tribune* financial editor Richard Longworth's experience while a correspondent in Europe is typical:

> My plane, a Boeing 737 of Belgium's Sabena Airlines, lands at Brussels Airport. I collect my baggage in an arrival hall, where the advertising signs (ITT, Chase Manhattan, Ramada Inn, Coke) are in English, although Belgium's two languages are French and Dutch. I pass up Hertz and Avis, hail a cab, and ride into the city past buildings owned by IBM, Goodyear, 3M, Culligan, and Champion Sparkplugs, past a Holiday Inn,...past the Shell garage, Kodak store, and Levi's shop, past my neighborhood supermarket (owned by J.C. Penney), and I'm home.
>
> Nearly every European city has its Sheraton and Hilton, its McDonald's and Colonel Sanders....More than a million of us are here, including soldiers. We probably should start thinking of this phenomenon as permanent.

We should. Others do. Raymond Georis, the secretary general of the European Cultural Foundation, for one, confided that one of his teenage children worked for an American-franchised fast-food outlet in the Netherlands.

"There's no point resisting," he said. "These places exist. They're popular. They provide a marvelous experience. We might as well draw from them what we can."

A flight over the United States makes a mirror-image point to Longworth's. Hour after hour, one's airliner passes over huge urban complexes, massive highway networks, sprawling industrial plants, car-choked parking lots, vast airports, ship-clogged waterways, immense bridges, and bountiful crops—not in the fragmented or small scale of elsewhere but in an endless profusion. Brazil, the Soviet Union, China, and India may emulate the vastness, but not the development. There is nothing else like it.

On the ground the sensation is similar. Industries, offices, shopping centers, apartment complexes, mansions, bungalows, schools, parks, highways, interchanges—again, all in infinite profusion. It is awesome, incredible, unique. We are the Paul Bunyan of nations. In the competition ahead, as one foreign commentator observed, we begin "with by far the biggest guns and the greatest stores of ammunition." Comparative data bear this out. Take several fields certain to be key determinants of global-age power.

First, science and technology prowess. We are the reigning superpower in science and technology. "In size and importance of the scientific establishment the U.S. now leads by far," as John Maddox of Britain's prestigious *Nature* told me in a far-ranging international science assessment. "Europe—including Britain—is next. Japan is obviously in third place. The Soviets are nowhere.

"The Japanese are superb workers but they lag in creativity. India is on the move. It is hard to be confident about China because it is so ideologically organized. In Latin America several countries—Brazil, for example—always have maintained a high quality of research in narrow fields like pharmacology. They have never applied even rudimentary physical science to industrial production, probably because their universities are poorly run. As monitors of the permissible and as engines of change, universities are crucial."

But more than formal education is involved. "In the U.S.," he added, "education is lackadaisical, inexpert, and dismissive of the idea that students have anything to learn. But in spite of the muddle there are many exceedingly bright young graduates. You have taken over science. And the American engineer is remarkably inventive compared with an engineer in Germany or Japan. That comes more from fixing hotrods than from formal education."

The evidence of our leadership is impressive:

- Since World War II, U.S. scientists have won more Nobel prizes (127) than the Europeans (98) and Japanese (5) together.
- Americans obtain more patents than the rest of the world combined.
- Americans write more than a third of all scientific and technical articles published.
- Government organizations such as the National Institutes of Health in Washington and Department of Energy labs in the West lead in defining frontiers in molecular biology, theoretical physics, and computer science.

- Some one hundred American research universities, which perform more than 60 per cent of the nation's basic science, are regarded as world-class—a resource nucleus unmatched elsewhere.
- Our research and development expenditures—$123 billion in 1987—are the world's highest.
- In the decade 1976-86, the National Science Foundation calculates, our cadre of scientists more than doubled, to 2.1 million.

This proliferation will continue, with immense impact. But so will others' progress. In 1965 we accounted for about 70 per cent of research-and-development outlay by the five-largest non-Communist spenders; twenty years later this had fallen to 55 per cent.* In basic research—tomorrow's technology—the Japanese, formerly marginal funders, now commit virtually the same ratio of research-and-development spending (12 per cent) to basic science as we do. West Germany allocates nearly twice that proportion.

The scale—and cost—of basic research is growing. But if anything this favors the United States. No single institution, and few if any other nations, alone could mount such megaprojects as a $4.4 billion atomic supercollider and other American programs—certainly not simultaneously. Our vast resources remain an inherent advantage.

The challenge is to maximize them, and this we are doing in unprecedented new partnerships among business, academia, and foreign companies. Despite historic inhibitions, for example, universities have opened funding doors to corporations—whose direct research support has tripled since 1980. At Carnegie-Mellon, one-fourth of the $100 million research budget comes from industry. At MIT and elsewhere, industrial support also has grown exponentially.

Potential conflicts of interest are worrisome, C. K. Gunsalus, associate vice chancellor for research at the University of Illinois, told the American Association for the Advancement of Science's 1990 annual meeting, but she and counterparts elsewhere have concluded that they must be risked. Indeed, she said, reduced federal research grants, the value of exposing students and faculty to real-world problems, and the importance of academic research to economic growth and competitiveness portend more such arrangements.

---

*Japan's share more than tripled (to 22 per cent). West Germany's doubled, to 11 per cent. Great Britain's fell by half, to rank with France at some half of Bonn's.

Increasingly, universities commercialize selected fruits of their research. The University of Utah, for instance, shares in more than two dozen ventures (including marketing of the Jarvik-7 artificial heart), and the Baylor College of Medicine participates in five businesses. In one year MIT obtained stock in six research spinoffs, and Harvard and the University of Chicago, among others, have venture-capital funds related to their own staffs' research. Despite trade-offs in independence, again, all sides expect the trend to grow.

Jointly funded institutes also are proliferating, including university-affiliated research parks such as Triangle in North Carolina and Technipark in Kansas. Under a 1984 easing of anti-trust restrictions for research collaboration, more than fifty commercial research consortia have been formed, in fields from biotechnology to telecommunications. One, Sematech, in semi-conductors, received a $100 million Congressional appropriation—nearly half its budget.

"A first-rate lab," says William L. Miller of the Stanford Research Institute, now "is too productive to belong to any one company."

The next plateau is multinational research, or techno-globalism. Here, too, our institutions are pivotal. Dozens of foreign firms, especially Japanese, support U.S. campus labs, including endowed professorships.* More than fifty Japanese companies pay up to $100,000 a year simply to participate in various university programs that preview papers before publication or offer other inside lab access. Among American companies, IBM in particular funds extensive research abroad, including over fifteen hundred researchers in Yamamoto City, Japan.

Space activity also is being internationalized, including a team space station to which the United States has committed some $12 billion, and Western Europe, Japan, and Canada up to $1 billion each. During the 1980s, NASA, Europe's Ariane, and the Soviet and Chinese space programs all sold payload launches to other nations, with India and Japan not far behind.

Even before the cold war died, Soviet-Western science cooperation—now obviously destined to grow—also took quiet root, to the parties' mutual benefit. "There may be a perception that the West gives knowledge to the Soviet Union and gets nothing back," says Michael Kenward of the *New Scientist* of London, "but the Tokamak Fusion Test Reactor

---

*At MIT this includes sixteen chairs, at some $1.5 million each, sponsored by Japanese firms such as Toyota, Fujitsu, Matsushita, TDK, and NEC.

at Princeton University is not called Tokamak for nothing; that is a Russian name for a design that came out of the Soviet Union."

A second prerequisite for Global Age power is a strong economy based on globalized industry. Here again our advantages are awesome. The Japanese have recorded impressive strides in globalization: Some 4 per cent of their industrial production now is overseas. By 1993 it may reach 8 per cent—and at least double that in autos, electronics, and selected other categories. Some sixty thousand Japanese live in metropolitan New York City, and at least ten thousand more in metropolitan London. Other Japanese colonies are growing.

But our economy and population are twice the size of Japan's, and we remain the undisputed globalization leader. In *Fortune*'s 1989 list of leading world industrial corporations, nineteen of the top fifty are American. These include six of the top ten.* All are exceedingly active overseas, and all are in the process of extending their global tentacles. This is apparent from continuing strong investment by American firms abroad—a record $22.6 billion net in 1987, for example, despite the weak dollar.**

Our percentage of corporate assets abroad surpasses that of virtually any other industrial nation—and is over triple Japan's. U.S. giants such as IBM, Ford, GM, and Motorola, which obtain more than a third of their revenues abroad, are only a vanguard, in both direct investment and joint ventures abroad. Over two thousand involving American firms now are recorded in Europe alone. Besides auto, electronics, and other partnerships noted, these include telecommunications, pharmaceutical, and scores of services ventures.

Europe's 1992 single-market target is one reason. There jockeying for status entails both expansion of owned assets plus joint ventures. Coca-Cola, for instance, has commissioned one of the world's largest bottling plants in France; AT&T, a $220 million semiconductor plant in Spain; and GE, a $1.7 million plastics factory in Spain and joint ventures in major appliances and electrical equipment with Great Britain's biggest electronics company. Among other major joint ventures, IBM and German giant Siemens cooperate in development and marketing of memory chips, and AT&T has acquired a one-fourth interest in Olivetti, which

---

*The six are: GM, Ford, Exxon, IBM, GE, and Mobil.

**Most of that consisted of our foreign affiliates' profits (never converted to dollars) reinvested outside our borders, mainly in Europe.

produces over $250 million in exports for sale here under the AT&T label.*

Developing nations' demand for services and high technology will further spur American overseas expansion. In 1990, according to one forecast, our services exports will surpass 1987's by over 60 per cent, quadrupling their surplus posted five years earlier. Here again we are destined to continue to lead.

"The U.S.," says Claude Barfield, supervisor of a study for the American Enterprise Institute, "tends to have comparative advantage in any area where the technological component is large."

International transportation—nearly one-third of our services account—is forecast to remain strong. Since fifteen of the largest software companies are American, and they obtain 20 to 40 per cent of their revenues abroad, that future also looks bright. Growing markets in office automation and temporary help further favor U.S. companies, which earn up to half their profits from abroad. Demand for American construction, health-care, and insurance expertise also continues to grow.

"As total world trade in services expands," a *Fortune* report titled "The Bright Future of Service Exports" concludes, "the U.S. may well find itself holding a somewhat smaller share of a much bigger pie." In absolutes, this means more—not less.

Meanwhile, we continue to reindustrialize at home. Here, despite pessimistic scenarios, a corner already has been turned. A few years ago the Great Lakes states, where I spent much of my life, were slow-growth, semi-depressed areas nicknamed "the Rust Belt." Layoffs, plant closings, and loss of population were endemic. Today all are stabilizing, with restructuring around downsized, efficient, automated, heavy industry and expanding high-technology and services suppliers attracted by its stable infrastructure and vast university complexes. Ohio and Michigan, which were losing population, showed net increases in the 1980s.

Michigan's example is especially impressive. In 1982 this longtime

---

*The Whirlpool Corp., Sara Lee, and Citicorp are among other aggressive players. Whirlpool has committed $60 million to 53 per cent ownership of the $2 billion appliance arm of Philips NV of the Netherlands; Sara Lee, $250 million for a Dutch coffee/tea firm plus purchase of pantyhose giant Dim of Paris; and Citicorp, which has eighteen thousand employees in Europe, multimillions to buy banks in Italy, Belgium, and Spain and introduce credit cards in West Germany, Belgium, and Greece.

auto-producing capital of the world had lost one-fourth of its manufacturing jobs in four years and recorded 17 per cent unemployment. By
1988, through reindustrialization it had regained fifty nine thousand high-
bracket factory jobs, created thousands in services, and cut unemployment to 7.6 per cent. This record is being replicated elsewhere. Further, it is being done with ecologically advanced processes—a costly
step most other nations have yet to take.

Within a decade, when early economic scar tissues have healed, we
may conclude that the Japanese and other Asian "tigers" were providential
catalysts—shocking us into reindustrializing for a new age.

A third requisite for Global Age power is geopolitical leverage. Here,
too, more than American public dialogue reflects, we remain the
heavyweight—more securely in the captain's chair than at any time since
the cold war's escalation. Our philosophy of democratic government and
human rights has become ascendant—heralding what one American, in
the hyperbole so disdained by more sober Europeans, pronounced to
be "the end of history."

Democracy's ascent is no accident. Logic dictates it; globalization imposes it. Surrounded by modern technology and entwined in economic
interdependence, no nation, regardless of rulers' fiats, can remain isolated.

The industrialization imperative is universal. Trade, tourism, and electronic communications can pierce any curtain. Transistor radios can be
concealed. TV dish antennas—100,000 in Mexico alone—provide anyone
within satellite range a television smorgasbord. In many authoritarian
nations audio and videocassettes serve as underground books.* In China,
phone-linked facsimile machines became substitute newspapers.

President Reagan's visit to Moscow marked the cold war's coda; the
fall of the Berlin Wall and East European Communism, the dawn of
post-postwar geopolitics. Communism as a viable ideology is dead; the
Soviet Union, for all its latent power, an unmasked Potemkin village,
culturally Balkanized, politically repressed, economically regressive.
Rent by ethnic conflicts, its destiny now is to resist self-destruction.

Kremlin hawks, like their minority of American counterparts, remain

---

*Audiocassettes from the Ayatollah Khomeini, smuggled from his exile in France,
helped bring down Iran's shah. Videocassette recorders—more than 100 million
worldwide—permeate even the Soviet Union. Poland has VCR clubs, some, as elsewhere
in Eastern Europe, featuring politics, others pornography. About nine-tenths of Saudi
Arabian TV homes have VCRs.

threats to a constructive international participation. But here again, the "objective circumstances," in Marxist terminology, leave the Kremlin little maneuvering room, with the United States holding the high cards: military, economic, demographic, technological, and political.

Inexorably, both nations must shift from superpower confrontation to world-order politics. That is, concern with issues less related to bilateral than multilateral welfare. The German unification question is one example. More than the Japanese "threat," it promises to be the West's Great Issue of the early 1990s. Mishandled, it could jeopardize the carefully nurtured postwar European power balance, the European Community's 1992 formula for global competitiveness, and East European as well as Soviet economic resuscitation. In the early months of unification dialogue, at least, Soviet-U.S. cooperation gave reason for cautious optimism.

Other areas for U.S.-Soviet cooperation include avoiding destabilization among developing nations. This translates into global economic development, human rights, territorial integrity, arms restraints, and containing religious extremism, drug traffic, population growth, ecological despoliation, and other legacies of the dying age.

This is an American agenda. We will continue to progress in promoting it, not by fiat or other bygone imperial prerogatives, but by Global Age power brokering. As the planet's most influential power, allied to other economic and geopolitical influentials—all interdependent—we can expect more than a minor share of successes.

Contrary to most impressions, this appears to be what Henry Luce envisioned when, in a 1941 *Life* editorial, he proclaimed "the American Century." The phrase usually is misconstrued to mean American hegemony. But Luce defined it as "our opportunity as the most powerful and vital nation...to exert upon the world the full impact of our influence." This, he said, would make "the twentieth century, if it is to come to life in any nobility of health and vigor,...be to a significant degree an American century."

The Global Age, then, offers a historic opportunity for leadership in a new American century.

# 6

# *Japan as Supernation*

An "American century?" ask the skeptics. What about Japan? No nation preoccupies us more. We are obsessed, haunted, traumatized by the Japanese. Many Americans—and some Japanese—see Japan as a kind of supernation, unique in culture and immune to the forces shaping other societies. Is it?

Listen first to historian Paul Kennedy. In *The Rise and Fall of the Great Powers,* he observes that nations tend to stabilize at natural power positions directly related to their population and economic resources. Great Britain, following the colonial era, settled into a natural power position consonant with its share of world GNP: about 4 per cent. By the same criterion the United States for some years will wield power based on at least 16 to 18 per cent of world GNP—well ahead of any other single nation, and expanding with international economic growth. Japan, a great power before World War II, is producing about one-tenth of global output, or slightly more than before the war.

Should its postwar ascent, then, surprise us? In hindsight, no. Nor does Japan merit the image of a supernation. As West Germany's Helmut Schmidt, the London School's Susan Strange, Harvard's Samuel Huntington, and others remind us, in Huntington's words it "has neither the size, natural resources, military strength, diplomatic affiliates, nor most important, the ideological appeal to be a twentieth-century superpower."

Given Global Age constraints on military conquest, it arguably is nearing its natural level of relative power. For all its dynamism, Japan is not immune to the forces working on other industrial nations. On the contrary.

Competition is proliferating for it as well as us. Domestic challenges impend. For various reasons, we have allowed a thoroughly logical and, in hindsight, predictable American-aided postwar recovery drama to become a horror thriller starring a latex Godzilla. Reflexively, we fixate on this monster's threatening qualities—its power, opportunism, and threats to perceived American interests—while ignoring other traits, including its limitations, both internally and externally imposed. These are genuine and significant.

Begin with its comparative structural handicaps of population, GNP, geography, and resources. That is, a population and economy only half the size of ours; largely mountainous home islands (only one-fifth arable or habitable), approximately the area of California; and almost no natural resources. These handicaps helped prompt its World War II adventurism, and render its achievements the more astounding. But they remain handicaps nonetheless.

There are others. We tend to perceive Japan's economic infrastructure as a mighty network of formidable, interlocked corporations—Japan, Inc. But this is only the most visible component. Living there, as I have, one becomes acutely aware that, in contrast to our economies of scale, except in its largest industries Japan practices the diseconomies of smallness and redundancy.*

Its railroad, farming, and hard-goods distribution systems are inhibited by waste, sloth, and obsolescence. Its retail sector is split-level, dominated by a mom-and-pop sector of some 1.6 million shops—more than in all of the United States. These are among its charms, contributing to its closely woven, relatively crime-free social fabric. They also are grave limitations.

Local shopkeepers hold de facto veto or delaying power over permits to open supermarkets or chain stores. Manufacturers are allowed their own hard-goods outlets—Matsushita alone has twenty-seven thousand—which can fix high fair-trade prices. This retards domestic markets and sends privileged shoppers scurrying abroad, where they can buy Japanese products more cheaply.

The quality of Japan's large, technology-based corporations is unquestioned. But these giants' power rests heavily on networks of tiny firms: captive suppliers that provide close, reliable intercompany liaison, with the quality control and just-in-time delivery system that have become famous. But a trade-off is a system that prevents Japan's small business from becoming the scrambling, entrepreneurial, yeasty innovators of American counterparts.

---

*One renowned diseconomy is innumerable small-plot rice farms. These remain extremely photogenic—and, like American small farms, heavily subsidized. This has kept some 18 per cent of the crowded Tokyo area as part-time farmland owned, thanks to farmland tax concessions, by city-dwellers.

Innovative technology and manufacturing? Here Japan's large corporations excell. But as the Japanese are acutely aware, their prowess rests on the sand of a notoriously weak basic-science establishment. Japanese scientists have won only 5 Nobel prizes, prewar and postwar, to Americans' 142. Government research grants are bestowed on a seniority, not merit, basis. These are limited to researchers' salaries, some research overhead costs, and some equipment. The peer-review process for most grants resides in committees of aging scientist referees who vote by mail, without discussion.

"It's a feudal system," says Kenichi Matsubara, head of Osaka University's Institute for Molecular and Cellular Biology. "We can't [even] hire secretaries and technicians."

Outstanding technologically as Japan's large corporations are, they still depend heavily on licensing (or in marginal instances still, pirating) discoveries from abroad. Only this and joint ventures enable them to demonstrate their true virtuosity in adapting, improving, manufacturing, and marketing—at which they are masters.

Japan's education system also is a contradiction. Confronted by swarms of black-uniformed schoolchildren on field trips, a visitor marvels at their discipline. But much of their learning is rote. This imparts enviable mass literacy and mathematics skills—but not creativity. As one observer noted, the Japanese "can make computers but cannot write software." Recognizing these shortcomings, the government, prodded by business, is striving for reforms.

In reality, however, Japan's government—read "political system"—is more a part of the problem than the solution. For behind its dynamic, high-technology facade, Japan is a nineteenth-century society akin to that of our own robber baron, Boss Tweed era. Its plodding, bureaucracy-ridden, corruption-prone young democracy fosters obstructionism and multi-billion-dollar boondoggles befitting our most notorious ninteenth-century political machines. Tokyo's remote, controversial Narita International Airport—uncompleted after more than a decade—is one example. Miles from the city, it must be patrolled constantly against protesters.

A similar virus infects several proud corporations and Japan's almost canonized (by foreigners) Ministry of International Trade and Industry. MITI, a civilian agency that various American reformers propose replicating, is justifiably respected for its postwar success in identifying areas of potential national competitiveness or supremacy, and orchestrating follow-ups. But it is far from infallible and, with major corporations growing in confidence and independence, now receding in importance.

Among MITI's many little-publicized faux pas, it choreographed a multi-billion-dollar aluminum-industry fiasco that, at full capacity in 1977, involved fourteen firms and over eleven thousand people. Eleven years later, after exponential electricity price increases, only 140 workers remained. Other notable blunders include an aborted nuclear-powered blast furnace for steelmaking, an undersea remote-controlled oil-drilling rig dropped as uncompetitive, and a costly jet engine rejected by All Nippon Airways for a GE model.

Among corporations' blunders, Sony's Betamax stands high. Who, aware of Sony's Tiffany image, would have predicted its obsession with a VCR system incompatible with the VHS mode that swept the world? A Mitsui consortium, meanwhile, courted a costly Waterloo in Iran, where it suffered $2.4 billion in losses on an unstrategically located, never-finished, joint-venture petrochemical plant leveled by Iraqi bombs. In 1989 the group offered over $1 billion to be released from the partnership.

Perhaps more than any other rich society, Japan is two nations: its clean, modern, crime-free, pulsating great-city centers, and a less gentrified sector beyond. The contrasts often astonish. Secondary rural roads, for example, are semiprimitive; sewers serve only one-third of its population; and six of every one hundred houses lack running water, compared to only one of every hundred in other rich nations. Journalist James Fallows, in a brief residency there recently, earned the scorn of many ex-GIs by expressing surprise to find that the effluent of even many affluent neighborhoods is stored behind houses for pickup in ubiquitous containers that, in my tenure there, were called "honeybuckets."

Such anomalies abound. Japan's high per-capita wealth notwithstanding, throughout its land-poor area residences are small and prices for land, per acre, about seventy-five times that of the United States. In 1986 Japan's official land valuation was triple that of the vastly larger United States: $9.3 trillion, to $3.2 trillion for us.

Like Japan's overvalued stock market, this reflects, as one observer noted, the yen as "Monopoly money." For who would pay such prices in other currency? Since land taxes are low, moreover, and comparable sites never will be cheap in Japan, ownership rarely changes.

Despite these handicaps, obviously Japan's system works—or at least has to date. Why?

One explanation surely is a homogeneous, work-oriented, group-first culture evolved over centuries of fiercely maintained isolation. Avery Fisher, whose hi-fi equipment then was a postwar world leader, sensed this work ethic in his first visit to a Japanese electronics plant. "The assembly workers, all women, hadn't seen that many Americans," he told me, "but when I walked down the line not one of them stopped to look up. My future was clear—selling my company to the Japanese."

I saw this ethic firsthand in a young Japanese executive who, though entitled to three weeks' vacation, confided that he never took more than long weekends. Submission of individual aspirations to the common good—of family, employer, and nation—is ingrained. This makes centralization—of corporate, financial, and government power—relatively easily achieved. Tragically, that resulted in the military-industrial-financial *zaibatsu* whose imperialism fueled World War II. But subsequently it also abetted the recovery and maximization of resources by Japan, Inc.

Another Japanese success secret: luck. Throughout this century its chief geographic rival, China, has floundered, while colonialism long inhibited Asia's now-thriving little tigers. Further, Japan's World War II militarists chose the right conquerer—the United States. Our benevolent occupation, with its implanting of a palatable mutation of democracy, and our mutually beneficial political, economic, and military relationships, all accelerated Japan's ascent.

The world is justified in its wariness of this dynamo. It is politically immature, unstable, and only partially integrated into the international system—geopolitically a potential loose cannon. It can be a powerful force either for progress or regression. Still, it is not a supernation.

Nor, as we are not in decline, is Japan necessarily in ascent beyond a curve extrapolatable from its prewar position. Like us, it seized its moment through postwar realignments. But also like us, it is only tasting Camelot.

A step-down already has begun. Japan's economic growth has slowed, to a rate resembling ours. Its labor-cost advantage over many competitors, including us, has vanished. Its steel, shipbuilding, and other industries have moved offshore, to South Korea, Taiwan, and Singapore—all rivals certain to impinge further.

Its ancient, rigid, ingrown society, too, is in disruptive transition. As in the West, affluence and hyperchange have fostered new values among its young. Many are increasingly hedonistic and materialistic, with a lassitude that exasperates their elders. "My wife and I don't know what to do about our son," one brilliant young computer expert told me. "He seems to want to sit around and play the guitar all day."

Another problem is demographics. Japan rigidly restricts immigration and mistrusts *gaijin*—foreigners—in its midst. This heightens and distorts a deep and sometimes destructive ethnic pride. Given decreasing birthrates, it also possesses an aging population. This soon will impose immense burdens for health care and other services.

I have met many Japanese, and become friends with few. They are hard to genuinely know. For all their success, this is a people peculiarly ill at ease in the world. They are torn between the old and new, traditional and technocratic, their peculiarily Asian and the West's seemingly irresistible mores. They strive to look outward, yet cannot surmount turning inward. This renders their overseas corporate empire a challenge to manage and staff.

They also sense increasing resistance to their presence. Their veneer of trust among outsiders is at best thin—especially among formerly subjugated neighbors. Throughout Asia, their geographically logical market, they remain hated.

The view confided by a Chinese government science official is typical. "The Japanese," he says, "are an aggressive people. They exploited us in the Forties with force, and now with finance....But Asians have memories that can't be rubbed out with money."

Japan has yet to confront this reality, as West Germany, faced with similar depths of postwar hostility, at least has tried to do. Indeed, says former West Germany chancellor Helmut Schmidt, "If I were a Japanese my top priority would be establishing friendly relations with my neighbors by learning to say 'I'm sorry.' They never have."

Perhaps they never can, at least not soon. As nationwide firestorms over sanitized portrayals of World War II in their textbooks, films, and other media show, supernationalist currents run strong. Like us, Japan must relearn how to face forward and outward.

Because of its history and culture, this will be achieved only by unremitting but tactful external pressure. Unlike other major powers Japan has no history of extensive peaceful international involvement. Reflexively it remains a "me" nation.

The United States, belatedly, has mounted reform-oriented pressure. Typically the response has been apparent assent, then delay, accompanied by protestations about our impatience or persecution. But change, albeit glacial, has begun in government policy restructuring.

Still, Japan's system militates against change. Japanese savings rates, for instance, are extraordinarily high. Two reasons are the lack of affordable housing and the high-priced domestic goods. In a land of dense population and rabbit-hutch dwellings, ownership of large products tends to be low—for autos, for example, half of our norm. Work, save, export—this has been the refrain.

For balanced development and diplomatic comity, such anomalies must be addressed. Recent consumption-fostering tax reforms and import promotion are a start. Basic market changes must follow.

As both we and Japan are unlikely to forget, the late 1970s and the 1980s were Japanese decades. The 1990s, in the view of many economists, cannot be. Much of the 1980s was distinguished by low costs for oil, coal, and other key Japanese imports and high prices for Japanese cars, computers, and other exports. Further, Japan's trade balance, formidable as it was, was magnified with "mirrors": Of a $90 billion "swing" in 1980-89—from a $10 billion deficit to an $80 billion surplus—three-fourths was due to currency realignments. As an early-1990 decline in yen and stock prices suggested, the sun already is setting on Camelot East.

Thus in Japanese publications one finds a mirror image of our own insecurities. Last winter, for example, the English-language edition of the *Nihon Keizai Shimbun*, regarded as "the *Wall Street Journal* of Japan," over a few weeks carried such stories as "Executives View Asian 'Tigers' as Technological Threat to Japan," "Will Current Economic Boom Fall Victim to Itself?", "Worker Shortage Likely to Worsen This Year," and "Chaos, Uncertainty to Mark Japan of the '90s."

If one looks away from political rhetoric and media sensationalism one finds such sentiments reflected outside Japan, in reports such as, in *Fortune,* "Japan's Troubled Future" and "Fear and Trembling in the Colossus"; in Hong Kong's *Far Eastern Economic Review,* "Japan: The Ground Trembles"; and in London's *Financial Times,* "Braced for the West's Disease."

"The country's current-account surplus already is on the wane," notes Bill Emmott, financial editor of *The Economist* and author of the book *The Sun Also Sets,* "helped by the risen yen and Japanese tourists; its savings rate is declining, thanks to better welfare systems, a new spendthrift generation, and an aging population; and the domestic demand for those savings is on the way up, thanks to desires to stimulate the economy and the cost of looking after the elderly. On this reasoning,

Japan's capital surplus has peaked. It may disappear altogether as early as 1995."

In fact, the case can be made that the United States and Japan will advance or decline together. We are not only competitors but, for mutually beneficial reasons, Pacific Rim partners. Our nations are economically and strategically symbiotic, as we have been with postwar Great Britain and West Germany.

The Japanese clambered to prosperity on our shoulders, with our enlightened postwar occupation, our sustained carte-blanche receptivity to exports, our sharing (for a price) of science and technology, and our pervasive military umbrella. These were no accident or miscalculation on our part. After our most bloody and costly foreign war, we sought a stable, democratic, friendly Japan. We foresaw opportunities in its markets plus a strategic anchor in Asia.

Now the two nations are interdependent. The Japanese need our mass market, scientific and technological virtuosity, and military protection. We need need their capital, political and economic stability, and strategic weight. The Japanese refer to this as *nichibei,* from the characters for sun and rice. It means that, for a bountiful harvest, the Japanese sun (industry and surplus capital) and American rice (mass-market and industrial, scientific, and military might) both are required.

The global power balance is shifting, and Japan is one lever. But in the medium if not long term, if we manage the sun-rice relationship effectively, Japan's success can support our own.

In fact, some authorities abroad already speak of a de facto new U.S.-Japan superstate: "Japerica" or "Amerippon." It could, in the words of one Australian political scholar, become "the most powerful economic, technical, and strategic force in world politics—one that could set the conditions under which most other countries, or groups of countries, would operate."

This is one reason the European Community is "running scared" toward 1992. It may be less of a concern in Asia. There the worry persists that Japan will rearm before it is housebroken into the global system. Will we really be enhanced by a rearmed Japan? That should be a policy consideration—and motivation to enlightened restraint—in Washington as well.

# 7

# *Living with Bashing*

Saying that the United States and Japan are both rivals and interdependent is one thing. Managing a relationship given that ambiguity is another. This is perhaps our greatest challenge vis-a-vis Japan. Like the feuding lovers in Shakespeare's *The Taming of the Shrew,* we continually seem at odds.

As Japan's wartime conquerer, we became accustomed to a victor's prerogatives. As a vanquished nation fearful of Soviet exploitation, a shattered Japan accepted subserviency. Now, like a former ward that has attained maturity, Japan not only resents but resists perceived overprotection or interference. We properly insist on preserving certain perquisities as leader of the world's dominant economic and political coalition.

Our mutual problem is to learn new roles, redefine an always-shifting relationship shot through with political, economic, and cultural contradictions, and, in light of *nichibei,* manage it constructively. This means acknowledging the existence of certain political hot buttons and treating them with care.

Several are especially conspicuous. One is Japanese rearmament. We hold that Japan has had a free ride economically under the U.S. military umbrella and should bear more of the burden of Pacific Rim defense. When we raise this the Japanese nod, sigh, and respond that their constitution, designed by us, imposes a limit of 1 per cent of GNP for defense, that Asian neighbors fear Japanese militarization, and that Japan contributes more to joint defense efforts than acknowledged.

They point to a military budget that, despite the constitutional limitation, with GNP growth has become second largest in the West—exceeding that of all of our NATO allies. They cite impressive chapter and verse, such as the role of Mitsubishi, maker of the renowned World War II Zero fighter, producing U.S.-designed F-86s, F-104s, F-4s, and F-15s under license and designing the FSX (tabled after approval to share advanced F-16 technology). Also, sea forces that include a huge, missile-equipped destroyer fleet and anti-submarine aircraft.

Their litany progresses to the substantial largess for America's security umbrella in Asia, including half of the support cost of 50,000 U.S. military personnel in Japan. That involves furnishing 130 facilities for American military activities, including ports for fifteen warships, the bases for their crews and families, and about half the labor costs of Japanese employees of the U.S. military.

We demand more. Japan gives slightly. So the dialogue goes.

Trade practices are an even touchier hot button. The issue approaches criticality over "dumping"—of, successively, cameras, consumer electronics items, cars, and exotica such as microchips. Defined as setting overseas prices far below those at home, dumping has antagonized almost every other industrial nation. When confronted, in ritual fashion Japanese nod, sigh, acknowledge minimal transgressions, and accept temporary embargoes or negotiated quotas. Over time, this reduces, but never totally eliminates, the problem, which the Japanese, with robber-baron-era reasoning, insist is simply an aggressive way of doing business.

Then there are Japanese import barriers. Year after year frustrated exporters cite Japanese offenses in almost endless profession. Japanese negotiators nod, sigh, and alternately deny and point to improvement, such as tax, regulatory, and budget reforms to spur imports and domestic consumption.

Each time around we demand more. Japan gives slightly. So the dialogue goes.

Does it change anything?

It is easy to assume not. But here more homework is required. Dispassionate observers such as *The Economist* of London declare "Fortress Japan" to be "more open now than most foreigners believe." And data reveal more export penetration there than most Americans realize. Japan's imports of American products, for instance, exceed the value of those by any other nation but Canada. Half of these are manufactured items—in value more than we sell to West Germany. Nonetheless, barriers such as rigged technical standards and certification procedures, links between Japanese manufacturers and suppliers, and impenetrable distribution labyrinths persist. All remain objects of continuing pressure and negotiation.

It is also true that Americans have penetrated the Japanese market far more than most U.S. critics concede. The modus has been the flip side of Japan's North American invasion: local and joint ventures involving some three thousand U.S. companies. These range from Exxon, Procter & Gamble, Texas Instruments, Coca-Cola, and IBM to small niche enterprises—some five hundred established in 1980-85 alone.

For fifteen years, our manufacturing investments in Japan have yielded roughly double the profits Americans realized in Canada, the United Kingdom, or France. IBM earns some 10 per cent of its overseas profits there—and Coca-Cola, more in Japan than at home. Indeed, American-owned firms reap such large earnings in Japan that, according to Kenichi Ohmae of the management consultants McKinsey & Co., in 1984 they sold the Japanese more than triple (some $44 billion) what we spent on Japanese products made in the United States.

These American ventures are expanding—by two-thirds in capital outlays in 1988 and half that again in 1989, according to Commerce Department figures. Included were a new $8 million W.R. Grace plant for meat-packaging materials, and new research-and-development facilities by a dozen U.S. firms such as Upjohn, Du Pont, and Eastman Kodak.

"The view of our headquarters," says an official of Schering Plough's Japanese subsidiary, "is that this is the second-largest market in the world, and we have to be here."

For years American auto-makers have complained of a one-way flow in vehicle trade. Japan asks why, if we sought customers there, we failed to offer cars for lefthand traffic flow—the rule in Japan, as in Great Britain. Chrysler's Lee Iacocca, in Tokyo, said it would not be "economically palatable."

Volvo, BMW, and other prestige European cars sell well in Japan. Why, the Japanese asked, did we not offer luxury models similarly suitable for Japan's narrow, sometimes rugged roads? Chrysler, Iacocca announced, was shipping Jeeps, and hoped to sell at least 1,000 a year there.

Washington cajoled and threatened over opening of Japan's construction market, notorious as a lucrative loop closed to outsiders. But our largest construction firm, Bechtel, professed no dissatisfaction with a two-year licensing process that ended in approval. The procedure was "time-consuming," acknowledged a senior manager, "but it was not unfair." In fact, note the Japanese, when bidding on a giant Osaka Airport project was announced, only one U.S. firm evinced interest in it.

Often, a U.S. Export Development official in Tokyo concedes, the main problem is lack of American businesses' interest. "We don't have a lot of people knocking at the door," he said. "We have to go get them."

Still another hot button is U.S. government deficits for which Japan provides financing. Americans lament a perceived susceptibility to economic blackmail. Japanese protest our indiscipline and insensitivity to sacrifices sometimes forced on them. During the dollar's mid-1980s decline Japanese investors were stunned by losses in dollar-denominated assets. Most deferred buying Treasury bills, but Japan's Finance Ministry stepped in, committing some $40 billion to dollar stabilization. Such intergovernmental cooperation continues.

Still, with the self-righteousness of the aggrieved, we perceive the cup of Japan-U.S. economic relationships to be half empty, not half full. This makes Japan-bashing easy, and results in replies in kind, through all media, including books. One of the most provocative best-sellers, published as 1980s controversies over autos, microchips, and dollar-propping mounted, was titled *Japan Is Not to Blame: It's America's Fault.*

In 1989 two more books advanced the theme. One, *The Japan That Can't Say No,* was co-authored by Akio Morita, chairman of the Sony Corp., and Shintaro Ishihara, novelist, Diet member, and former Cabinet minister. The other, *Japan as the Enemy: A New Scenario for U.S. Strategy,* was the product of military strategist Kazuhisa Ogawa. In the former volume, Ishihara complained of "inerasable arrogance" by Americans and other whites who "built the modern era," and called for a U.S.-Japan summit "to let Japan's status be recognized" and provide "more of a chance to say 'no' to the U.S." Morita, whose co-authorship consisted of contributing speech texts, lamented that Japan is blamed for an America that has become lazy and complacent. In the latter book Ogawa contended that America now considers Japan "the third enemy," behind the Soviet Union and China, and only the Japanese "do not know about this."

Even casual perusal of our media reveals the size of our "understanding gap." It also suggests the source of many exaggerated fears and insecurities about competitiveness and status compared to Japan. Oversimplifications and hyperbole abound. A few examples:

• *Trading Places: How We Allowed Japan to Take the Lead.* (Clyde V. Prestowitz, Jr., Basic Books, 1988).

This is an arresting title that plays skillfully on our insecurities. But "take the lead" in what? "In industry after industry," this former trade official writes; in specific "multiplier" fields (including certain but not all or even most) microchip fields; and in size of banking and securities firms, and so on. But *the* lead? Trading what *places?* Who among us, after a comparison of positions, would swap?

- "Japanese Assets in '87 Reportedly Surpassed U.S. for First Time." (*Wall Street Journal,* Aug. 22, 1989).

Again, an eye-catching angle that reinforces the U.S. decline theme. "Japan," reports this Associated Press story from Tokyo, "became the world's richest nation on paper in 1987, surpassing the U.S. for the first time with $43.7 trillion in national assets." The story's source is the *Nihon Keizai Shimbun,* the *Wall Street Journal* of Japan, whose stated sources were compilations by Japan's Economic Planning Agency and the U.S. Federal Reserve Board. Missing was any reference to U.S. assets being calculated at acquisition, not market, values—and the relevance of comparing inflated Japanese real estate valuations to levels of other industrialized countries.

- "Japan Science Activity Seen as Matching U.S." (*New York Times,* Dec. 27, 1988).

Here, if it is accurate, is a legitimate scare headline in a credible newspaper, based on a study by the National Science Foundation (NSF). "Japan's scientific enterprise," we are told, has "achieved 'relative parity' with that of the United States." But upon examination, it develops that the NSF report claims only that "Japan now spends money and supports scientists in the same proportions as does the U.S., when the different sizes of national economies and populations are taken into account." Japan's economy and population, of course, are only half the size of ours. Thus, it "matches" us only by half. Some "match!"*

- "Technology Report Finds U.S. Lagging." (*New York Times,* May 16, 1989).

"The Defense Department," states the lead, "says Japan has a significant lead in six of the twenty-two technologies that the Pentagon considers crucial to national security and 'the long-term qualitative superiori-

---

*The story also notes that, while Japan's "share of the world's scientific literature rose to 7.6 per cent from 5.1 per cent" in 1973-84, ours is 36.8 per cent—only 1.4 per cent less than in 1973.

ty' of Americans weapons systems. 'In key niches of microelectronics and information-systems technologies, Japan either holds or shares a worldwide lead.'" Is leadership in sixteen of twenty-two crucial technologies lagging? In the last paragraph, moreover, we find that Japan is not carte blanche "significantly ahead of the United States," but "in some niches" of the six technologies.

• "The Chip Industry Is Sliding Again. Concern Grows About the Nation's Competitiveness." (*New York Times,* Jan. 27, 1989).

Here is vintage reason for confusion. The microchip industry is only one measure of competitiveness, and, as the headline suggests, an ever-changing one. Closer reading, moreover, shows that the story does not report red ink, but that "the robust growth of 35 per cent last year is expected to dip to 10 per cent this year." Indeed, it concedes later, some experts see the industry as "healthier than it appears," the declining world market share as "a distortion produced by changes in currency exchange rates," and "a few poorly managed companies [as reflecting on] the whole group."

The more critically one reads such stories, the more soundly one can sleep. But only until the next one—never long in coming.

What can be done about such conditioning? Little, apparently, at the supply end, which either serves special interests or is cast in that mold by media superficiality and oversimplification. Again, much of the solution must lie with the consumer. This means accepting the burden of understanding high technology better, and reading or viewing all reports, print or electronic, with mental zoomar lenses and second thoughts.

Begin with the microchip. A fingernail-size silicon wafer into which circuitry equivalent to 10 million transistors can be etched, it is an electronic-age commodity that directly affects both strategic and economic competitiveness. But there is no discernible limit to its permutations and product derivatives. Consequently no company or nation can excel in every aspect, and "wars" for supremacy—corporate and national—are unending. To minimize fear, exploitation, and heartburn, we must accept these realities.

Early microchips made possible LCD watches, hand calculators, personal computers, miniature TV sets, and tiny computers for auto engine and washing-machine controls. Future chips will drive devices that understand and translate spoken language, extend human senses through robots, and create artificial intelligence. There is, says Jack Kilby, Texas Instruments engineer who was co-inventor of integrated circuits three decades ago with Intel's Robert Noyce, no predicting their end evolution.

"Most people who have tried to set limits," he chuckles, "have missed pretty badly."

The design of one sophisticated chip resembles a map of the United States with every street. Quantum leaps beyond that require costly and complex advanced design tools, new computer software, and new materials. Every advance, obviously, bestows instant competitive advantage and renders many products obsolete. Since advances are inevitable and no one can monopolize them, single companies—or consortia from any one nation—are increasingly pressed to keep pace. Hence, choices of specialization and alliances must be made.

Add permutations such as supercomputers and high-definition television, and the confusion mounts. But the implications of these, too, must be understood.

Supercomputers are fast, high-capacity machines capable of far speedier calculations than the ordinary—billions per second. They are used for design of aircraft, autos, and nuclear weapons, electronic surveillance, cryptology, antisubmarine warfare, and for fabricating advanced materials, and medical and other scientific experimentation.

High-definition television provides color-slide clarity, delivered by a picture with some 1,000 instead of the U.S. standard 525 lines of electronic dots, on a one-fourth wider screen. It also has military applications, from radar to weapons fire-control displays. If achieved with digital rather than existing signal technology, it could be part of a sophisticated, multipurpose computer network. Unlike supercomputers, which are already in use, HDTV remains experimental, including test broadcasts of systems incompatible with present transmitting or receiving equipment.

From government and industry statements and the tone of media reporting, one easily could conclude that the Japanese lead in these three fields. Or that at least they are on the verge. Is this true?

The fact is that in microchips, Japan's great lead—and a not insignificant one—is based mainly on one of the simplest, most pervasive circuits. That is, the one-megabit memory chips, also known as DRAM (direct random access memory), used in high volume for personal computers and the like. Japan's world sales share: 90 per cent.

Overall, for semiconductors of all types, in 1988 the world's largest single chipmaker was American—IBM, which manufactures only for itself. In this all-inclusive sweepstakes Japan had half the international market, the United States and Europe the rest.

The history of the "chip wars" and our resiliency in them also is revealing. As the birthplace of the microchip, of course, we once led sui generis. But one-megabit DRAMs (pronounced dee-rams) in particular proved ideal for production in Asia, and Japan pounced. It became so efficient and aggressive that soon it was charged with dumping—price-cutting—to submerge European and American competitors. We retaliated, including imposing voluntary quotas on Japan. That raised prices and interrupted supplies. When shortages occurred, Japanese firms satisfied Japanese demand first, causing delays to others. This raised a question beyond leadership: dependence. That was a turning point.

The Defense Science Board responded with a task force report that urged reviving U.S. memory-chip production with a manufacturing consortium. Typically, the report was cast in doomsday terms—"designed to shed the worst possible light on the situation," as the *Financial Times* of London observed.* But it achieved its purpose.

Industry and government funded the research consortium Sematech. Shortly after, IBM provided another surprise: announcement that it was producing four-megabit chips "in volume," for new products to follow within months, thus leapfrogging Japanese competitors.** IBM would license its technology for sales to American and European firms, but not the Japanese. Next the Sarnoff Research Center announced a circuit combining electronic and optical functions in a chip likely to be standard by the mid-1990s. And two U.S. firms entered into joint ventures with Japanese chipmakers: Motorola with Toshiba; Texas Instruments with Hitachi. Subsequently IBM announced a memory-chip joint venture with West Germany's Siemens, and others U.S. firms, alliances with Japanese companies.

A chip-industry revival was on—based in part, it should be noted, on the Global Age realism of cross-national joint ventures, which will increase, not decline. All the while, it should be added, we never lost our margin in another crucial computer component, microprocessors. Indeed, as *The Economist* reported, "Japan, for all its lead in commodity

---

*One example, noted the *New York Times*, was the "relatively little scrutiny given to logic chips, where most experts consider American designers to hold a substantial lead."

**In February, 1990, IBM announced the first sixteen-megabit chip fabricated on an existing production line.

chips, is way behind in advanced soft microprocessors and has no software industry with which chipmakers can consult in designing the next generation. Even in commodity chips it is being challenged by other Asian countries."

Should Japan, then, be worried? "No," *The Economist* advised. "It is perfectly natural to have an international division of labor in chipmaking. For the same reason, American chip firms shouldn't worry, either."

What about supercomputers? Here the U.S. long has held an overwhelming lead. But here, too, panic dominated headlines when our number two firm, Control Data Corp., in 1989 announced withdrawal from the field, citing the threat of Japanese competition. "Supercomputers Worry U.S. as Japan Challenges American Dominance," said one headline *(New York Times)*. "Supercomputer Market Feels a Japanese Threat," said another *(Wall Street Journal)*.

What were the facts?

The U.S. lead was mainly due to one firm, the IBM of its small, specialized field: Cray Research Inc. Of the 409 supercomputers worldwide, Cray, of Chippewa Falls, Wis., had installed 220—three times more than anyone else. Three Japanese firms (NEC, Hitachi, and Fujitsu) had installed 132, mostly in Japan. But the three were spending $100 million a year each to develop faster machines, and had promised to introduce the world's fastest within a year.

In uncomfortable succession before the Control Data announcement, Cray had lost a protege, Steve S. Chen, to a new firm (Supercomputer Systems) started by Chen with IBM backing; and Cray's founder, Seymour R. Cray, resigned to open his own firm (Cray Computer Corp.). This shook the world supercomputer community.

But several mitigating points should be noted. Seymour Cray left his namesake firm with a strong team—fifty-four hundred employees—and nearly $1 billion in assets, successful products, and 10 per cent cross-ownership in his new firm. The parting, actually a spinoff with minority ownership by his former firm, arguably rejuvenated Seymour Cray, who like many geniuses, chafes under bureaucracy to the point he had left two previous jobs because success had bureaucratized them.* Further, protege Chen's firm, sustained by IBM, provided a third mainstream

---

*One former colleague remembers Cray's classic response to a request for one-year and five-year plans: one binder with a sheet inscribed "Five-Year Development Plan," accompanied by another binder with a sheet reading, "To complete one-fifth of the five-year plan."

U.S. supercomputer force, with other entries expected; the subsidiary killed by Control Data had never attained flight altitude;* and experts questioned the significance of higher-speed Japanese machines without the software to exploit them.

Software for supercomputers is one of our long suits. We also lead in parallel computing—dividing problems to enable simultaneous handling by several processing units—and in mini-supercomputers. As the 1980s ended, "mini's," which sell for $1 million—one-twentieth the price of a supercomputer—were the hot segment of the field, with no Japanese representation.

This is not to say that there is no supercomputer competitiveness issue. In all high-technology fields leadership must be earned and continually revalidated. As in other areas, Japan has protected its supercomputer industry by excluding outsiders—in 1989 only thirteen machines there were Crays. Also typically, one Japanese firm tried to shake our industry with prices two-thirds below market. (Offered to MIT, which cited anti-dumping rules and declined.)

The point is, we must keep micro-events in a macro-context, and plan accordingly. A next grand strategy in supercomputers, for instance, might be a nationwide network, building on the Pentagon-financed Arpanet system begun in the 1970s. Linking universities, corporate research facilities, and military laboratories, this could both enlarge the market and allow integrated research involving thousands of scientists nationwide.

High-definition television is the subject of an even louder clamor. Here, on paper, both Japan and Western Europe appear ahead. Both have invested over a decade and some $500 million in systems ready for demonstration while the United States, it appears, has dawdled.

Where does this leave us?

In trouble, contend HDTV boosters. In the 1970s and 1980s, American firms dismissed television as a low-tech, low-profit business and opted for computers and defense contracts. Japan then swept to supremacy in TV technology and parlayed that into leadership in videocassette recorders, compact disc players, and the like. Now, Asia's economic tigers all produce TV sets, VCRs, and the like.** HDTV is seen as yet another potential multi-billion-dollar industry in which we will trail.

*In six years it delivered fewer than three dozen machines, mostly small, and usually late; its software was below par; and it lost $100 million in its last year alone.

**Only one U.S. firm, Zenith, manufactures as well as assembles TV sets in the United States, and none makes VCRs.

Other implications are portrayed as ominous: inferiority in some military applications for one; loss of microchip markets, another. The HDTV industry, by some estimates, will become the largest consumer of chips. It also involves markets for graphics and video screen technology in computers, medical, and printing equipment, and the like—fields in which we now lead but could lag.

The outlook for HDTV as a bonanza, however, remains murky. First, there are doubts about demand for the European and Japanese systems. Makers of conventional sets already can enhance picture quality with computer chips. HDTV's benefits are apparent mainly on screens forty inches or larger—hardly candidates for most living rooms. And price tags are stratospheric—$21,000 for Sony's first forty-five-inch HDTV sets in Japan, and an expected $4,000 to $7,000 for smaller ones, even in the mid-1990s.

Perhaps the greatest initial handicap is systems incompatability. Any new system, the Federal Communications Commission (FCC) has ordained, must be compatible with our present over-the-air TV. Neither Japanese nor European technology meets this criterion.

A longer-term question is the systems base. By the mid-1990s, if not sooner, digital technology will be feasible. This will replace analog, high-voltage, electron-gun picture tubes, high-frequency antennas, and transponders with an energy-efficient, solid-state TV receiver-computer-telecomputer. Fiber-optics distribution eventually will allow its use for integrated phone, home-education, TV games, and other interactive services. Screens, up to seventy-two inches in size, will be flat for wall-mounting. Price tags may be $1,000 or less.

"HDTV," as publisher M. S. Forbes, Jr., declared in *Forbes* magazine, then "may be the equivalent of a horse-drawn carriage in an era of automobiles."

Achieving and marketing such breakthroughs may take years. In that case Japan and Europe may have bet right technologically, but wrong financially. Reaching 10 per cent color-TV penetration of U.S. households took thirteen years. The HDTV investments required for research and new transmission and receiving equipment will be immense. This is apart from special programming probably needed as a sales incentive.

This means uncertain returns even for the medium run—a counterpart of the supersonic *Concorde*. This seemed implicit in a mid-1989 Congressional Budget Office report, which concluded, "It seems counterintuitive to suggest that such a small market that may exist in the future is a more important driver of economies of scale, technology, and competitive success than is the growth in the present market. It would be a case of the tail wagging the dog."

A little-reported Second Annual Conference and Exhibition on HDTV in Arlington, Va., in 1990 affirmed these caveats. Sponsored by two trade newsletters, its expert panel on the subject was summarized in the monthly 300,000-circulation newspaper of the Institute of Electrical and Electronics Engineers as postulating: There is no HDTV boom; HDTV will not drive the semiconductor industry; HDTV costs to stations are high; HDTV is not just around the corner; a "U.S." company needs defining; and government support of HDTV is not needed.

American strategy—sound, skeptics believe—has been to hedge. We are not without defenses. One is American firms' joint ventures, first, between U.S. giants such as AT&T and Zenith, and second, with foreign HDTV developers, such as NBC and Europe's Thomson and Philips, one of several such cross-national efforts. Another, sharply focused research on high-resolution screens, computer technology, and other HDTV components, some with Pentagon funding. Still another, FCC control of HDTV standards for U.S. broadcasting, bound to exclude system-incompatible innovations by others.

Even as we hedge, we are not undermining certain strengths. Among them are our DRAM chip-industry revival and our prowess in software and the custom chips sure to be integral to HDTV success. Here we hold clear leads. Another is our TV-set manufacturing system. Though maligned as "dead" or mainly offshore, it is structured so that over two-thirds of the value of TV sets bought here is added here. Then there is TV programming, which in the end drives the consumer TV market, which we dominate.

Thus, as *The Economist* notes, "Jobs and investment will not fly away abroad, even if success in HDTV does....Before American taxpayers are asked to enrich electronics firms in the name of HDTV nationalism, Congress should take a skeptical look at the arguments put forward by this lobby. Few of them stand close scrutiny."

Always, we must remember that technological innovation, competitiveness, and economic and military security encompass far more than the contentious, highly publicized fields associated with Japan. The Japanese do not even manufacture mini-supercomputers, trail significantly in computerized work stations, still cannot write software, and lag in lucrative realms such as fiber optics, computer-aided design, aerospace, genetic engineering, and medical technology.

Further, even industry group leaders do not agree on competitiveness issues. J. Richard Iverson, president of the American Electronics Association (viewed as Silicon Valley's industry voice), told an editor of the professional monthly *IEEE Spectrum* in 1990, "The biggest problem for the [U.S.] electronics industry is survival." Peter F. McCloskey, president of the older Electronics Industries Association, said, "There is a perception that the [U.S.] electronics industry is dying. I don't see it that way."

From now on, when reading, hearing, or viewing stories comparing the United States and Japan, or American and Japanese industries, self-interest dictates that we envision three flashing signs:

- CAUTION: INTEREST GROUPS AT WORK
- WE CANNOT AND NEED NOT LEAD IN EVERYTHING
- REMEMBER, CROSS-NATIONAL JOINT VENTURES ARE HERE TO STAY

# 8

# *Foreign Corporate Bodies — Ours and Theirs*

Return now to another aspect of globalization in American life: foreign-owned industries in our midst. Since they now are fixtures, we should ponder their impact. Are they, as opponents contend, hazardous to our economic health? What does their presence mean for their employees, communities, and government? Might their modus operandi undermine our own companies?

Some answers are revealed in mirror image of the curve of American corporate expansion. At first the arrival of foreigners is perceived as an invasion. Then events unfold in predictable sequence. As in Western Europe with Jean-Jacques Servan-Schreiber's *The American Challenge,* alarms are sounded. Then come caveats to seek and exploit potential benefits. Finally, a synthesis.

Corporations' habit is to launch foreign ventures on tight reins. They begin with only one or a few bases, supervised extremely closely. Outposts may engage foreign line employees, but import top executives from home. With time this changes. Foreign nationals win increasing authority, and within management the international side becomes an accepted upward mobility route. So it has been with American expatriate firms.

IBM provides one model. From its earliest overseas ventures the company's philosophy was devolution of authority. Its postwar overseas arm, IBM World Trade Corp., focused on Western Europe, with a Frenchman in charge. Now its more than 300,000 employees are dispersed through 132 countries. Its overseas investments include over thirty manufacturing plants, sixty research-and-development laboratories, and a hundred educational centers staffed by seven thousand professionals. Six of its foreign subsidiaries ranked among *Fortune*'s 500 largest industrial corporations abroad.

"Top-quality nationals," believes IBM chairman John F. Akers, "have a unique feel for their home country's language, culture, economy, and needs." IBM's manager in Spain, for instance, "not only understands the Spanish economy and unique needs of that market—the King knows [him] well enough to kid him about the long hours he puts in at the office...." Similarly, IBM-UK's president "understands Britain's drive for more jobs, better quality, and international competitiveness as only a British citizen could."

The same curve applies to outsiders here. West European and Canadian firms, the first large investors, began gingerly, managing with executive imports. With time and sales growth, they promoted Americans. In many cases home-office presence now is virtually invisible. American managers responsible to headquarters preside; American corporate customs reign.

This is not to imply that foreign ownership means business as usual. Far from it. All communities prefer local to absentee ownership. A foreign proprietor seems distressingly remote. As a resident of one small midwestern town said when Swedish interests bought a division of *Fortune* 500 industry there, "With us over here and them over there how do we know what they'll do with us?"

If the acquisition is profitable, nothing may change, at least not immediately. If the acquisition is sick or redundant with the parent company's other interests, all bets are off. But frequently the new owner provides a happy ending. The venerable A & P, for instance, near death when half its stock was sold to West Germany's Tengelmann Group in the 1970s, underwent a complete reorganization that saved it and raised equity values sevenfold.

Indeed, while union leaders, defense planners, and others decry foreign "invasions," especially by the Japanese, state and local officials openly seek more, for identical reasons—jobs, investment, and area development. At least forty of our fifty states now have promotion offices in Tokyo, and some two dozen, bases in Taiwan. More than one hundred cities, port authorities, and development agencies, plus the Federal Savings Loan and Insurance Corp. (FSLIC), also solicit foreign investment.*

Tennessee has led the charge, with a parade of government and business

---

*In spring 1989, the FSLIC held a London seminar to showcase $10 billion in real estate from failed savings and loan associations. Included were a $7.2-million shopping center, a $9.5-million hotel, and office buildings, bowling alleys, and motels.

executives to Tokyo, resettlement assistance for Japanese families, and multi-million-dollar tax abatements. Its reward through 1987: more than $1.5 billion in investment by sixty Japanese companies, creating ten thousand jobs directly, and another twenty thousand indirectly. Besides grits and fried chicken, many Tennessee localities also now feature sushi.

"When word leaks out that a Japanese company is considering a U.S. investment," says a Tokyo magazine report titled "The War Between the States," "the firm is besieged by a pack of state representatives hoping for the prize."

The prize frequently comes high. In Flat Rock, Mich., near Detroit, it was $150 million in inducements for Mazda—now 25 per cent owned by Ford—to build a $450 million plant. In Indiana, $26 million for GM-related Isuzu to build in Lafayette. This included management training for several hundred Americans in Japan, new highways and sewers, even English lessons for arriving Japanese.

Four months before official announcement of Isuzu's plant, local officials were besieged by job inquiries. In Bloomington, Ill., almost two years before opening of a Mitsubishi-Chrysler plant, a shelter for the homeless was filled with arriving job-seekers. A year before Toyota's plant in Georgetown, Ky., opened, fifty thousand applications had arrived for fourteen hundred jobs.

"I've never had sushi before," one development official proclaimed, "but I'm going to learn to like it."

He is not alone. At the ground-breaking for Mazda's Michigan plant, where a Shinto priest blessed the site, the governor bowed before a Japanese altar and a band played Japan's national anthem. In nearby Southfield, meanwhile, a Japanese video-grocery store featured squid, five kinds of tofu, and samurai movies.

There is also an ugly side. In Detroit in the early 1980s, for instance, a Chinese-American mistaken for Japanese was fatally beaten by two unemployed auto workers. Some incidents are union related. In Tonawanda, New York, when some two thousand construction workers protested hiring of nonunion labor to expand a unionized Sumitomo Rubber Industries' tire plant, several donned Japanese military uniforms, shouted World War II epithets, and burned a Japanese flag.

The Japanese, of course, are only manifestations, not creators, of the triple revolution they epitomize. Neither they nor cloddish American management decimated our auto, steel, or other heavy industries. Post-Industrial Third Wave technology and globalization did. Nor is their invasion unique. As we have seen, other foreign investors arrived earlier, and American businesses blanket the planet.

But the antipathy toward them is understandable. Like Europeans in their "Yankee Go Home" days, we see such outsiders as threats, or at least agents of unwelcome change. Older Americans remember the Japanese as an aggressor in, and loser of, World War II. Theirs seems an exotic, non-Western culture.

Japanese globalization, unlike our broad-based corporate thrust, has been high profile in the specialized fields of autos and electronics. Japan's ascent has been sudden. In just eight years, for example, Japanese firms created a massive auto-manufacturing complex here.*

A further complication is that, like our early European ventures depicted by Jean-Jacques Servan-Schreiber, the Japanese have brought not only new investment and jobs, but strong competition and new ways. As Servan-Schreiber advised his European colleagues, the intelligent response is to adapt, combining the best of both worlds. This we have begun to do.

Toyota's joint venture with General Motors, NUUMI, in Fremont, Calif., illustrates. NUUMI operates a former GM problem plant which had five thousand employees with low productivity, 20 per cent absenteeism, and rampant drug and alcohol abuse. When closed in 1982, the plant had eight hundred union grievances pending.

Shortly thereafter, a curious Toyota invested $150 million in a revival attempt, and a dubious GM $20 million plus the existing plant. Toyota took charge. The United Auto Workers (UAW) agreed to a complete reorganization, including new job flexibility. Of three thousand laid-off

---

*This includes:

- Honda Motor, Marysville and East Liberty, Ohio (opened 1982), planned employment 8,000, planned production capacity 510,000 vehicles yearly.
- Nissan Motor, Smyrna, Tenn. (1983), planned employment 5,100, capacity 440,000.
- Toyota/General Motors (New United Motor Manufacturing, fifty-fifty venture), Fremont, Calif. (1984), planned employment 3,400, capacity 300,000.
- Mazda Motor (25 per cent Ford ownership), Flat Rock, Mich. (1987), planned employment 3,400, capacity 240,000.
- Toyota Motor, Georgetown, Ky. (1988), planned employment 3,500, capacity 200,000.
- Mitsubishi/Chrysler (Diamond Star Motors), Bloomington/Normal, Ill. (1988), planned employment 2,900, capacity 240,000.
- Subaru/Isuzu, Lafayette, Ind. (1989), planned employment 1,700, capacity 120,000.

employees who reapplied, twenty-two hundred survived a rigorous selection procedure, including oral, written, and physical dexterity tests. All were provided with hundreds of hours of training, nearly five hundred people in part in Japan.

When the plant reopened, an executive cafeteria, priority parking places, and enclosed offices were gone. There were only four levels of management.

Everyone received identical work uniforms. The former two hundred job categories for hourly workers were telescoped into three (assembly line, general maintenance, and tool and die) at two beginning salaries: $11.29 hourly for unskilled, $15.05 for skilled workers.

Now both the old executive and shop-floor hierarchies are memories. Workers, in units of six to eight, are team members, each under a team leader. Three to five teams comprise a group, under a group leader. Every team member is cross-trained and, to reduce tedium, as often as every two hours during shifts rotated among team functions.

Teams meet regularly, at their discretion, for problem-solving. They, not engineers, revise the standardized work sheets outlining their tasks. All are trained in minor repairs and enjoined to monitor and correct malfunctions. Assembly lines are designed to eliminate heavy lifting, bending, and stretching.

Overhead alert cords hang along the assembly line. Anyone unable to fulfill his or her task is authorized—obligated—to pull a cord rather than send a defective vehicle forward. If team and group leaders cannot solve the problem in roughly a minute, the line is halted until they do.

Issue-resolution is relegated to the lowest possible level. If a worker calls a union representative, rather than generating a formal grievance that may languish, he or she can expect to see the representative and a company labor-relations officer. All three will try to resolve the problem there. Allowable absences are minimal: More than three are "offense"; four offenses in a year, cause for firing.

The object is not to enshrine production quotas, but an efficient, humane system, from which it is assumed optimum output will flow. This is presumed to require teamwork, pride, and trust. To abet this, NUUMI pledged to avoid layoffs. When sales of Chevrolet Novas slumped and the plant cut production by one-third, it assigned workers, one hundred at a time at full pay, to extra training in problem-solving and interpersonal relationships.

All Japanese plants share several traits: reorganized staffing, systematic training, employee involvement, and a commitment to quality. Many also bring imported suppliers—a closed circle now increasingly being penetrated by combined pressure and enhanced performance. Most plants also are non-union—and, as Nissan workers' celebrated two-to-one rebuff to the UAW in Smyrna, Tenn., suggests, they and more American plants may stay that way.

The work pace is demanding. But while bemoaning that, employees on the whole seem to approve their experiences. As one put it, "I have a job." Most also find the participatory aspects, openness, and climate of respect refreshing. "These people," went one typical comment, "treat us like human beings."

All this has had a refreshing impact on U.S. management. While laying off blue-collar workers, for example, our Big Three auto-makers also have pruned white-collar ranks and given new priority to quality, flexibility, and efficiency. GM, which more than competitors reflected financial rather than engineering or marketing expertise at the top, was perceived as the most rigid. It also has unbent, shuttling executives in and out of NUUMI and other joint ventures to gawk, gasp, and assimilate.

The Japanese, meanwhile, have undergone counterpart shocks, in relations with local officials, regulatory bodies, the media, shop-floor workers, and union organizers. One of their most difficult, redolent of our early postwar experiences in Europe, is a clash of management cultures.

*Business Month* encapsulated the problem in one subheading: "American executives in Japanese companies are well paid, but they so often lack real authority that many quit in despair. That bodes ill for Japan's U.S. strategy." A few large Japanese firms, it found, are advanced in Americanizing their U.S. subsidiaries. But on the whole newcomers lag on industrial nations' curve of corporate decentralizing,* and on the whole an estimated twenty-five thousand American managers in Japanese companies here "seem to be an unhappy and demoralized lot." They lament "subtle and debilitating discrimination," withholding of authority to get things done, and lack of upward mobility in a consensus-based environment.The ambition, independence, and risk-taking admired in American firms are handicaps.

---

*Of twenty-five Japanese subsidiaries here in one sampling, only three had American executives in charge: Subaru, Kyocera International, and Bridgestone (the parent of Firestone). All of the other twenty-three were run by Japanese. These included Toyota, Honda, Nissan, Sony, Matushita, Toshiba, Hitachi, Sharp, NEC, and Ricoh.

A common complaint is that Japanese managers focus on good relations with headquarters. Even when Americans are put in charge, salaries and benefits of Japanese underlings usually are dictated by headquarters.

Richard Kraft, president of Matsushita Electronic Corp. of America, for one, counsels patience. "Autonomous local management will take maybe ten to twenty years," he says. "But the Japanese will do it, just as [the U.S.] did."

Like American counterparts abroad, Japanese companies quickly have adapted to an alien politics. By 1986 they were spending some $60 million annually for officially registered lobbying here, and millions more for unregulated activities. That total since has grown. Many of their lobbyists are political VIPs—a fact that some commentators portray as sinister.* 'Twas ever thus, here and abroad. At all levels, as one would expect from the stakes, Japan's intermediaries, like ours abroad, tend to be effective.

A Reagan-era contretemps over a Toshiba sale of U.S. technology to Moscow illustrates. The Senate, in retaliation, banned all Toshiba imports for up to five years. Toshiba exhorted all U.S. divisions' employees to "speak out" to save their jobs, and its customers to protect product pipelines. One Toshiba office reportedly generated some six thousand letters in a week. The sanctions soon were modified to defense-related imports only.

Similarly, efforts by a Japanese pulp mill in Alaska were regarded as instrumental in the 1985 defeat of the Clean Water Act. Increasingly, debates on Capitol Hill reflect these realities. "Looking around the Senate," says Senator Jim Sasser of Tennessee, "I would say that having a substantial amount of foreign investment or foreign industry in your state can have an inhibiting effect."

---

*These include former Commerce Secretary Peter G. Peterson, who heads the prestigious Council on Foreign Relations and his own investment firm; Bill Brock, Reagan-administration U.S. Trade Representative; and Robert Ingersoll, former U.S. ambassador to Japan, now chairman of the $12-million Matsushita Foundation.

# 9

# *Global Village— or Media Oligopoly?*

For many of us, the most worrisome investment influxes are not in manufacturing, real estate, or finance but in the news media, books, and mass entertainment enterprises that mold our politics and culture. This, too, is a concomitant of globalization—and, since a wave of well-publicized media mega-mergers, an increasingly pervasive one.

Worldwide, ten firms now are massive enough to be described as Lords of the Global Village. Of these, only two are American based. The other eight have carved deep inroads into the United States. Should this minority position among the Lords and their potential for compromising our information/entertainment stream trouble us?

Consider first the eight non-Americans in this titanic ten. They are:

* Sony (Japan). Annual revenues: $17.9 billion.*Perhaps the world's most famous consumer-electronics producer, this Japanese giant became an instant global power in entertainment software with bold purchases of CBS Records and Columbia Pictures.
* Bertelsmann A.G. (West Germany). Annual revenues: $6.8 billion. This diversified giant, the parent of the huge Gruner & Jahr, publishes some three dozen periodicals; owns RCA Records and Bantam, Doubleday, Dell, and the Literary Guild and other book clubs with twenty-two million members in twenty-two countries; and has European newspaper and TV interests.

   Its magazines include West Germany's *Stern* and, in the United States, *Parents* and *Young Miss;* newspapers, Germany's *Hamburger* and *Morgenpost;* TV, Europe's RTL-PLus satellite network; and records, besides RCA, Ariola and Arista Records.

---

*Estimated 1989 totals.

- Fininvest (Italy). Annual revenues: $6.4 million. Headed by master political maneuverer Silvio Berlusconi, it owns four Italian TV channels; TV partnerships in France and West Germany; a twenty-studio production company; and TV interests in Spain, Yugoslavia, and Tunisia. Other holdings include the Italian daily *Il Giornale,* magazines, nearly three hundred theaters, and an advertising agency.
- Thomson (Canada). Annual revenues: $4.7 billion. Also prominent in travel and business services, this media empire, named for the late Lord Thomson of Fleet, encompasses 116 U.S. dailies and, among others, Canada's prestigious *Toronto Globe & Mail* and *Winnipeg Free Press.* It also publishes trade magazines and books.
- News Corp. (Australia). Annual revenues: $4.4 billion. The domain of Rupert Murdoch, Australian magnate who took U.S. citizenship after buying broadcast properties that required it, this Australia-based venture encompasses some of the best-known media in the United States, United Kingdom, and Australia.

In newspapers these include *The Times, Sunday Times, Sun, News of the World,* and *Today* in London; two-thirds of all newspaper circulation and 40 per cent of the Australian Associated Press in Australia; a stake in almost half the circulation in New Zealand; the *South China Morning Post* in Hong Kong; and the U.S. tabloid *Star* and dailies in Boston and elsewhere.

In magazines, *TV Guide, Seventeen, New York, New Woman,* and others in the United States, *Times* Supplements in London, and others. It also owns 7 per cent of the world's number two news service, Reuters, and 20 per cent of the giant Pearson PLC.

In TV, properties include the satellite Sky Channel (Europe's largest system) and, in the United States, Fox Broadcasting. In films, 20th Century Fox. In books, Harper & Row, Times Books, and William Collins.

- Hachette S.A. (France). Annual revenues: $4.1 billion. With its affiliate Publications Filipacchi, this is the world's largest purveyor of magazines—seventy-four in ten nations—and France's number one communications firm. Photographer Daniel Filipacchi, a picture-magazine aficionado, directs media operations.

In magazines, its holdings in France include *Paris-Match, Elle,* and *Tele 7 Jours,* and in the United States, Diamandis Communications (*Woman's Day, Elle, Car & Driver,* and others). Book properties include Grolier Publications (*Encyclopedia Americana,* Disney's

Wonderful World of Reading, Dr. Seuss's Beginning Reader's Program, and so on), all in the United States. It also owns the number two American periodical distributor (Curtis Circulation); the largest print distributor in Spanish-language nations (Salvat of Spain); and French newspaper and broadcasting interests.

- Pearson PLC (United Kingdom) Annual revenues: $2 billion. This fast-growing firm owns the *Financial Times* of London, *The Economist* magazine, Penguin Books, the economic daily *Les Echos* of Paris, and other admirably profitable, prestigious properties—and avowedly wants more.

- Maxwell Communications Corp. (United Kingdom). Annual revenues: $1.4 billion. Headed by Czech-born chairman Robert Maxwell, its holdings include London popular newspapers, Pergamon Journals, Macmillan (also owner of the Berlitz language schools), and TV services such as Movie Channel and MTV.

The only two American-based firms in the titanic ten:
- Time Warner. Annual revenues: $10.9 billion. Founded by publisher Henry Luce and filmmaker Jack Warner, this multimedia giant is the largest magazine publisher in the United States, with the greatest single share of magazine revenues, second-largest record company, second-largest cable TV presence, and one of the world's leading film producers. It has subsidiaries in Europe, Asia, Australia, and Latin America.

Its empire includes, in magazines: *Time, Life, Fortune, People, Sports Illustrated,* and *Entertainment Weekly.* In cable TV, the Home Box Office, Amex, and Cinemax systems. In films, Warner Brothers. In books, Time-Life, Little Brown Warner, Scott Foresman, and the Book-of-the-Month Club. In records, Warner, Electra, Asylum, Atlantic, and Repriso.

- Capital Cities/ABC. Annual revenues: $4.7 billion. One of the largest media conglomerates still largely national, it is a quintessential faceless corporation operated by professional managers.

Broadcasting properties include the ABC-TV and radio networks, eight TV and twenty-one radio stations, 80 per cent of ESPN, 38 per cent of Arts & Entertainment, and 33 per cent of Lifetime cable channel. In print, nine dailies (in Kansas City, Fort Worth, and elsewhere), Fairchild Publications; and Word Inc., largest U.S. publisher of religious material.

But these ten giants constitute only one echelon of global media power.

Among others, the Gannett Co., America's largest newspaper publisher, with 6.3 million circulation, ranks high. It owns the internationally distributed *USA Today,* eighty-five other dailies, sixteen radio and ten TV stations, and our second-largest billboard company, and became active in TV co-production through Grant Tinker/Gannett.

Also in the United States, Ted Turner's media empire, with $5 billion in assets, remains a potentially powerful global player. It includes the around-the-clock Cable News Network (CNN) and Headline News; twenty-four-hour superstation TBS; Turner Entertainment, a syndication and licensing subsidiary owning thirty-seven hundred MGM and other films and hundreds of hours of TV programming and cartoons; Turner Network Television (TNT), a cable entertainment system reaching twenty-nine million homes; and baseball's Atlanta Braves and basketball's Atlanta Hawks.

South of the border, Roberto Irinu Marinho's Globo empire includes TV Globo, one of the world's leading producers of TV soap operas; seven TV stations; the giant Brazilian daily *O Globo;* and a Monte Carlo station that beams TV programs to Italy. In Mexico, the Televisa complex monopolizes commercial TV with four channels, plus five radio stations; and, among other ventures, publishes the U.S. sports daily *The National.*

The two largest worldwide news services, the Associated Press and Reuters, cooperatively owned by their media members, also might be added. The AP is American; Reuters, British. Then there are internationally distributed publications independent of global conglomerates, such as the *International Herald Tribune, Wall Street Journal,* and *Newsweek.* Most of the largest are American.

The Paris-based *Herald Tribune,* jointly owned by the *New York Times, Washington Post,* and Whitney Communications, publishes in nearly a dozen cities around the globe. The *Journal,* also using multiple printing plants, edits separate editions for North America, Europe, and Asia. *Newsweek,* like *Time,* prints an international edition in English and, in a joint venture with TBS Britannica, is translated into Japanese for publication in Tokyo.

Television and movie distributors also are spreading tentacles. Here the United States overwhelmingly dominates. Our Big Four networks— CBS, NBC, ABC, and CNN—are well known. All are represented worldwide, if not in direct broadcasts such as CNN's, in syndicated programs. In films, the world has seven major libraries/studios. All are in the United States. They are: Paramount, MGM/United Artists, Warner Brothers, 20th Century Fox, Universal Studios, Columbia Pictures, and the Walt Disney Company. Of these, three are foreign owned: 20th Century Fox, by Rupert Murdoch's News Corp; Columbia Pictures, by Sony; and United Artists, by the Australian Quintex Corp.

Media support functions such as advertising also are international. Here Madison Avenue remained king until 1986. Then Saatchi & Saatchi PLC of London bought three New York giants to become the world's largest. The next year Saatchi was challenged by its former financial strategist, Martin Sorrell, whose WPP PLC of London spent $1.4 billion for Madison Avenue's JWT Group—itself a former world-leading nucleus of affiliates—and the longtime model Ogilvy Group. This gave the fast-growing WPP a vast domain of blue-chip agencies plus the largest public relations company on the globe, the number-one direct-marketing firm, and some three dozen other subsidiaries in sales promotion, graphic design, and audio-visual communication.

Both British behemoths since have suffered digestive problems, including mini-revolts among merged creative talent and, in Saatchi's case, a financial crunch predicted to end in divestitures or even the company's demise. But together Saatchi and WPP controlled nearly 10 per cent of $350 billion spent annually worldwide on marketing, far surpassing America's Interpublic, Young & Rubicam, Japan's Dentsu, and other giants.

This is not to say that Madison Avenue has been eclipsed. Far from it. The United States still is considered the planet's center of advertising, and American-owned agencies rank high. Further, the British, though they temporarily may have overreached, undeniably have seized some industry high ground.

Do these developments, as some observers warn, portend loss of control of our information and entertainment streams?

Again, beware of overreacting. In a diverse market economy, the case can be made that readers (or viewers or listeners) and advertisers, not the principal owners of thousands or millions of shares of stock, ultimately determine what is acceptable content—and it is not, as we are discovering, necessarily admirable or elevating, only indigenous. Also, as in other fields, our perception of the numbers and prominence of foreign ownership may deceive. In our Country of Big Shoulders, foreign acquisitions, compared to our media whole, have been minuscule except in book publishing. There, the foreign presence is disproportionately large.

Yet of all media fields, books, in both publication and distribution, are the most pluralistic, idiosyncratic, and open. The smallest, most individualistic participants can, and do, carve niches and create best-sellers. For now this field's most pressing pragmatic issue, involving entirely American ownership, is the antitrust implications of powerful mass-distribution retail book chains.

What about the vulnerability of national opinion-leading media to foreign takeover? True in theory; false in practice.

In broadcasting, the Federal Communications Commission must approve all license transactions, from which foreigners are excluded. Hence, cynics note, Rupert Murdoch's rush to obtain citizenship after contracting to buy a broadcast chain. Networks, not subject to FCC licensing, could be made so. Meanwhile, because they depend on acceptance by advertisers and affiliated stations, only majority American ownership is likely.

Among America's sixteen hundred dailies, foreigners already own small or medium-size properties. Witness Canada's Thomson chain, with over one hundred U.S. newspapers. But as in every industrialized nation except Great Britain, opinion-leading dailies are, by law or tacit understanding, off-limits to foreigners. In Great Britain, the not-insignificant exception of Murdoch's purchase of *The Times* and *Sunday Times* was attributable to his Commonwealth provenance and, as London's tabloid czar, unique leverage over a Thatcher government disdainful of monopoly restraints.

In the United States, it also should be noted, the *New York Times* is family owned, with poison-pill family-held preferred shares to inhibit takeovers. The *Washington Post, Los Angeles Times,* and other family-controlled, opinion-leading dailies are themselves part of large media conglomerates. At these or at other thought-leading papers, asset values rest in part on the credibility—read, among other criteria, nationality—of ownership.

In our information and entertainment media, the deeper policy concerns lie elsewhere. Press critic Ben H. Bagdikian, author of *The Media Monopoly,* puts the case for one set.

"The lords of the global village," he says "have their own political agenda. All resist economic changes that do not support their own financial interests. Together, they exert a homogenizing power over ideas, culture, and commerce that affects populations larger than any in history."

A more evident impact is the Greshamesque consequence of megascale. As media reach grows, common denominators of taste fall and profit stakes rise. Bagdikian puts it this way: "The global reach of the largest media firms, and their grand strategy of synergism, increases what is already a drug on the market: commercially safe, generic, all-purpose books, films, and TV programs. The bigger the corporation, the fewer risks it is likely to take."

For example, he adds, "American commercial broadcasting has produced much that is important in public affairs, programs with genuine humanistic values; it has also given us entertainment that is harmless and occasionally even uplifting. But most programming conforms to the imperative to freeze the hand that reaches for the switch...[with] constant violence, gratuitous sex, and deliberate manipulation of split-second change of images and sounds to make an emotional or sensory impact that leaves no time for reflection....Commercial television has also degraded the electoral process....[And] children's programming...is an enduring national scandal."

The issue, then, is more than nationality of media ownership. It is the venerable anti-trust problem of preserving competition, plus the institutional nature of megamedia, with their escapist, trivialized product in a market-driven, supermass age.

# 10

# *Lost in a Witchy Thicket?*

Even if one grants that present threats to our leadership and cultural, economic, and political integrity are exaggerated, what about the future? Globalization is gathering speed. Economic competitors are proliferating. The international economy seems precarious. Who can be sanguine?

No one should be. It is a dangerous and troubling world. But it best can be dealt with by understanding its perils and promise.

Consider first the potential of new competitors on the horizon. Four large nations are evolving fast. They are:

- India.

Here by a clear consensus among authorities abroad, if not in the United States, is an imminent "junior superpower." By the middle of the next century, says John Maddox, editor of London's prestigious *Nature,* this Asian giant could be another Japan. "The Indians," he points out, "have some excellent universities. Their electronics industry has grown at a pace unthinkable a few years ago. In spite of its status as a Third World country, India is on the move."

Girilal Jain, courtly, articulate editor of the powerful *Times of India,* enumerates how quickly. "In the past two decades," he says, "nobody has died of starvation in India, where famines were routine in the eighteenth and nineteenth centuries. We also have eliminated mass killers like malaria, plague, and smallpox. We have raised the average lifespan from twenty-six at the time of independence to fifty-two. We have raised literacy from 12 to 36 per cent in the past thirty-five years.

"India can build a nuclear plant, communications satellites, and missile launchers; it manufactures steam engines and diesel engines for its railways. There is hardly a machine we need that we cannot build ourselves. For a largely agricultural country with a very small industrial base at the time of independence a generation ago these are major achievements. And our press is among the finest."

In 1986, the newsmagazine *India Today* calculated, India had twice as many doctors as a decade earlier, more than triple the number of owners of industrial establishments, and 40 per cent more factory workers. Its post-colonial education system graduates 160,000 scientists and technical personnel annually. Every fourth Indian lives in a city or town. Some 100 million citizens—equal to two-fifths of the U.S. population—are defined as middle class, and some 63 per cent of the population is above the government's poverty line.

"The poor," as *India Today,* an impressive, *Time*-like weekly that itself exemplifies the progress, has observed, "will always be with us, but so will the middle class."

- Brazil.

The achievements of this South American colossus also have been obscured. Its continent's largest nation—number six in world population and number eight economically in the West—it, too, suffers awesome problems: a swelling population, immense debt, and a precarious post-military elected government. Nonetheless, *The Economist* observed in one of a spate of glowing business-magazine reports, it remains "a potential United States [of] the next century."

Like us, it possesses scale—nearly half the land area of South America. Between 1972 and 1980 it almost doubled industrial production, and almost tripled hydroelectric energy. In ten years it has created at least thirteen million new jobs, and more than doubled per capita income.

It possesses sophisticated industry and technology, including computer firms and space capabilities (e.g., its own communications satellite). In recent decades its manufactured-export increases have compared with those of South Korea and Taiwan. Its population includes about a million citizens of Japanese extraction, and Japanese firms invest heavily there. One of their most ambitious ventures: a controversial highway from the Amazon to the Pacific, via Peru. Much of the nation's immense debt, unlike that of peers, represents potentially sound development: highways, energy complexes, industry.

- The Soviet Union.

This now-faltering behemoth encompasses the world's largest land area—one-sixth of the total and two and a half times that of the United States. Its backward economy and peasant-steppe image notwithstanding, it trails only the United States and Japan in national product. It leads the world in oil and steel production and is second only to the United States in heavy industry. Like Brazil with its Amazon, it also possesses one of the planet's great untapped treasure houses: Siberia. The Soviets have a 99 per cent literacy rate. Two-thirds of their populace is urban. Selective technological prowess is indisputable. Their transition from Communism may be debilitating and painful, including loss of a number of previously conquered border states, but given their human and natural resources and the West's needs for markets, they, too, could surprise.

- China.

This evolving Communist colossus also is advancing. Despite low per capita income, China now compares to democratic industrial societies in several social indicators. For more than three decades its industry grew at 10 per cent annually, and in 1978-83 its rural income rose 70 per cent. It possesses both nuclear-missile and space capabilities. Given its culture-instilled drive and a receptivity to outside investment and expertise that predated Moscow's, once it stabilizes even faster progress than the Soviets' could occur.*

One reason is the imminent emergence of a "Greater China." Hong Kong, one of Asia's four little tigers of postwar development, is destined to shift from British to Chinese jurisdiction in 1997. Already, thousands of Hong Kong residents commute daily to China's adjacent Kwangtung Province, where some 1.5 million Chinese work in electronics, textile, and toy factories operated by Hong Kong capitalists.

Ultimately another tiger, longtime adversary Taiwan, is expected to be largely merged into the Mainland's economy. With the blessing of Taipei's mellowing Nationalist Chinese government, indirect Taiwan-China trade through Hong Kong exceeds some $2 billion annually, and indirect Taiwanese investment reached nearly $100 million in 1988.

Integration of these three Chinas, fostered by proximity, a shared language, and blood ties, will create a formidable force—an economic superpower whose components now aggregate twice South Korea's export volume, operate the world's largest container port and fourth-largest

---

*U.S.-China trade now exceeds $7 billion, and we have $3.1 billion invested in 408 enterprises there. Foreigners can buy land and run factories in Hainan, where McDonnell-Douglas and Occidental Oil are reported "happy" with recent ventures. Kentucky Fried Chicken operates its largest facility in Beijing. Before the Tiananmen Square upheaval, 300,000 Americans visited China annually.

financial center, hold $90 billion in foreign exchange, and have scientific establishments involved in biotechnology, lasers, space, and superconductivity.

Other potentially influential new players are in ascent. These include:

Malaysia. This populous former British colony obtains one-fifth of its gross product from industry and records a per capita income of $2,000. By the early 1980s it was second only to Japan in semiconductor export volume to the United States.

Indonesia. The world's fifth-most-populous country spread over three thousand islands, it profits from oil, petrochemical, and other new industries. By 1995, according to one forecast, it "will have scored the strongest gains of any Asian nation."

These and other nascent competitors' advances will complicate our lives. But in the high-technology Global Age, competition is no longer a zero-sum game. To the degree that new achievers abet economic growth and geopolitical stability they will enrich us. World economic stagnation, not competition, is our greatest enemy. For only continuing international growth can ensure our prosperity and the quickening global march toward order and democracy.

Here, too, we must look beyond current problems, especially in trade. Inevitably, trade must expand. If debt, dictatorships, and protectionist sentiments inhibit it, their inhibitions will be circumvented. One already apparent method is a variation on managed trade known as regional free-trade blocs. The contours of three now are visible:

1) North America. The U.S.-Canada Free Trade Agreement has formally entwined the two countries economically. It requires elimination of major mutual trade barriers and accelerated integration of Canadian-U.S. industries from banking and energy to transportation. In the event of trade embargoes, investment restrictions, or retaliatory measures against "foreign" firms by either country, these two nations' companies are to be treated identically.

Previously the same principle was written into a proposed Caribbean Basin Initiative, applying to Central America and the Caribbean islands. We also are edging in that direction with Mexico. With an open U.S.-Mexican border, and our security tied to south-border stability, Mexican participation in our free-trade area seems inevitable.

2) Europe. Internal European trade already surpasses that across the
Atlantic. With the European Community's single-market plan for 1992,
an even greater all-European flow of people, goods, and services is projected. The opening of Eastern Europe and the Soviet Union promises
still more growth.

3) East Asia. From Australia to South Korea, Japanese investment,
industrial transplants, and opening to imports have accelerated regional
integration. Within ten years North-South trade within East Asia may
surpass transpacific commerce.

The regional advantages of these arrangements are clear. Unfortunately,
they also facilitate protectionism against outsiders. This long has been
suspected as a tacit motive for Europe's single-market plan. Historically, the continent and protectionism have seemed synonymous. When
Japan's export explosion hit, for example, EC nations promptly batten-
ed down, restricting Japanese imports (especially autos and electronics
products) and low-price dumping.*

Such protectionism always fails. Japan responded with new assembly
plants in both Europe and North America, from which exports could
be classified as North American. Similarly, when we imposed "voluntary" auto and microchip quotas on Japan, the result was, for autos,
more expensive American cars that invited an influx of Japanese assembly
plants, and for chips, a shortage that drove up our own prices and made
Japan's chips even more attractive.

Chicken Little forecasts for both the world and the United States are
plentiful—and popular: Three of America's seven top-selling business
books of the past decade turned on prognoses of economic collapse.**
Throughout most of the 1980s economic expansion, most forecasters
polled annually by the National Association of Business Economists
predicted a downturn within two years. It didn't happen.

The fact is that, despite troubling problems, long-term the world
economic outlook seldom has been more promising. Downturns are in-

---

*Italy and France were especially aggressive, with the Italians allowing only two thou-
sand car imports annually and the French delaying electronics items over border
technicalities.
***The Great Depression of 1990, How to Prosper During the Coming Bad Years,* and
*Crisis Investing.*

evitable. Business cycles persist. Nonetheless, new-wave economics provides rational reason for optimism. It holds that macro-economic management has evolved to the point that recessions, for the most part, now may be mini-crashes or, in Alvin Toffler's term, "eco-spasms." That is, unsynchronized mini-recessions affecting distinct industrial or farm sectors or regions. For various reasons, including rolling reindustrialization that selectively tunes business cycles, we now are seen as immune to prolonged, nationwide economic cataclysms.

If that is true, globalization is one factor. Our 1981-82 recession left almost one-third of manufacturing capacity idle and unemployment at nearly 11 per cent. But services growth and overseas affiliates' profits kept us afloat.

Reaganomics—Keynesianism squared—then helped lift the rest of the world without triggering inflation. With the dollar's mid-1980s fall, our export markets revived enough to set several sectors booming.

Three other anti-recession elements contribute: A "birth dearth" that decreases pressure on the labor market; a growing services sector, which offers insulation from manufacturing downturns; and global confidence in the Federal Reserve's independence and acumen. Thus, new-wave theory holds, when a recession does occur, it can end in a "soft" rather than "hard" landing, with revival in as little as a year.

One of the great imponderables is debt. This includes our own, both public and private sector, plus potentially calamitous fallout from savings-and-loan scandals, plus mountains of Southern and Eastern bloc obligations. Since surfacing in the Polish and Mexican financial crises, these have cast a pall. But again, there is a bright side. For nearly a decade, while conditions in most debtor countries worsened, forecasts of a domino collapse remained forecasts.

On the macro-level, levitation has been aided by stretch-out strategies. These gave creditor banks and their governments time to tighten procedures and build reserves (albeit inadequate). President Reagan's unforeseen Keynesianism partly compensated for debtors' lost purchasing power. International agencies contrived often surprising coordination. And even the most burdened debtors proved poignantly resilient. But the picture remains an ugly one of corruption, exploitation, and peril, darkened by the potentially catastrophic U.S. regulatory scandals.

The current global slowdown need neither worsen nor persist. Industrialized nations' demand has continued upward, exports of all major countries surged in late 1988, and in Western Europe, partly in anticipation of 1992's single market, business confidence and capital investment reached highs.

Theodore Levitt, former editor of the *Harvard Business Review,* for one, is not surprised. "I see no reason why world economic growth should not be sustainable," he says. "We don't necessarily have to fall off the cliff. We can just be tired for awhile."

We need not be tired for long. Every problem is said to contain an equivalent opportunity. That is demonstrably true here.

On the one hand, the problem is not simply destabilizing debt and economic slumps. It is a taproot: such abject poverty in the majority of the world that every day at least thirty-five thousand persons die of hunger. That is the equivalent of more than seventy fatal five-hundred-passenger jumbo jet crashes daily. This is intolerable morally, destructive politically, socially, and economically—and, in the Global Age, unnecessary.

The equivalent opportunity is a gift of science—an ability to feed everyone—and a symbiosis between North and South. While the industrialized North has excess production and too few markets, the South needs almost everything and lacks only purchasing power. The solution may be a page from Henry Ford that could exploit this synergy.

In the auto industry's pre-World-War I infancy, Ford was impaled on a dilemma: His new assembly line could build many more Model-T's than people could afford. His solution: Make assembly-line workers his market by guaranteeing a $5-a-day wage. The idea was revolutionary—and it worked. His employees' new purchasing power, replicated elsewhere, financed the volume production that put Ford—and American—prosperity on wheels.

This rationale also underlay two other great twentieth-century innovations: the New Deal and the Marshall Plan. In the 1930s the Roosevelt administration, faced with mass hunger and unemployment, reasoned that jobs—of any sort—were prerequisites to stability and recovery. It created them, making government the employer-of-last-resort in a vast public works program, until World War II created the demand required for revival.

In the case of the Marshall Plan, the problem was to resuscitate war-shattered Western Europe quickly enough to neutralize extremists. The solution, proposed by Secretary of State George C. Marshall in 1947, was massive grants and loans—$13.6 billion over five years—to governments that would coordinate recovery projects with neighbors.

This complemented some $20 billion in U.S. support through UN relief assistance and occupied-areas aid to Austria and Germany. The aggregate of $5.5 billion annually, when our gross product was some $250 billion, at today's GNP would translate to $80 billion.

In hindsight it was a bargain. It forged Western Europe into a fortress of democracy and market economies that helped ignite the postwar American and world booms. Its conception and execution, as Harvard historian Charles Maier told a fortieth-anniversary commemorative conference in Berlin, "required a loftiness of American vision that has not been demonstrated since."

We could reincarnate that loftiness in a multinational, Global Age Marshall Plan II. Various foresighted officials, including Sen. Bill Bradley of New Jersey, vigorously champion it as part of a resolution of the debt crisis. "We must be clear about the stakes," Bradley emphasizes. "We are talking about economic growth and prosperity, about security, and about democracy. This is not charity. It is self-interest. The aging societies of Europe and Japan need the developing countries with young populations and high growth potential to thrive in order to avoid their own economic stagnation."

Japan is the world's number-one capital-surplus nation. We finance much of its military umbrella. We must increase the pressure on it to lead. The Japanese already have announced programs making them the world's number one foreign-aid donor. Given their titanic surpluses and our disproportionate military and trade-deficit contributions, we and others are justified in expecting them to provide Marshall-scale redevelopment funds.

Should this happen, Japan would at one stroke have won the global respectability now denied it, and both we and it would benefit. We, for example, forget at our peril that no other large industrialized country shares a long and porous border with a developing nation—Mexico— and a hemisphere of other largely poor, struggling neighbors. Cuba, Nicaragua, Haiti, and Panama are only early warnings.

A chronically unstable backyard is not conducive to progress. Our hemispheric neighbors' economic instability could, if we are not prudent, become our Global Age Achilles' heel.

# 11

# *Needed: A New Periscope*

This, then, is the anatomy of the new age, some of the perils and opportunities it presents, and why we can be said to possess a winning hand that only awaits our playing it. Are we prepared to play it successfully?

Our public dialogue suggests not. Our obsession with decline reveals a narcissism, lack of self-knowledge, and skewed perspective only marginally related to who we are, what forces actually are driving human affairs, and our relation to them. We seem, as the popular song says, to be "always chasing rainbows"—in this case, Camelot. We lack a worldview relevant to the new age that we, more than anyone else, have molded and that requires our leadership.

This new worldview will not come easily. As a society, we are renowned parochialists. The monarchs of our continent, sheltered by oceans, insulated from old-empire conflicts, united by a common language and culture—we found it easy to turn inward. We came late to international power and in the great colonization era were the colonized, not the colonizers, who, as a French editor told me, "had to understand and manage" other peoples. Indeed, except in confrontations, we seem reluctant to wield political—as opposed to economic—power.

Our intelligentsia in academia, the arts, and publishing tends to turn outward only along well-worn paths. As author Edward Hoagland observed in connection with an international authors' meeting, our writers, "like other affluent citizens here, do make the rounds of the countries that were regularly visited, for example, by Henry James....[But] in no other developed country, I suspect, has the intellectual community remained so unfamiliar with and uninterested in the changing postwar world"—especially developing nations.

Our journalism and political discourse reflect this. Abroad they are viewed as appallingly crabbed and narcissistic. Forty of the world's fifty top newspapers, and at least a dozen leading radio-television networks, are foreign. Yet except for Soviet propaganda and British TV drama, for the most part we ignore them. Only about a hundred of our sixteen hundred daily newspapers employ full-time foreign editors. Despite record media profits, since the 1950s American foreign correspondents have declined, not increased. For us our continent, long a comfortable haven, remains our "world."

Our daily journalism's universe is "news," defined as crisis, conflict, disaster, titillation. Contexts are slighted, follow-ups sporadic, tides obscured by waves. This leaves blurred snapshots inferior to the broader panoramas of West European and, at times, others' newspapers and broadcasts. Such deprivation fosters a chronic befuddlement over what really is happening in the world and how we relate to it. This means, as the *New York Times'* James Reston has said, that we are constantly surprised and "often out of touch with the violent forces that threaten the security of our people and the order of the world." Islam is one example. It is, he points out, difficult to ignore a movement "which commands the allegiance of sixty-seven countries and one-fifth of the world's population," but we long have managed to—"we are still innocents abroad."

This is sadly true. We see history as episodic and Amerocentric, not a flow in which we are but part of the mainstream. Thus we are nonplussed by inevitable results of decolonization such as the ascent of Asia's economic "dragons"—and if we do not change, we will be again by the Global Age.

The same could be said of image versus the reality of four decades of Soviet bumbles, of the inexorable deflation of the Communist menace, and of American ignorance about the UN. Americans were the UN's chief progenitor. It is based here. Polls perennially affirm high American "generic support"—nearly 90 per cent in a 1985 Gallup poll. Yet the same survey revealed 80 per cent unable to name any UN agency. We remain abysmally uninformed.

The UN has achieved far more than it is generally credited with by our media and political establishments. In fact, Therese P. Sevigny, under secretary general for public information, insists, "Despite its well-publicized flaws, it has been overall a quite remarkable success."

In regional conflict, for example, the UN's auspices provided for the Soviet withdrawal from Afghanistan, facilitated the cease-fire in the Iran-Iraq war, and remains instrumental in peacekeeping in Cyprus and the front-line Middle East. On disarmament, most arms control agreements, except on nuclear weapons, and nuclear prohibitions for the deep sea and outer space have roots in the UN framework. So do bans on bacteriological weapons and modifications of our environment for military purposes.

On human rights, the UN has put and kept the issue on the international agenda, adopting universal standards and binding covenants and helping focus on mass violations such as South Africa's. On international law, the UN, the under secretary general notes, "has codified and created more international law than was done in all previous history," including registering some thirty thousand treaties and helping negotiate provisions on the seas, ocean floors, and outer space.

On population, its World Population Conference in 1974 became a watershed, producing an action plan and unprecedented cooperation through the UN Fund for Population Activities. On ecology, the UN Environmental Programme, among many achievements, negotiated treaties on the Mediterranean and, in 1987, the planet's ozone layer.

"Even more visible achievements," the under secretary general adds, "include the worldwide elimination of smallpox, under the aegis of the World Health Organization. Or the dramatic increase—from under 5 to over 50 per cent in the past decade—in infants immunized against the worst killer diseases. Or the role of the UN High Commissioner for Refugees in helping some 10 million dispossessed annually. Or UNICEF's feeding and care of millions of children every day. Or the role of the entire UN system in dealing with famines and other mass disasters."

If we saw the UN even partly in this light, how much healthier might our relationship with it be? But we so seldom hear such viewpoints, even if for the purpose of disagreement, because they are consigned to media "black holes." Such chasms are not necessarily ideological. Greed, rigidity, and failures of professionalism bring the same result.

We suffer from all three, partly for structural reasons. Both newspapers and radio-TV are among our most lucrative businesses. But most daily papers, now chain owned, exist to export local monopoly profits, which they bolster by editorial understaffing, underpaying, and shrinking "newsholes," especially for international commentary and analysis.

Television, freed by deregulation to ignore all but high-profit trivia, generally restricts foreign coverage to crises and controversies, with almost no prime-time analyses and documentaries such as those formerly aired under public-interest-service and fairness requirements. Local radio, for which networks have become marginal, now programs to special interest audiences. Public radio and TV, unable to realize hopes for funding through fees for commercial licenses (now free), or levies on commercial broadcast profits, languish in semipoverty.

Our journalism's definition of news derives directly from *The Front Page*—what is "new," immediate, surprising, outrageous, entertaining (and accessible). As former World Bank consultant John Maxwell Hamilton observes, it encompasses "an unwritten rule"—that "local news is news and foreign news is foreign, and that people want plenty of the former and will tolerate only small doses of the latter."

Like others extensively exposed to the outside world, I often puzzle over this. Many of our journalists have exceptional pride and talent. But for various reasons they accept inherited mores with largely intramural, if any, complaint. The media rarely analyze or critique one another, and support is only marginal for journalism reviews or scholarly institutes that might.

Control of major media increasingly is concentrated in publicly traded stock-owned companies. This makes managements beholden to pension-fund and other instant-profit-oriented institutional investors now in the majority on Wall Street. And, unlike major European nations, we never have evinced an inclination to fund quality noncommercial media. Thus, the common denominators of megascale rule.

Our educational system sustains comparable black holes. Foreign-language teaching is one example. While second- or third-language study is common abroad, fewer than 3 per cent of our high-school graduates reach "meaningful foreign-language competence," according to the President's Commission on Foreign Language and International Studies. In two decades the number of colleges with foreign-language entrance requirements dropped fourfold—to fewer than 8 per cent. "There is," said the commission, "a widening gap between...needs and the American competence to understand and deal successfully with other peoples in a world of flux."

Ironically, deficiencies are particularly acute in two langages with the greatest strategic and competitiveness ramifications: Russian and Japanese. Fewer than a dozen Americans are thought to know fully any languages of Soviet Central Asia. No more than four hundred can translate Japanese scientific and technological information. Only about ten American students a year with technical expertise study Japanese. A small fraction of some ten thousand Japanese scientific and technical journals get translated into English, many in a stilted style that, an aerospace engineer told me, "is worth your life to unravel."

"We have yet to learn a critical lesson," a study for the Southern Governors' Association declared. "The language of trade is the language of the customer."

Further, the study lamented, "We do not adequately know the globe, nor the cultures of the people that inhabit it." A commission headed by retired educator Clark Kerr called this "global illiteracy." It pervades our schools.*

Global illiteracy is costly. It was part of the reason for our Indochinese, Iranian, and Lebanon debacles. It also underlies many of our current economic problems, real and imagined. The extent is illustrated by several potentially costly business mistranslations.

GM, for instance, found belatedly that its Chevrolet model Nova, when spoken as two Spanish words, means, "It doesn't go." "Body by Fisher" translates as "Corpse by Fisher." Schweppes Tonic Water was translated into Italian as "bathroom water." And "Come Alive with Pepsi" almost was translated into a Chinese advertisement as "Pepsi Brings Your Ancestors Back from the Grave."

Global illiteracy need not continue. Polls repeatedly show residual interest in world affairs. We are, after all, a nation of immigrants.

More and more we travel abroad—to find ourselves surrounded by other Americans. The world is infinitely interesting. A visit to one country whets the appetite for another.

Indeed, former World Bank consultant Hamilton has proved Americans to be receptive to information about communities' international socioeconomic links.

Using his experience as a onetime *Milwaukee Journal* newsman, he designed a reporting project on varieties of global interdependence and obtained support from the Ford, Carnegie, and Benton foundations. Then he worked with the *Christian Science Monitor* and a score of other newspapers to stimulate features on specific local, regional, and national links with developing nations.

From Hattiesburg, Miss., to Richmond, Va., Aurora, Ill., Middletown, N.Y., Everett, Wash., and other cities, his project left a trail of informative stories. The variety is suggested by a sampling of chapters from his book, *Main Street America and the Third World,* summarizing the experience.

---

*In a nine-country UNESCO study of ten- and fourteen-year-olds, Americans ranked next to last in comprehension of foreign cultures. In another study, over 40 per cent of American high-school seniors could not locate Egypt accurately, and over 20 per cent failed to locate France or China. This, says the National Council on Foreign Language and International Studies, should not surprise. "At most," it says, "only 5 per cent of our prospective teachers take any course relating to international affairs or foreign peoples and cultures."

In "Manufacturing Trade: The Two-Way Street," he tells of the small Keene, N.H., company that in 1963 set out to sell printing equipment in Europe, increased exports to 25 per cent of its sales, and has expanded into Australia and developing nations such as China, Brazil, and Singapore. Home-base employment has doubled to seven hundred, with seven hundred more on payrolls abroad.

In "Third World Imports: Good Business," he analyzes how imports of foreign parts or finished products have kept American firms competitive, saved consumers money, revived ports such as Bridgeport, New Haven, and New London, Conn., and increased payrolls outside their industries. "Commerce Department figures," he notes, "show an estimated 3.4 million Americans' jobs depend on imports."

Other chapters ranging from "When the Third World Sneezes" to "Global Drug Addiction" detail other aspects of interdependence. "As surely as communities have Third World connections," he concludes, "they have people who can talk about them....The central question for journalists is whether they will put such questions on the public's agenda."

Postproject surveys confirmed its impact: At the *Hattiesburg American* alone, the editor received five times the calls usually made about the "hottest stories." Subsequently the Society of Professional Journalists helped fund briefings and panels on emulating his work elsewhere.

Many ongoing efforts could be cited. The medium-size Stanley Foundation of Muscatine, Ia., for instance, for which I edited *World Press Review,* also sponsors a syndicated radio series, multinational conferences on global issues, a schools program, and similar activities. The Danforth Foundation of St. Louis funds pilot programs in teacher training and curricula in international studies. The American Forum for Global Education provides conferences, publications, and classroom materials. A network of councils on foreign relations and world affairs councils sponsors speeches, conferences, and opinion-leader briefings.

The United Nations Association U.S.A. and other efforts could be added. All that I have encountered are heartening. But their aggregate impact approximates that of a lawn sprinkler in the Sahara. In the United States of America—the richest, most productive, most powerful nation in the world, is this to be recorded as our best? Not if we wish to continue to prosper and lead the world.

# 12

# *Our True Decline Problem*

This brings us to our true decline problem. That is not our economic performance nor our international status but our national spirit—our values, perspectives, resource allocation, even our popular culture. We are the richest and most secure in our history. Yet despite these riches and this security our national quality of life is falling. This is the root of our declinist syndrome.

The look and scent of decline envelop us. They are manifest in our hordes of homeless, malnourished, and alienated inner-city underclasses. In our drug culture. In the bankruptcy of a prison system that we cannot expand fast enough. In random violence that appears endemic. In all the ugliness, noise, and crudities of taste and manners that assail us.

We may sing "America, the Beautiful," but we are not creating it. On the contrary. Such beauty as survives tends to be the old, not the new. Architecture, art, music, entertainment, and public projects no longer usually are grand in concept and execution, but contrived, demeaning, repugnant.

Like Detroit in its disgraceful shoddy-product days, we live by and for a short-term bottom line. On the whole, this philosophy has brought neither pride nor satisfaction, but the cheap, the tawdry, the crumbling, and ultimately the unfulfilling—and uneconomic. We sense this. Yet it persists—and worsens. Except for a fortunate elite, our school system is a failure. Our "spacious skies"—and shores and waterways and often our soil—are despoiled. The income disparity between America's rich and poor, for a time closing, is widening.

Affordable housing, even for the middle class, has become an exception.

Single-parent families are multiplying. One of every five of our children lives in poverty.

Over two decades, net real investment in roads, bridges, mass transit, and other public works fell by three-fourths. The results are blight and peril. Even a partial summary is shocking:

117

- One of every four American bridges is regarded as dangerous; more than forty-five thousand are closed; every two days one collapses.
- Two-thirds of our interstate highway system and nearly that ratio of all paved roads need rehabilitation.
- Some three thousand dams in populated regions are hazardous.
- Airports and airways are congested, and air-traffic control systems need upgrading.
- Water-system storage and distribution deterioration wastes more than one-fourth of daily supplies in some major cities.
- More than $100 billion in new sewage treatment plants may be required by 1999.

And so on, for schools, parks, housing, city streets, and more.

What is wrong? In a preoccupation with pleasure, acquisitiveness, and individual or special-interest rights, we have lost a sense of community, history, and shared obligations. Since the Kennedy assassination—a psychic demarcation for us and the world—we have been a fragmented, contentious society, sundered over values, definitions, and purposes. It is an age of discontinuity, evident in national life from our political processes, industrial structure, and generational relationships to our entertainment and arts.

Rock music, for instance, unlike its predecessors' musical form, is not simply a derivative of the instrumental and rhythmic structures it followed. It is a discontinuity, eschewing the rich tonalities of brass for strings—mainly guitar, percussion, and electronic effects. Its pounding, high-decibel, monosyllabic nature make it a further anomaly—and repugnance to most in the generations that knew different. To these multimillions its poverty reaffirms the magnitude of our decline.

Similarly, the scale of divorce, drug dependency, religious alienation, pseudo education, extreme longevity, and aimless, jobless but well-clothed, well-fed young are discontinuities. These all have roots in the 1960s, a demarcation when dreams died, purposes fled, and consensus collapsed. Culturally, that, too, marked the end of an age.

Like the Soviets, Eastern Europe, and newly industrializing nations, we need a *perestroika*—national restructuring and renewal. The 1990s then can be the next divide, when we revive dreams, recover communal purposes, and relearn the art and necessity of compromise and consensus-building.

This may not be as dubious a proposition as it seems. Historically, there has been unity in adversity, and adversity has begun to intrude. The Monopoly-money era of postwar growth is over. We have returned to the more moderate progress of earlier decades. We have no choice but to begin living within these new national means.

We can do this with relatively minor sacrifice. Both our own and the world economies are basically strong. We have immense residual resources and infrastructure. Political rhetoric notwithstanding, we are among the lowest-taxed nations in the world. And fortuitously, despite pressing needs for new public programs, two major areas can sustain non-destructive cutbacks. These are the military and federal entitlements.

Begin with the military. For years we have sensed that it was over-funded. In Camelot and the cold war we could justify that. No more. Now we must reexamine our military's mission and design a strategy to achieve it. We may have difficulty agreeing on that—but we start with the advantage of knowing what it is not.

It is not, a majority in surveys now acknowledge, an obsession with the arms and bipolar competition that distinguished the cold war. This reached its apogee in the 1980s, when Pentagon budgets—some $300 billion annually—set peacetime records. More than one-fourth of federal expenditures went for military purposes. Their cost, historian Paul Kennedy calculates, aggregated a greater share of gross product than did Great Britain's military at the height of its empire, even in wartime.

Military forces always will require major appropriations. But we have made "Pentagon" synonymous with waste and muddled priorities. With Nixon-era detente, the likelihood of a superpower nuclear exchange waned. Yet the "Great Reagan Buildup" of some $2 trillion in Pentagon appropriations allocated nearly one-fourth for nuclear weaponry.*

Meanwhile conventional forces were only peripherally strengthened: Total military personnel of 2.1 million increased by only 100,000. Reserve forces fared even worse: In one Congressional Budget Office study, most Army reserve units—mandated to provide 40 per cent of our initial forces in any major European conflict—were ranked only "marginally ready" or "not ready" for combat. Former NATO commander Bernard W. Rogers, in post-buildup testimony to Congress, conveyed dismay that U.S. conventional forces possessed only two weeks of firepower. Former

---

*This included $50 billion alone for the MX missile, Trident II, and other megaprograms. Some, like the B-1 and MX, were advanced without adequate design and testing.

defense secretary Robert S. McNamara was even more vehement. "It's a disgrace," he said, "spending $2 trillion and getting two weeks of firepower."

In President Reagan's closing year, the President's Commission on Integrated Long-Term Strategy warned that, notwithstanding our record expenditures, we remain unprepared for precisely the type of challenges most likely to occur. That is, terrorist, guerrilla, and small-nation actions. The commission included former secretary of state Henry Kissinger, two former national security advisers, and two retired generals. It recommended upgrading conventional forces, with flexible options such as "smart" (extraordinarily accurate) weapons and radar-evading aircraft and missiles.

"If tighter budgets impose an increase in risks," it concluded, "we should, for the near term, accept a greater risk of the unlikely extreme attacks, to bring about a reduced risk of the more probable conflicts."

Before the buildup, congressional Republicans estimated that mismanagement wasted at least $15 billion annually. In 1984, before a Senate subcommittee, an Air Force systems management deputy doubled that total, to $30 billion a year, or nearly one-third of military contracts. In 1983 the President's Private Sector Survey on Cost Control, headed by J. Peter Grace, put the waste total at one-fourth of all defense budgets spent since 1981.

In one 1987 analysis, Congress' General Accounting Office (GAO) found, nearly half of 114 Pentagon accounting systems failed to meet GAO requirements. In the Foreign Military Sales Program alone, over $600 million in advance payments could not be accounted for. Even sophisticated weapons tend to "disappear." For nearly a year, two dozen Stinger missiles in Germany were erroneously presumed missing.

Sergeant Bilko, Beetle Bailey, and Trapper John are fictional in name only. As internationally respected British military expert John Keegan says, "The U.S. military cries out for reform....If the bureaucracy of the conventional and the mediocre stifles [the] impulse for reform, there will be more Beiruts, more *Desert Ones,* perhaps even another Vietnam."

This, not money alone, is the issue. President Eisenhower, in his now-famous "military-industrial complex" speech, diagnosed its genesis— the "conjunction of an immense military establishment and a large arms industry that is 'new in the American experience.'" We must, he warned, "be on guard [against the] acquisition of unwarranted influence, whether sought or unsought," by this complex. "The potential for the disastrous rise of misplaced power exists and will persist."*

That is the cancer with which we must cope. Military contracts, jobs, bases, and other aspects of Pentagon activity mystically have been converted into corporate or community entitlements, unrelated to objective national security needs. Much of this alchemy is skillfully contrived.

Since World War II, for instance, there has been no significant dispute about our need never to be militarily inferior to anyone. We never have been—nor remotely close to it. Yet "shifting-target" propaganda continually panics us into fear that we might be.

Should the standard of comparison be force capabilities? If so, focus on the two superpowers only and start with "raw force" numbers. These obscure facts such as the civilian-support functions of many Soviet troops, the age and inferior capabilities of many Soviet weapons, or in naval comparisons, the Soviet coastal, merchant-marine, or fishing vessels equated with our long-range warships, where we are clearly superior— especially in number and size of aircraft carriers.

The alliances factor? Our allies spend six times more on defense than Moscow's Warsaw Pact allies. The power of NATO's non-American conventional forces—land and sea—far surpasses that of non-Soviet Warsaw Pact counterparts. "Fuzz" that. Never, ever discuss our overarching advantage in spheres of influence. When all else fails, switch to "gaps." If none sounds sufficiently ominous, invent some. Thus:

- The "missile gap" (1960s)**
- The "antiballistic missile (ABM) gap" (1970s)***

---

*This was not an atypical comment. Previously, in a letter rebutting hawkish columnists Joseph and Stewart Alsops' call for "a crash program" in missiles and bombers, he wrote a publisher friend, "I have spent my life in the study of military strength as a deterrent to war, and...military armaments necessary to win a war. War implies a contest; when [a contest] is no longer involved and the outlook comes close to destruction of the enemy and suicide for ourselves—an outlook that either side can ignore— then arguments as to the exact amount of available strength as compared to somebody else's are no longer the vital issues....Safety cannot be assured by arms alone."

**The Soviets were expected to have five hundred to one thousand intercontinental ballistic missiles (ICBMs) by 1961. "Later," notes Ruth Leger Sivard, formerly of the U.S. Arms Control and Disarmament Agency, "it developed that what they actually had then were ten while the U.S. had two hundred."

***By the early 1970s the Soviets were to have ten thousand interceptors in a nationwide ABM system. "The actual count," she says, "proved to be sixty-four interceptors and essentially a defense against bombers rather than missiles."

- The "hard-target kill gap" (1970s)*
- The "spending gap" (1980s)**

The latest shifting target? The percentage of GNP allocated to military budgets compared to the Soviets' or our own for other years, or our own actual budgets for one year compared to another. Regardless of NATO-Soviet force comparisons and the objective sufficiency of ours, failure to hold the line or continue raising ours then is said to reflect lack of resolve. Reductions become weakness, woolly-headedness, or endangering national security.

Is there no end to this? No. It works—and it pays. The history of Pentagon budgets demonstrates the former; a General Accounting Office study, the latter. In 1980-83, it showed, military contracting became 120 per cent more profitable than commercial manufacturing.

The tragedy is that, beyond a point, military spending weakens, not strengthens. Some weakening is quantifiable. In research and development, for example, we allocate 40 per cent of all funds to the military. West Germany allocates only 4 per cent; Japan, 1 per cent. Another 10 per cent of our R & D is committed to other government programs—in health, space, energy, and the like. Thus, only half of our R & D spending has what the Commission on Industrial Competitiveness calls "competitiveness as a primary consideration." This saps us.

The talent diversion alone is enormous. Fully one-sixth of our scientists and engineers are employed in some seven hundred federal laboratories—seventy-two, employing twenty-seven thousand engineers and scientists, run by the Pentagon. Some 30 per cent of all U.S. scientists and engineers—including three of every ten electronics engineers— are estimated to work on Pentagon-related projects.

A few years ago, when technologies from jet engines to computers flowed from military research, this balance might have been defensible. But as weaponry became more exotic, commercial fallout declined. Only

---

*Such new Soviet missiles as the SS-19 were judged accurate enough to destroy all our land-based missiles (ICBMs). But "assessments in the 1980s found this unrealistic for several reasons: among them the 'Silo-killer' SS-19 was...less accurate than originally gauged by more than one-third."

**Dramatic growth in Soviet military spending, plus the "danger" to our ICBMs, had opened a "window of vulnerability." But a CIA reassessment in 1983 "showed that Soviet procurement had leveled off during 1977-81" and the spending increase was half that of the alarmist projections.

about a third of defense-related innovations lead to claims for commercial title.

Thus, notes the president's commission, in many key technologies "the Government has become a net user." In civilian R & D, "from which we can reap the greatest commercial reward," we trail both Germany and Japan. Hence "the question of how the Government manages its R & D becomes critical."

Another study, for the Council on Economic Priorities, in a two-decade comparison of seventeen advanced industrial nations found that "those devoting large portions of gross domestic product to arms typically had weakening economies, decreasing technological prowess, and spreading industrial lethargy associated with low investment rates." Compared to alternative spending, military appropriations are among the least effective in spurring job creation—especially of the blue-collar type. A billion dollars for military procurement, the study found, creates some 28,000 jobs, but, spent elsewhere, many more—32,000 in public transit, for example, or 71,000 in education.

"Nations which have devoted a larger share of output to civilian investment," it concluded, "have experienced faster overall economic growth and, prior to the energy crisis, higher productivity growth as well."

Closing of obsolete or redundant military installations also pays. In a 1977 study of the effects of one hundred base closings since 1961, the Pentagon's Office of Economic Adjustment found a 47 per cent increase in civilian jobs on facilities transferred to local governments or the private sector.* The last major installation closed, Kincheloe Air Force Base in Michigan, became an industrial park where forty businesses employ two thousand people—three times its previous civilian total.

"Closing bases poses a threat to individual members of Congress," says Republican Rep. Richard Armey of Texas, author of an act empowering a nonpartisan commission to make such decisions, "because bases mean federal money and jobs back home. But the business of defense should be defense. Keeping obsolete bases open as a government jobs program is a terribly inefficient allocation of defense dollars that are becoming more scarce every year."

*Office-industrial parks were established at seventy-five; civilian airports at forty-two; community colleges or post-secondary vocational schools at thirty-two; and four-year colleges at twelve.

Political and economic realities also require reform of federal "entitlements." Like the military, our entitlements (benefit payments directly to individuals) "just growed." All are for good purposes: Social Security, Medicare, pensions, farm subsidies, veterans' benefits. But they amount to 47 per cent of federal outlays and are growing twice as fast as the economy.

Further, contrary to our traditional values, most (85 per cent) are not distributed according to need. Of some $455 billion in 1986:

- Most ($271 billion) consisted of Social Security and Medicare payments;
- $47 billion, largess for what former commerce secretary Peter G. Peterson calls "the two most generous pension systems in America," civil service and military retirement;
- $26 billion, for agricultural subsidies;
- $43 billion, for veterans' health care and assorted other programs;
- $18 billion, for unemployment compensation.

What can be done?

In logic, the issue, now joined in Washington, turns heavily on equity. The elderly, with total benefit income included, have the lowest poverty rate of any age group—under 3 per cent. In 1986 federal benefits per elderly American (about $9,130) exceeded benefits plus education aid per American child by elevenfold. Meanwhile, in 1979-86, the poverty rate for American children rose by nearly one-third, to 20 per cent.

Other aspects of entitlements are equally controversial. Many federal retirees, for instance, work at other jobs and receive second (double-dip) pensions. Farm subsidies go mainly to owners enjoying the largest sales and to banks to service debt. And most veterans'-care recipients are elderly with above-average incomes and no service-related ailments. Meanwhile, nonpoverty benefit programs—"our true 'social safety net,'" according to Peterson, who co-authored a study of the problem—over a decade have shrunk as a ratio of the federal budget and experienced almost no growth as a ratio of GNP.*

---

*More than three-fourths of all retiring enlisted men, according to a recent General Accounting Office study, served for twenty years without any combat experience, and less than 10 per cent of their service time was spent on "hazardous duty"—which in any case is accompanied by a special bonus. Meanwhile, millions of short-term enlistees have experienced combat in war without receiving a pension.

Skilled single-issue lobbies exploit our political fragmentation to prevent military and entitlements reform. Can we rise above them? If we do not, but continue posturing and scapegoating, we will have invited any blight that this brings to our Global Age future.

# 13

# *The Education Imperative*

A relevant worldview, reformed military, and rationalized entitlement programs are only the beginning of our needed *perestroika.* In Asia's dynamic new-achiever economies, it has been observed, education is "the stem that winds the watch." So in this high-technology age it must be here.

Corporations no longer are bound by national borders. Capital flows freely. The only wholly American asset is its people. Ultimately, it is in this realm—human capital—that future competitiveness and leadership will be determined. This means that, above all, we must become an education society.

We have spoken glowingly of this idea for years. But it has been paid only lip service. Now a litany of our problems is staggering.

- About one-tenth of our people—some twenty-six million—are functionally illiterate.
- More than a fourth of our young people never have completed high school.
- Almost 13 per cent of all seventeen-year-olds in school are functionally illiterate—and 44 per cent are marginally so.
- In one sampling, fewer than one in five eleventh-graders could compose a note asking for a summer job, and in another, only one of every five young adults could read a bus schedule.

Other studies, from the Department of Education's *A Nation at Risk* to *What Do Our 17-Year-Olds Know?,* based on a sampling of 8,000 seventeen-year-olds, document shocking deficiencies:

- In the seventeen years through 1980, College Board verbal and math scores dropped by more than 40 per cent. Science and math results also fell steadily.

- In 1982 even the top 5 per cent of our twelfth-grade math students scored last among peers from nine developed countries.
- Foreign-language ability and "global cultural literacy," as already noted, are even greater wastelands.

All this reflects deeper systemic ills. Since the 1960s colleges and universities, in pursuit of relevance, have eased admissions criteria. High schools have pared graduation requirements. Homework shrank—by nearly a third among high-school seniors in the 1970s.

Teachers' salaries also have lagged. While school budgets rose 12 per cent in a decade, the proportion allocated to teachers' pay fell by 10 per cent. New opportunities, especially for women, siphoned potential teaching talent. Teacher quality, as measured by College Board verbal and math results, also has fallen steadily.

Shortages are especially acute in science and mathematics. One-third of our science classes, the National Science Teachers Association estimates, now are taught by nonspecialists such as athletic coaches. More than 80 per cent of our seventh- and eleventh-grade students never take field trips—and half have no access to a lab. Nationwide, from the eighth grade on, with each successive year the ratio of students taking mathematics drops by half.

The implications of these failings are enormous. For, as Dr. Shirley A. Hill, chairman of a National Research Council study group, observed, "Those who do not learn basic mathematics problem-solving skills will be left behind in the world of the future. And this is just as true for nations as individuals."

Vocational guidance remains a desert. Specialties such as masters in law or business administration (MBA) suddenly become fashionable—and flooded—while others languish. Thus, we end up having twenty lawyers per ten thousand people, compared to Japan's one—and forty accountants per ten thousand, versus Japan's three, while critical fields such as engineering and computer science are short an aggregate 200,000 graduates.

Who outside the field knows how many engineering and computer-science opportunities there are? Who besides engineers even know what an engineer does, and how many subspecialties there are, from electrical to electronic, hydraulic, and construction? Where are the career films and videos or publicity campaigns about such opportunities?

Priorities within curricula also are skewed. As Derek C. Bok, president of Harvard University, lamented, business schools overemphasize finance and analytic skills to the detriment of manufacturing, motivation of workers, and international business. As a result managements are more easily swayed to manipulate rather than create wealth. Universities also focus too little on core social issues such as the causes of poverty and their potential correctives.

Are these the causes or consequences of an age of greed? Either way they must be corrected. Both pragmatic and ethical imperatives require it.

It is sobering to see Help Wanted signs everywhere or read columns of classifieds offering jobs and, in the same newspapers, stories of inner-city or migrant masses without jobs or, in many instances, apparent purposes in life. It is equally troubling to be confronted, as all who manage enterprises have been, with potential recruits of almost uniformly dismal qualifications, in education, general skills, maturity, and general responsibility. One of Manhattan's largest banks, Chemical, reports that it must interview forty high-school graduates to find one to train as a teller. It is not alone.

Japan, Western Europe, and even the Soviet Union and China have functional literacy rates exceeding 95 per cent. Ours hovers around 80. In 1959-71 our spending per student through high school—public and private—increased about one-fifth faster (4.7 per cent) annually than GNP growth. But through 1985 the total slipped to about even (2.7 per cent) with GNP growth—while teachers' salaries, which had been rising about 2.8 per cent yearly, fell by 1.25 per cent annually.

"We have a situation in the world," says Maurice F. Strong, former UN under secretary general who now heads the World Economic Forum, "where everybody—politicians, businessmen—pays lip service to the fact that knowledge, operating through technology, through design, through management, is the major source of wealth creation—competitive advantage, added value, etc. But while they acknowledge that at the level of rhetoric, they allow what you might call the knowledge industry—the institutions through which we produce and learn how to supply knowledge—to be starved. Our universities, our school systems, our research institutions...are the prime source of wealth creation today."

Cosmetic gestures no longer will suffice. We need an education system oriented around the new real world. This means shattering the strictures that bind us to hereditary, agrarian-era forms of educational structures and instituting lifetime learning, from pre-school through retirement years.

Reading, writing, foreign languages, and other knowledge come easiest in the immediate post-toddler years. Japan capitalizes on this with subsidized private kindergartens, attended by more than four-fifths of pre-school-age children. Why not emphasize this more, especially as pre-school daycare expands?

Particularly in disadvantaged areas, such programs pay dividends. For every dollar invested in pre-school efforts such as Head Start, more than four dollars is saved in other areas, such as public assistance and special education. We spend some $20 billion a year—a demonstrably inadequate total—on prisons and only $2.4 billion on government care and education of pre-schoolers. Shouldn't we begin reaping the competitiveness—and social—benefits of earlier intervention?

Given changes in blue-collar employment, improved vocational training and retraining is vital. A vast network of community and junior colleges blankets the country. Why not strengthen their efforts?

Business must help. American corporations spend $30 billion annually on schooling, from basic literacy to college studies. More than 80 per cent offer tuition reimbursements. They must do more, with tax credits or subsidies if necessary. This includes increased collaboration with both high schools and community colleges.

Germany has a renowned dual, or vocational, education system that we might emulate. An extension of public education operated by the private sector and partly financed by the government, it serves about four-fifths of Germany's youths. The sequence begins at age fifteen, when students in two of the three public education tracks register for apprenticeships in any of four hundred fields. For the next three years they work four days a week at one of the 500,000 firms that offer apprenticeships. On the fifth day they attend regular school, studying theoretical principles of their chosen vocation. The curriculum is monitored by a government vocational agency.

Approximately five of every one hundred West German workers participate in the program. Over 90 per cent of the participants earn school or apprenticeship certificates. Local business organizations, including the Chamber of Commerce and Industry, are responsible for ensuring apprenticeship quality.

"The dual system," says MIT labor economist Paul Osterman, "creates workers who are 'overqualified' for their initial entry jobs and perhaps even for many of the positions along the promotion trajectory normally associated with their jobs. This has helped to ease the incorporation of new technology into production and hence has made more flexible deployment possible."

Most American schools are poorly equipped. They need modern technical equipment, including computers and televised teaching aids. Indeed, it has been observed, our most fateful long-term competition with Japan may be who first succeeds in wiring its classrooms nationwide. This is not wholly fanciful.

In the end, the success of any approach rests on teachers. We will need more, and higher-quality, classroom talent, with rewards for excellence. Then, following the model of business, we need to debureaucratize schools' management and free teachers to teach.

These are only the beginning of needed reforms. Why, for example, should our schools, as in agrarian days, continue operating less than half the year—180 days? The school year in Japan is one-fourth longer—240 days—and in West Germany, the Soviet Union, Great Britain, and France, about one-seventh greater: up to 210 days. Our schools could offer classes year-round, with remedial programs and staggered staffing.

Colleges and universities compete for students, faculty, and funds. Why not extend the competitive ethic to lower- and secondary-school districts? We might expand pilot "student-choice" programs that give subsidy "credit vouchers" that enable parents to choose among a given pool of schools. In the end this rewards stronger schools and gives weaker ones incentives.

Japan goes a step further, subsidizing successful private high schools— now some 30 per cent of its total. Paying about half of a well-accepted (judged by attendance) school's cost, the government has found, results in more than 40 per cent of urban parents' choosing these over nearby weaker public institutions. Motivation is provided by entrance exams tied to subsidized "cram" courses called *juku*.

We also need more adult education, for young dropouts, mothers preparing to reenter the work force, retirees wanting part-time careers, or simple life enrichment. Many "young old" want to work, but not necessarily full-time. As baby bust labor shortages intensify, many will be needed.

Great Britain has pioneered with an Open University that links radio-TV courses and other teaching aids with local study centers. This system has been cloned in Africa, China, India, Japan, and elsewhere. South Korea also offers an impressive model with lessons piped into factories after hours.

Such reforms will not come easily. We have fifteen thousand public school districts, which change glacially and, reflecting local tax bases, usually penuriously. But as business' Committee for Economic Development observes, "Any call for comprehensive improvement in the public schools that does not recognize the need for additional resources is destined for failure." Thus far this has been the missing link in President Bush's campaign to be known as an education president.

Only the kind of Kennedyesque commitment that reenergized our space program will revitalize education. The job can be done. As *Business Week* observed in a special report, "In a $4-trillion economy with a $1-trillion federal budget, there surely is room for some shifts in spending: away from plant and equipment and toward workers; away from the aged and toward the very young; and even away from guns and toward people."

The resources are there. We need only reallocate them. For the $3.6 billion spent on just one of our five nuclear aircraft carrier task forces, for instance, we could pay four years' full tuition for ninety thousand private-college students—in science, engineering, or any other chosen field. Eliminating one year's Social Security cost-of-living increase could add $3,260 to the average salary of our 2.3 million public-school teachers.

School reform is scarcely off the starting blocks. But national consciousness-raising is. Private sector commissions abound, and business associations are stirring. The National Alliance of Business, for one, has mounted a nationwide campaign, including advertising supplements with Harvard president Derek Bok's admonition, "If you think education is expensive, try ignorance."

Some concrete changes have been made. A National Board of Professional Teaching Standards, organized by a Carnegie Foundation affiliate, has initiated competency tests and supplemental certification to upgrade teachers. Several states have raised admission standards for teacher trainees, and some two dozen allow accelerated accreditation of non-education majors. New Jersey is perhaps the most advanced, accrediting retirees and others from non-school fields who can pass equivalency tests and training tryouts.

Alternative certification programs, says Nancy Adelman of the Policy Studies Association in Washington, D.C., "attract some highly qualified people and turn out teachers that are as good as or better than those trained in traditional programs."

A start has been made, too, in strengthening curriculum content, with

reinstatement of core requirements obliterated in the 1960s. These include revised foreign-language requirements in some thirty states and
about one hundred major colleges.

North Carolina, for one, mandates foreign-language teaching for every
district from kindergarten through high school. New York has tripled
high-school enrollment in foreign languages since 1981, and Texas' enrollment has doubled. But teaching shortages remain acute.

In global studies, more than a dozen states have commissioned
task forces or issued reports on the subject. New York has mandated
global segments for social studies in all districts; Minnesota has allocated
funds for teacher training in the field; and California has established
six regional centers to assist local school districts, and Florida four—
three publicly funded, one by a foundation. Innovations include such
lessons as "The World in a Chocolate Bar." An elementary-school teacher
holds up a bar and asks its origin. Rejecting the obvious answer, "The
candy store," the teacher explains that the cocoa comes from Ghana,
peanuts from the Sudan, corn syrup from Iowa, coconuts from the Philip-
pines, and sugar from Ecuador. Then, the wrapper, from Canada; the
tinfoil, from Thailand; and the truck that delivered the bar to market,
from Japan.

At the junior-high level the metaphor might be cars, with components
from three dozen countries, or tennis shoes, pencils, and bicycles from
elsewhere. Math lessons may deal with the metric system and foreign
currency; music, with songs or dances from Africa; and so on.

"Global education," says Andrew F. Smith, president of the American
Forum for Global Education, "has matured from the latest 'educational
fad' to a major educational reform movement."

In year-round schooling, Los Angeles, among other places, operates
some public schools—over ninety of six hundred—all year, as a prelude
to 100 per cent twelve-month operation by 1992. It uses nine-week terms
separated by three-week breaks. Teachers have thirty-six-week contracts,
with an option for forty-eight.

In several cities business cooperates in public-private efforts. These
include such large corporate centers as Minneapolis, Philadelphia, Pitts-
burgh, Atlanta, Boston, and Dallas. In Minneapolis, Honeywell sponsors a summer Teacher Academy for high-school math and science in-
structors. In Dallas, over one thousand businesses have "adopted" public
schools, providing volunteers, equipment, and money for upgrading. In
Boston, under a compact involving the Private Industry Council, near-

ly seven hundred firms provide summer jobs for three thousand students at more than $5 an hour.

In South Carolina business went even further, helping spearhead adoption of a one-cent sales tax increase to finance an Education Improvement Act. Since its passage in 1984, combined math and verbal SAT scores in the state have increased thirty five points—the greatest in the nation—and teachers' salaries, previously among the nation's lowest, have risen by nearly half.

Vocational education is flowering in new forms in Ohio, California, Oklahoma, and elsewhere. In Ohio, forty-nine area vocational centers pool money and equipment from participating school districts to provide relevant advanced technical training. In California, some two dozen career academies in some twenty communities offer three-year vocational programs in computers, electronics, and similar subjects.

In Oklahoma, five school districts in Oklahoma City operate a joint $20 million complex called the Francis Tuttle Adult Education Center, offering over two dozen programs for students aged sixteen to sixty. Courses range from building maintenance to more technical subjects. High-school students attend free; full-time adults, for less than $400 a semester. Enrollment totals some ten thousand annually.

Arkansas has pioneered a statewide effort called Home Instruction Program for Preschool Youngsters (HIPPY). Modeled on an Israeli program to integrate immigrants into public schools, with the help of paraprofessionals it trains parents as teachers and provides books and worksheets for fifteen-minute home sessions daily, thirty weeks a year for two years. Tests after sixteen months in one district revealed a thirty-three-month gain in educational level among HIPPY students.

Student-choice programs also are spreading. Minnesota has led the way, with primary- and high-school students allowed to apply for attendance at any school in the state. More than thirty-five hundred did so for the 1989-90 school year, and, under another program, six thousand high-schoolers took courses in local colleges. Since the college attendance option began, high schools' own course offerings for college credit have quadrupled.

Other states with major choice plans include Massachusetts, Iowa, Nebraska, and Arkansas. Such plans—over 120 nationwide, dating to the 1970s—use various enrollment arrangements, from lotteries and first come-first enrolled to preference for siblings already admitted to a school. Transportation usually is provided.

Action also may be imminent against illiteracy. Under an Illiteracy Elimination Act proposed by Senator Paul Simon of Illinois in 1989, a Cabinet-level council would coordinate federal efforts, including a national center for research and information sharing. The act also would expand funding for teaching, supplies, and volunteer services under current programs.

The Working Group on Adult Literacy, consisting of eleven education groups, is among those rallying support. Federal programs, it calculates, reach only one-eighth of the twenty-three million people believed to need such services, and combined federal and state spending totals only $20 a year for every adult without a high-school diploma. Only doubling of federal expenditures, to $270 million a year, it says, will "begin to meet the need."

"Fighting illiteracy," Senator Simon points out, "is not just an issue of fairness and equity—it is an issue of economics," directly linked to welfare dependency, parenting skills, international competitiveness, productivity, job creation, and crime. Three of every four prison inmates are functionally illiterate, "and American taxpayers pay the price—$14,000 a year to keep a prisoner in jail, versus $4,200 it would cost to send a child to school."

The next move depends on citizen groups' applying enough pressure to spur—and pay for—meaningful nationwide action.

# 14

# *Rx for Renewal*

Education is partly an investment in the future—and a critical one. What about the present? What must be done now to ensure competitiveness and a chance for an enhanced quality of life?

Begin with American business. During the mid-1980s David Halberstam produced a much discussed book, *The Reckoning*. It chronicled a panoply of industry sins to which he ascribed Detroit's fall from auto-making dominance. One sin was blindness to market changes. Others included structural rigidities—failure to modernize employee relationships, training practices, factory organization, and manufacturing processes.

Like other seers, Halberstam underestimated the impact of globalization, which portended Detroit's decline. But his basic point remains valid: American industry must operate at the cutting edge of change. This requires attitude and policy reforms from boardroom to work place.

Here the Japanese manufacturing model already has proved useful. Improved design, engineering, and quality control; shortened product-development cycles; higher priority for long-term market-share and profit goals; greater attention to labor-management trust and cooperation—all are part of Japan's manufacturing and marketing success formula.

Can they be widely adapted here? Not without a nationwide change in investor, manager, and worker attitudes. Start with management-labor relations. For decades they have rested on a prevailing Dickensian-era management view of labor as an inanimate body of interchangeable parts, to be bought, used, and disposed of as cheaply as possible. This triggered the Newtonian reaction of adverserial labor union cartels. Spurred by Japan's example of worker participation and shop-floor teamwork, this has begun to change.

It must change more, with what New York Governor Mario Cuomo calls "some sort of intelligent engagement of working people in the economic process." This means not only greater worker participation in production planning and organization, but also bonus and ownership arrangements.

Lynn Williams, president of the United Steelworkers of America, in a variation on economist Schumpeter, calls the process "creative construction"—seeing workers not as liabilities but as "assets, whose talents, experiences and energies are as indispensable…as modern equipment and capital."

Ironically, it was an American, consultant W. Edwards Deming, who implanted this idea in Japan after World War II after being largely ignored here. Now it may be Japan's most significant "re-export." Perhaps its most dramatic demonstration is the strife-plagued GM works in Fremont, Calif., which in its reincarnation as NUUMI, under Toyota management doubled output per employee and revolutionized quality.

There are many examples. At National Steel, for instance, in just one year workers in redefined job classifications cut the labor for a ton of steel from five to four man-hours. At an inefficient transmission plant in Ohio, Ford and the United Auto Workers devised such efficient team concepts that the plant repatriated orders from a Mazda affiliate in Japan. The new system, without foremen, empowers any worker suspecting a quality defect to halt the assembly line. In some plants even managers join in assembly-line work.

Teamwork, however, remains the exception, and few American workers—9 per cent in one survey—expect direct benefits from improving their job performance. This compares to 93 per cent in Japan, where productivity bonuses are standard. The exception, as the President's Commission on Competitiveness says, must become the rule: "Share prosperity as well as austerity."

This means greater emphasis on job security and worker training. Collective bargaining already has gravitated in that direction—a trend, employee polls suggest, that inevitably must continue.* "Workers," says the United Steelworkers' Williams, "will support change, including plant closings, if they [alone] don't bear the burden."

Yet, the President's Commission on Industrial Competitivenes found, workers in declining industries "are not provided with sufficient incen-

---

*One of the largest programs, negotiated at General Motors in the early 1980s, retrained more than eleven thousand employees in six years. Others, particularly several involving the Communications Workers of America, have enabled internal transfer or external placement of hundreds of phone-company employees.

tives and opportunities to retrain." Labor-management contracts "inhibit allocations of jobs...that would boost productivity"; some employers invest too little in the skills-upgrading that would facilitate their own employee redeployment; and some workers assume too little responsibility for retraining.

Other nations do better. At least seven—West Germany, France, Great Britain, Sweden, Italy, Canada, and Japan—formally assist in adjustment of the displaced (casualties of trade or technological change). Techniques include mandatory advance notice of plant closings, guaranteed income during retraining, required severance benefits, and early-retirement incentives.*

Here, California is perhaps the most advanced, with subsidized retraining encompassing more than one thousand firms. Through a tax tied to unemployment insurance, it raises a pool exceeding $50 million annually, financing up to eighteen months of retraining. The state also subsidizes work-sharing, involving shortened hours to help reduce layoffs during adjustments.

At least a half-dozen other states have work-sharing laws.

Why shouldn't such policies be national?

Most Americans little appreciate the psychological toll of work place change. I know from the travails of my former home, Rock Island, Ill., a historic Mississippi Valley farm-implement center with a federal arsenal. While a downsized John Deere thrives in neighboring Moline, Rock Island's International Harvester and J.I. Case are gone, and its arsenal is steadily contracting, bringing lasting trauma to the region.

Such strains can be eased—and they must be if we are to progress.

American managers also are barely out of the starting blocks in widening marketing horizons. For years, concentrating on the vast, rich United States was sufficient. No more. Competition is global, and the fastest-growing markets are elsewhere, including Asia, Europe, and Canada. We must export more. If firms that could export did so, the president's

---

*In France, employers must allocate 1.5 per cent of their revenue for job retraining. West Germany mandates vocational education. In Japan, a "structurally depressed industries" law provides aid to entire sectors if half or more of their companies petittion for it. The aid applies to shutdowns or conversions, reducing payrolls through early retirement, and similar adjustments. More than three dozen industries, from shipbuilding to aluminum, have received such help. In Canada, a respected Manpower Consultive Service assists all parties in plant closings, conversions, and worker retraining and relocation.

competitiveness commission estimates, it could create 125,000 new jobs.*

Another imperative is longer attention spans in development of new products and services. Stories of U.S. firms handing over innovations to foreign firms are legion. The videocassette recorder is one example. An American company, Ampex, invented a bulky version for business use. But blind to a consumer application and eliciting no support for development, it offered rights to Japanese firms. Several snapped them up and created a multi-billion-dollar business that they dominate.

Managers aren't entirely culpable for such miscalculations. We worship instant profits. Tax laws and our stock market, where institutional investors control over half of portfolio values, foster short-term vision. If companies are to look beyond short-term earnings and stock fluctuations, we must enact laws that reward long views.

There is no magic in Japanese managers' techniques. They systematically assess products' marketability, concentrate on several, and bet heavily on these. They emphasize top design, engineering quality, and efficient manufacturing. For several decades Japan's Ministry of International Trade and Development was integral to the formula, guiding giant corporations' choices by funneling money to chosen fields. But its role steadily has waned—in 1988 Hitachi's research and development budget alone exceeded MITI's by half.

Ironically, simultaneous with this the Pentagon has sought more and more power to orchestrate private American research and development, from microchips to high-definition television. Its Defense Advanced Research Projects Agency, with a $1 billion annual budget, has become a major venture capitalist for high-technology industry. Its 1989 appropriation included $100 million for the Sematech microchip consortium, $40 million over three years for high-definition TV, and $25 million for superconductivity technology.

Because of high technology's military ramifications, some Pentagon role in its development is inevitable. But Pentagon emphasis is not what is commercial but, in its conception, militarily strategic.

Government, the Commission on Industrial Competitiveness properly

---

*Of 100,000 companies that export from the United States, only 3,600 make it a priority. They average over four thousand shipments a year. The other 96,400 exporters, averaging as few as nine shipments yearly, could step up activity. Still another 11,000 firms whose products are adjudged to have export potential could start. Over 1,500 export-management companies, many of them small and specialized, now are available to help.

points out, "cannot legislate success in world markets." But it can help even the game. Across the board, we must make it an ally, not an enemy, of other sectors' competitiveness efforts.

We are not without policy alternatives. Are executives, for example, rewarded too highly for short-term priorities? Provide tax reasons for management to link pay and incentives to long-term performance.

Do managers of pension funds and other institutional portfolios oriented toward short-run profits distort the market? Enact tax disincentives on short-term trading.

Are research and development for new technologies too risky? Raise tax credits for R & D and restore tax subsidies for investment in new plants and machines.

Are plant downsizing or closings, worker mobility, and labor-management relations in general hindered by lack of protection of pension funds? Legislate pension-holders' rights, including government-guaranteed "portability."

Then there is the sacred cow of federal deficits. Mega-deficits are more than a mortgage; they are a millstone on public and private sector maneuverability. For fiscal 1989 more than $150 billion of the federal budget was allocated purely for interest. This is some $14 of every $100 of all federal outlays—and more than the aggregate budgets of nine departments.*

Arms and space priorities provide a further ripe opportunity. As the Competitiveness Commission notes, both siphon R & D resources into "agencies and organizations with no common management...[where] commercial spillover is not a prime objective."

Then there are export controls. Foreign policy restrictions cost us nearly $1.23 billion in aborted exports annually. Nearly two-thirds of that is attributable to national security controls, greatly expanded in the Reagan years. All need review.

Such provisions, the competitiveness board affirms, "rarely achieve their desired result...[while creating] a reputation for American industry as an unreliable supplier." Indeed, in one investigation into security-embargo overzealousness the Commerce Department disagreed with some 65 per cent of the Pentagon's export-license rejections. We gave away business—for no return. We should require a heavy burden of proof for any embargoes.

---

*Agriculture, Commerce, Education, Energy, Interior, Justice, Labor, State, and Transportation.

Reorganization of some functions also is essential. Trade and investment policymaking, for instance, are fragmented—at least two dozen executive agencies and nineteen congressional subcommittees share decisionmaking, often at cross purposes. The White House Office of Science and Technology Policy, once a potent coordinating force, has only half the budget of a decade ago—and throughout the Reagan years, had no direct access to the President. We should, as the competitiveness commission suggests, centralize both trade/investment and science/technology activities and might grant both Cabinet-equivalent status.

Trade barriers are two-way streets. Thus, we should recognize and act against our own. A "dirty little secret," a small *cause celebre* abroad seldom mentioned here, is that these now affect an estimated one-fourth of our products and services traded.

To some outsiders, the list resembles Japan's. Begin with agricultural-import quotas—for sugar, products containing sugar, and cheese. Add superfund import taxes on petroleum products and chemical derivatives. Then take customs fees on boats, planes, trucks, vessels, and passengers, mix in tariffs on clothing, footwear, ceramic tile, and glassware, and one level is complete.

But there is more. Sprinkle in military-procurement preferences for American industries and transportation firms, steel lobbies' insistence on state contracts' specifications for American steel only, bureaucratic delays in testing office-switching equipment, voluntary restraints and quotas on autos and other products. The result: more than $80 billion a year in higher prices to U.S. consumers—and inevitable retaliation abroad.

This is championing open markets?

More than we recognize, much of our fate remains in our hands. Take research and product development. Japan, Inc., need not have a monopoly on inter-corporate coordination and collaboration. We can ease anti-trust strictures. In 1984, the National Cooperative Research Act did just that for R & D consortia, resulting in dozens being formed.

The size of Japanese banks and securities giants? By three or four mergers of our own institutions we could outstrip theirs. Where greater size is required to compete—in financial services and banking, for instance—a congressional vote plus a stroke of the president's pen can alter policy.

Foreign theft of U.S. innovations? We lose $40-$60 billion a year through pirating of U.S. innovations. In a high-technology era, this is plundering of our national wealth. We have placed protection of intellectual property on conference agendas for years. We must be more persistently Machiavellian about it.

America's governors, in their association's report *Jobs, Growth & Competitiveness,* urged action on many such fronts. Indeed, several states have far surpassed Washington's ingenuity. At least forty have pooled federal, state, and local funds for campus research and separate technology centers and research parks. Nearly two dozen aid in targeted development for selected industries.

Connecticut, through its Product Development Corp., has put over $27 million from a venture capital fund into developing new products, which, if successful, return royalties to replenish the fund. Over five years, Pennsylvania oversaw investment of $1.4 billion in government and private funds in such ventures as robotics, biotechnology, and restructuring of old industries. The Port Authority of New York-New Jersey formed a trading agency, XPORT, to assist in marketing and distribution abroad.

"We're not waiting on Washington," says Governor Gerald I. Baliles of Virginia, one of thirteen members who prepared the association's report. "We are laying the foundation for the future of America's domestic policy."

Finally, we must acknowledge that youth alienation, unemployment, and drug addiction mandate more than business as usual. There are no cure-alls. But one program could ameliorate all three and serve other needs as well. That is a national service corps.

The depression era's Civilian Conservation Corps and Works Progress Administration are two models. There are others. Metamorphosed into a new cross-class national service program, they could change the nation's face, mood, and prospects.

Recent generations never have known a compulsory military draft. Many of us who have known it recognize it, in hindsight, as more than a military staffing expedient. It imparts discipline, fitness, and practical experience. For upper- and middle-class recruits, it provides one of the great cross-regional, cross-class, democratizing opportunities of a lifetime.

Israelis, with their kibbutzim service requirements, know this. West Germany, among others, does also. There young men have the option of fifteen months' military service, three years with the police or border patrol, two years overseas in a peace corps, or ten years part-time as civil-defense and disaster-relief volunteers.

A dozen states and dozens of localities now provide variations on youth corps service. California is most prominent, with a CCC (California Conservation Corps) in which forty thousand members since 1976 have developed parks, planted trees, built trails, fought forest fires, battled floods, and performed other "low-priority" services that might have gone wanting. At least four school systems—Detroit, Atlanta, Springfield, Mass., and the Denver suburb of Cherry Creek—require community service for graduation.

Youth alienation and isolation, and unmet public needs, are growing. Youth service programs at all governmental levels could address both problems. These could encompass tutoring, counseling, health-care assistance, child care, conservation and ecological assistance, and dozens of other tasks. Here, surely, is yet another idea whose time has come.

# 15

# *Optimism or Pessimism?*

What are the odds on our achieving this *perestroika?*

Our history gives mixed signals. More than any other large country, we have proved our ability to change. But we tend to move slowly, only as far and as fast as pushed, and in spurts. Historian Arthur M. Schlesinger, Jr., a chief student of this phenomenon, calls these public and private interest-serving cycles. He calculates their oscillations at approximately thirty-year intervals. During each oscillation, problems in the counterpart sector build.* If he is correct, by the early 1990s we will swing from our current private interest to a public interest-serving cycle. Already, intimations of this are evident in the Bush administration. This is the good news.

The bad news is that often we change only in response to a detonating event—an economic crash, mass disturbances, and the like. We draw political energy from the apocalyptic—what historian Richard Hofstadter calls "the politics of paranoia." Japan's ascent and our competitiveness scares may serve that purpose. But unless we accelerate our *perestroika,* we are courting the whirlwind.

Despite our prosperity, American social peace rests on a thin veneer. Gaps between rich and poor, educated and uneducated, white and non-white, have grown. Our homeless and jobless, single-parent families, drug-dependent, armed and violent, unassimilated immigrants, and other problem groups have proliferated.

We suffer immense ideological strains—witness schisms over conceptions of life focused on legal and ethical codes for contraception, abortion, and voluntary euthanasia. There are innumerable others:

---

*The most renowned public interest-serving cycle of this century was the New Deal. Thirty years later came the next, the Kennedy-Johnson administration. The 1960s' upheavals and Vietnam truncated that, ushering in the mirror-image private sector phase.

- With drugs a transnational, multi-class scourge, for example, what kind of realistic treatment, prevention, and supply-limiting or legalizing policies can we adopt?
- With medical care becoming technology-dependent, costly, and malapportioned, how can we reorganize and finance what we need?
- Given restrictive building and craft codes, how can we restore the prospect of affordable housing for the masses?
- Given millions of working mothers, and more who want to (and will be needed for) work, how can we achieve a quantum advance in daycare?

The list could be extended.

Economic issues are said to be negotiable, moral issues not. Yet in a democracy, in the end all must be. This means enlisting the soundest contributions of our best and brightest to achieve the kinder, gentler mood of which President Bush has spoken.

Here another gap exists. Many of our best and brightest seem amorally devoted to greed, in law, finance, and other activities that they have made semi-parasitic. In our great cities especially, selfishness, surliness, mistrust, and violence seem in ascent. Nationwide the tone of public information and discourse often inhibits rather than fosters a constructive climate.

The 1960s demonstrated this climate's importance. Ethnic, ideological, generational, and class elements fused with apathy, arrogance, and ineptitude to produce anarchy. This need not recur. But avoiding it will require a rediscovery of civility, reason, and fairness by public officials, interest-group spokesmen, and our communications media. Especially the latter. For it is they—print and electronic—through which public actors' images, words, and actions are filtered.

America's news media have become our national opiate. More than ever, in the McLuhanesque environment of an information age, pervasive media determine public perceptions. Yet our supermass media—electronic in particular—too readily trivialize and distort policy-related issues and agendas.

The 1988 election campaign offers an example. Now largely forgotten, it then was widely regarded as one of the most dispiriting ever. Why? In part because our media—both print and electronic—abdicated their social obligation to act as a referee. Skillfully manipulated by agenda-twisters and spin doctors such as Bush guru Roger Ailes, media coverage became redolent of the McCarthy era, when reporters, in the thrall of a simplistic definition of "news" as merely "what happens," conveyed extravagant, unsubstantiated charges without a logical follow-up: independent research and evaluation.

Not that this would—or should—have changed the 1988 outcome. But it could have elevated the dialogue (and perhaps accountability in the administration), reduced public cynicism, and helped arrest a disturbing trend. That is the increasingly influential role of calculated, manipulative, TV-friendly disinformation.

The culprit is a simplistic, consumer-driven, sound-bite-oriented definition of news. Charges—controversy—are its core. As President Bush justly noted in one interview, one can devote an entire day to concrete policy pronouncements, yet a single accusation preempts the coverage. Campaign managers exploit that with skill.

One consequence of such manipulability is to distort reality. This corrupts the democratic process. Another—sometimes by provocateurs' design—is to stimulate or escalate violence. This further corrupts.

Radio call-in and talk shows are perhaps the most egregious. In the guise of providing exemplary electronic soapboxes, nonjournalistic hosts grind ideological axes to the lowest common denominator of self-selected audiences who crave (and, in broadcast call-ins, spread) the most base prejudices, mischief, and misinformation. These forums' role in defeating a congressional pay increase illustrates. The disgrace was not the result they triggered (a separate issue), but the oversimplifications, know-nothingism, and hate defeated over licensed channels.

Media preoccupation with controversy is understandable. It is the cheapest grist for journalistic mills. Mass audiences, especially, are conditioned to accept it. Institutions and processes are more costly and complex to cover. Yet their impact on most lives and futures surpasses that of most formula police, fire, and other "blotter" stories.

Jack Benny remarked about mastering the violin, "You have to practice seven hours a day just to play lousy." Journalism is equally demanding. In many ways it has improved. But megascale society, its commercial-based media structures, and the profit-maximizing mores of attracting supermass audiences have debased most mainline media.

Television, with its commercial-oriented, readily manipulated tabloid format, seems particularly exploitable. As former CBS-TV president Fred W. Friendly has observed, "How can we expect television to do its best when it can make so money much doing its worst?" Every week over five thousand network TV commercials interlaced through endless trivia and escapism affirm this.*

We can't expect commercial TV to do its best. What we can do is recognize that commercial pressures to attract and hold ever-larger audiences—eventually global—will, without checks and balances, further debase the medium. The ultimate choice then may be censorship or anarchy.

A middle ground of intervention that can ensure alternative values is infinitely more palatable. This should include revived public service and fairness requirements—swept away by deregulation—and strengthened nonprofit radio and TV, now severely hampered by lack of funding. Fees for now-free (but lucrative) commercial broadcast franchises could help rectify that. More generous foundation and corporate underwriting also are essential. And, since paid radio-TV political commercials corrupt by escalating campaign costs and trivializing and distorting issues, we should prohibit them. Especially coupled with free TV time, as several other major democracies allocate to candidates, this could restore TV to a constructive role.**

Another hope lies in greater reporting and self-criticism of media practices and institutions. As pioneer critics such as *The New Yorker*'s A. J. Liebling observed, the media are their own number one sacred cow. Yet they continue to grow in power and importance. The *Columbia Journalism Review,* which I was privileged to edit, and other ventures have demonstrated the feasibility and value of media analysis and criticism. Information, like sunlight, disinfects. With foundation help, a cadre of analysts/critics and appropriate outlets could be broadened, in print and radio-TV.

More than four decades ago the ad-hoc Hutchins Commission on Freedom of the Press, convened by Henry Luce and University of Chicago chancellor Robert M. Hutchins, offered an agenda for achieving such goals. It included all this and more. If we are serious about improving our public information stream, such prescriptions must be heeded.

Public civility, order, and a quality popular culture are not esoteric concerns. Social and cultural climates matter. They help set the tone, texture, and possibilities of daily living. This is why living in the

*A quarter-century ago under tighter regulation and voluntary codes the total was one-third that number, and programming was of higher quality.

**This includes Great Britain, France, West Germany, and Japan.

pre-1960s' social and cultural *belle epoque* was exhilirating and its collapse calamitous. The good old days were indeed that: in the flowering of our classical arts and the heyday of Broadway, the Hollywood studios, big bands, *Life,* network radio, and early television. Even when arduous, life seemed fulfilling, purposeful, suffused with a sense of progress.

No more. Boom boxes, avarice, drugs, and violence seem the symbols of the 1980s. We appear satisfied to act, and be acted upon, as primarily economic animals. Priorities become valid if they attract, please, and elicit money or approval from large subgroups regardless of their impact on others.

This is the marketplace, or what-will-assemble-an-audience, test. It is synthesized in the "no-tomorrow-accounting" of the bottom line: the criterion of immediacy that determines how and what we see, hear, build, discard, or ignore. Thus, large minorities—even a majority—spend much time being intruded upon, or offended by, actions directed at others.

In the long run this variation on dictatorship-by-the-proletariat is destructive. Almost inevitably, it magnifies the repugnant, which, Gresham-like, then drives out the fulfilling. This is evidenced in the architectural sameness, mass-marketing gaucheries, and collapse of public amenities around us. Not that enclaves of quality can't exist—only that their opposite, an apotheosis of commercialism, tends to overwhelm. This is now The American Way.

We who have known better may lament this and weep. But the future need not hold a straight-line projection of tawdriness, tastelessness, and materialism. As every action has an equal reaction, so do many trends.

We may hope that our present gilded age is no exception. For the issue is not only the uglification, commercialization, and dehumanization of American life but the world's. More than any other nation's, our values— political, economic, cultural—are dominant. If we wish to live in a world uncoated with slime, like beaches despoiled by an oil spill, by our own laissez-faire, consumerist, mega-mass popular culture, we must arrest the pollution at its source.

Can we? Cynicism is tempting, but shortsighted. Ralph Nader, John Gardner, and other citizen-group leaders have demonstrated that people power works. Western Europe has shown that spectacular scenery, distinctive architecture, comfortable cafes, and high art can be saved.

Europe's model may ultimately shame, or inspire, us to emulation. We have, after all, banished billboards from interstate highways, preserved historic buildings and districts, saved parkland, and nurtured a global ecology movement. If it is true that things sometimes must worsen before improving, a turning in national esthetics and popular culture may impend.

But a turning will not just happen. Americans who care must cause it, starting with awakenings in such flaccid institutions as our universities, foundations, and professional associations. Engulfed by cyclical tides, they cheerfully have abandoned their agenda-setting, value-preserving, taste-elevating functions. Yet it is they on whom society bestows the privileged roles and resources of public interest guardians; they who are presumed secular arbiters and catalysts of humane values; they who must instill the will to light candles rather than curse darkness.

Americans supposedly Think Big. We haven't lately. With some $250 million in grants over several years, the Ford Foundation almost singlehandedly created American public television. It also was instrumental in fostering grassroots social-action movements. Since then it has demonstrated no hint of grand commitments. Nor have other giants such as Rockefeller, Carnegie, or MacArthur, or smaller foundations—which must, like business, subordinate preoccupations with "turf" to the need for alliances and coalitions that can make an impact on megascale instituitions. As with government, we do not lack the private sector means, only the vision and the will.

Given our global weight, if no other reason, a renaissance of such vision and will is imperative. Our nation was founded to exude more than materialism, escapism, and self-gratification. If we are to do so, we must rediscover how to do it at home.

A vacuum exists. This is evident in the astounding reception to such jeremiads as *The Closing of the American Mind.* Neither Allen Bloom's reactionary elitism nor other academics' lamentations alone provide answers. But judged by their reception, such critiques strike receptive ears.

America can afford social, cultural, and economic quality. Americans can appreciate and support it. But someone must lead, persuade, and provide role models. The challenge is for enough members of the media, academia, business, and philanthropy who decry our materialistic malaise to act.

Oases of enlightenment, taste, and high-culture alternatives matter—and will increasingly amid the esthetic acid rain of megascale. With a renaissance of vision, we could—dare one hope?—surprise ourselves.

# 16
# *Afterword*

Should we, then, be optimists or pessimists about our future?

Based on our history and our present status, one should hesitate to bet against us. We command lofty pinnacles. We hold a winning hand. We have a history of overcoming by change.

Admittedly, more than ever our fate is entwined with that of the global community. But over time that community has progressed. Now all humanity is hostage to the Law of Acceleration. Scientific miracles notwithstanding, we seem condemned to live on the brink. That is humanity's lot.

Hunger, poverty, and injustice are endemic. Ecological, nuclear, or lesser catastrophes threaten. Increasingly, like the Red Queen, we seem fated to run fast "just to stand still."

Clearly, if one is to choose optimism it must be relative. For as André Malraux observed, "We are evolving from the far reaches of time, and I don't know if what impresses me most is the enormity of what is behind us or the enormity of what lies ahead."

What lies ahead can intimidate. For in human affairs, the light at the end of the tunnel inevitably is...another tunnel. And history's clock contradicts human impatience.

The fact is that progress on any scale is arduous, uneven, slow. It occurs strangely and unpredictably. But despite all of history's blood, pain, and tragedy, the thrust has been inexorably forward. Slowly but surely, over time we have spread freedom, security, an enhanced quality of life, and greater longevity.

One vehicle has been successive changes of scale. The late Jean Monnet, the father of the European Community, viewed these as milestones of human progress. Monnet, recalls columnist James Reston, "saw history as a series of ever-expanding units—from the village to the region, from the region to the nation-state, and from the nation-state to the integration of continents."

In each case larger scale triumphed over smaller. Every progression altered the existing order. Every one imposed trade-offs—and, as we have noted, in the environment of megascale some trade-offs are sharp. But the negatives do not negate the positives.

Perhaps the greatest positive is, in globalization, a structure for resolving many of humanity's and our own most intractable problems. Since World War II human affairs often have seemed out of control. But it now is apparent that this was a transition, a turbulent strait that marked a passage between eras.

That strait has been traversed. Quakes and tidal waves are waning. Fault lines are stabilizing. Nuclear war's shadow is receding. The threat of superpower combat is the lowest in years. A post-hegemonist world holds perils—as terrorism, arms proliferation, and other afflictions attest. But we can dare to contemplate global cooperation.

Indeed, the climactic trauma of the period, globalization, may be the key to historic advances. In a world so complex and interdependent, with institutions so vast and their action so circumscribed, the imperatives of an extended community—a global one—obtain. The globalization of institutions—industry, communications, transportation, and trade—with its denationalization and interdependence, ensure this. It is analagous to the industrialization of a nation.

With industrialization all of society changes. It becomes urbanized. It reorients economics, agriculture, education, law, religion, transportation, communications, population distribution, and foreign relations. Conflict—ethnic, religious, regional, class—finds new channels of accommodation. Charity—social welfare—is institutionalized. The enlightened self-interest of the interdependent prevails. The processes of nation-building also apply to world order.

National narcissism blinds us to certain truths. The decades since World War II constitute one of humanity's great leaps forward. In the long view of history, decolonization is a quantum advance. It lifted an ancient yoke from all but Soviet colonies and southern Africa. It unshackled the world economy. It broadened democracy's constituency.

Industrialization, science/technology, and trade further contributed. Beyond a point they incubate—mandate—democracy. "There can be and are dictatorships in primitive tribal or landlord-dominated societies," economist John Kenneth Galbraith has pointed out, "and perhaps for a while in the early stages of industrial development or in times of economic regression and hardship, as in Germany and Italy in the 1930s....All this changes with economic and industrial development."

This reality has undermined authoritarianism everywhere, most spectacularly in Eastern Europe, the Soviet Union, South Korea, and China. Technology, from modern communications to the infrastructures of mass marketing, similarly democratizes. In a global village of instant communications and quick transportation, no society can remain closed.

Beyond a point technology inhibits conflicts. It escalates destructive power—but also its costs and consequences. Nuclear arms, for all their terror, have forestalled blunders into great-power wars. Except as deterrents, such weapons are operationally useless. The superpowers' reluctance to acknowledge this has only sapped both.

Global reindustrialization, seen by us and other developed nations as an economic threat, ultimately may prove our salvation. For combined with capital infusions into the South it can solve a root North-South problem: the economic consummation of decolonization. It can accelerate global development, create critical new markets, and reduce contagious destabilization. This already is apparent in relative calms everywhere but in the Mideast, still convulsed by religion-based animosity.

A truly integrated economic system then will, as Republican internationalist Wendell Willkie held in his visionary 1940s book *One World,* bring global political integration.

We will need it. For some of our deepest problems can be solved only on a global scale. Again, globalization may have occurred just in time. For awesome as many problems are, globalization may make them more manageable.

Consider arms proliferation. Of annual global military spending of $1 trillion, over half is attributable to the superpowers. They finance four-fifths of all arms research and development. Since just two nations are the chief catalysts of this spiral, and its excesses bleed both, improvement in their relations should slow the arms forest's spread. Further breakthroughs await advanced globalization and refining of regional and international organizations.

Though poverty remains a blight, the rise of newly industrializing nations, plus scientific advances and a global economy, promise continuing improvement. Progress, it now is apparent, neither thrusts up nor trickles down. It germinates in clusters and pushes outward to receptive soil.

This usually is accompanied by a harsh developmental period, like our own robber baron era or modern statist dictatorships. The larger the clusters of development, the faster progress spreads. Today's industrialized nations are the largest critical mass ever, and almost no colonial relationships remain. Hence the spate of economic takeoffs.

John Maynard Keynes, among others, foresaw this acceleration in 1930. "I would predict," he wrote, "that the standard of life in progressive countries 100 years hence will be between four and eight times as high as it is today."

To many, Keynes' forecast now seems conservative. The increase, former *Times* of London editor William Rees Mogg has estimated, more likely will be six to twenty times 1930s' levels. The rule in advanced countries, he says, "was that 20 per cent were prosperous and 80 per cent were poor. These proportions have now almost been reversed....By 2030 or a little later, 60 per cent of the people in 60 per cent of the world's national populations may [reach middle-class levels]."

Food production has no ceiling. Since 1950 Asia has doubled its production of rice, Europe has tripled wheat output, and the United States nearly tripled corn yields. In 1986 world reserves of rice—the diet staple for 40 per cent of humanity—reached 300,000 tons. New technologies will increase that further. Aquaculture and other advances also await.

In fact, predicts Peter Drucker, "the true revolution on the farm" lies ahead. "Vast tracts of land that hitherto were practically barren are being made fertile, either through new methods of cultivation or through adding trace minerals to the soil: the sour clays in the Brazilian highlands, for instance, or aluminum-contaminated soils in neighboring Peru, which never produced anything before and which now produce substantial quantities of high-quality rice. Even greater advances are being registered in biotechnology."

Even the most uniformly deprived continent, Africa, whose bete noire has been agriculture, may see dawn. With biotechnology's Green Revolution, enabling almost infinite adaptation of crops to conditions, its agricultural-development impasse can be broken. Since agricultural success is a traditional prerequisite of industrialization, providing needed surplus labor, trade, and monetary exchange options, this can help overcome the regression left by colonial exploitation.*

---

*Ghana is one example. For a quarter-century after independence from Great Britain, it sank in an economic morass of mismanagement, inflating civil-service rolls tenfold and placing nearly half its modern sector under state control. That ended with the regime of Flight Lt. Jerry Rawlings, who took power in 1981.

In coordination with the World Bank, his government tripled prices to growers of Ghana's largest export crop, cocoa. With improved methods of growing and marketing, Ghana moved from importing half its food to 15 per cent. By 1988 it possessed Africa's highest growth rate—a five-year average of 6 per cent.

"There are no magic solutions," says BankAmericorp's A. W. Clausen before leaving the World Bank. "[But] history should have taught us never to despair."

Clausen's optimism seems most strained when applied to population. His World Bank predecessor's analogy of overpopulation to nuclear war was justified. But again, there is no revising history. Exponential population increases were bequeathed to us. Yet here, too, there is qualified hope.

"On the global level," says the eminent demographer Paul Demeny, "the 1960s and 1970s represent a major demographic watershed: the culmination of several centuries of accelerating natural increase, and the beginning of what promises to be a...downward course [in growth rate] for at least the next half century." But, he warns, the next two decades are crucial. "Failure to achieve a decisive decline of fertility would have grave implications."

The keys are economic growth and family-planning programs. National birthrates fall with income improvement. The poor see children as "Social Security"—extra help in the house and fields. A destitute African or Indian family must have six children to be 95 per cent sure of one surviving son. Thus, disincentives remain strong.

But dramatic progress has resulted from saturation campaigns in even India's poorest regions. And experience shows that "satisfying," not necessarily spectacular, economic advances, lower birthrates. Hence the indispensability of steady improvement—and a worldwide breakthrough attempt such as Marshall Plan II.

Medical research also offers hope. Abortions are global givens. Nearly fifty million are performed each year. Thousands are bungled so badly that the mother dies. But advances such as the French RU 486 abortion, or contragestive, pill can avert many tragedies of both unwanted births and maternal deaths.*

The next goal is a completely safe, inexpensive successor to the existing, partially discredited Pill. With intensified effort, says the Population Council's George Zeidenstein, a breakthrough to provide it, either as a drug or intrauterine device, is possible by the mid-1990s.

Meanwhile, with some twenty million couples a year attaining reproductive ages, the population timebomb ticks. Its ticks grow increasingly ominous. From 1985 to 2020, just thirty years from now, they

---

*Taken with another drug (total cost $80), it has proved over 95 per cent effective in terminating pregnancies in the first two months.

will have added 3.2 billion people to the planet, for a population of 8 billion—double that of 1900. This lends urgency to one problem about which sanguinity is perhaps most difficult: ecological degradation. The projected scale of population and economic development clearly can jeopardize our planet's life-support systems. Some degradation already is irreversible.

Fossil fuels' and other pollutants' impact on the ozone layer, for example, has led many scientists to regard a greenhouse-effect global warming as inevitable. With that, farming and desert areas, exposure to sun-caused cancer, and rising sea levels and coastal flooding will spread. This could be disastrous for the United States. We take agricultural bread-baskets, coastal resorts, and other climatic gifts for granted. We no longer can.

The case for countermeasures seems unassailable. At the very least, they could prevent the potentially most cataclysmic effects. Slowing the pace of ozone-layer destruction, for example, could allow time for research, forecasts of regional impacts, and strategies to adjust.

Most American funding for such research was a casualty of Reagan arms priorities. But at least one major earth-sciences project is being revived: multinational climatic research and monitoring by NASA, the National Science Foundation, and other agencies. Though complex and costly, this clearly is essential.

Yet all is not gloom. In two decades the environmental movement has brought many advances. They include:

- Signing of a global treaty to help prevent ozone depletion;
- Post-Chernobyl tightening of multinational nuclear-contamination controls;
- Pollution control for the Mediterranean, Persian Gulf, Rhine basin, and other regions;
- Spreading of vehicle, industrial, and residential pollution-control regulations;
- National and multinational programs to protect endangered species—land, sea, and air;
- Agendas covering acid rain, hazardous waste transport and disposal, oil-spill, and other industry-related menaces.

Ecological action conferences are proliferating. So is relevant research. For CFCs, a substitute chemical may be near. For depleted rain forests, fast-growing trees to be planted en masse throughout the developed world. And for acid rain and other industrial or vehicle pollution problems, chemical suppressors and alternate energy sources.

All these are merely a start—and sad consolation for lost opportunities. But their significance should not be minimized. As the late Barbara Ward of the International Institute for the Environment observed, they represent "a profound step" ahead. "We still," she concluded, "have a chance."

To paraphrase an old lament, "If things are so good, then how come so many of us feel so bad?"

The quick answer is, because so many things *are* so bad. The human condition persists. Progress does not mean Utopia. The world remains difficult and dangerous. Further, there is the Law of Unintended Consequences, or Rule of Perverse Results. That is, that every improvement has unpredictable, and sometimes undesirable, side effects. As change accelerates, so do these.

Take shifts in scale. A village or small town provides a constricted range of activities; a megalopolis, a plethora. But this plenty imposes a penalty in crowding, blight, noise, pollution, violence, depersonalization, and living costs. As the scale and complexity of forces, masses, and interactions keep growing, so do a feeling of alienation and lack of personal power and control. Mass automobile ownership, a boon, creates congestion, pollution, accidents, and scrap dumps. Jumbo jets, which provide economies of volume, in aggregate produce the delays, discomfort, and invitation to terrorists of current air travel. Modern hospitals, which can reconstruct bodies and prolong life, also dehumanize and bankrupt.

Modern communications, too, are two edged. Miracles of convenience, they can enrich and debase, distract and distort. Their incessant and vivid depiction of problems also can depress.

Then there is future shock. Any change inconveniences. Macro or hyperchange debilitates. On paper the coming new world may be an improvement; in practice, unfulfilling.

But here, too, we should beware straight-line projections. Indeed, we should consider the possibility that a post-Modern *belle epoque,* informed by a new world culture, may lie ahead. From my cross-cultural editing parapet, I detected fragments of it in a diversity of foreign prose, films, television, theater, and music. A richness exists, awaiting only collection and dissemination.

Here, too, globalization may be the key. Many newspapers and magazines abroad are of impressive quality and diversity. Satellite-relay and cable TV networks also can be. Latin American, Asian, and African novelists have attained world prominence. Even humor is alive and well abroad, in *Punch* of London, Paris's *Le Canârd Enchâine,* Moscow's *Krokodil,* and assorted essays, books, films, and broadcasts.

Americans were introduced to this in British films' *Lavender Hill Mob* period. French, Italian, Czech, German, and others' cinematic gems followed. Soviet geniuses, long repressed, may provide the next wave.

Given an unending but unexposed supply of foreign masters in literature, films, music, theater, and ballet, who can despair of humanity's cultural prospects? Not, for one, Jeremy Treglown, editor of *The Times Literary Supplement* of London.

"There never has been a time," he says, "when there have not been people saying everything is in decline and decay. I honestly believe it is impossible to make such a generalization. There is a flood of good work. There rarely have been so many new and successful literary magazines.

"Ideas travel more quickly and are more easily assimilated than one hundred years ago. Ordinary people have easy access to wonderful musical performances in their home. This is miraculous." It is, he adds, "important for the growth of a culture that people should be optimistic about it."

What of the threat of a homogenized, global, rock'n'roll, Coca-Cola esthetic? For a time it appeared plausible. Now its limits are more evident. If stubborn distinctions of American regional cultures, clearly discernable away from our urban centers, are not sufficient proof, consider Italy, France, or other idiosyncratic survivors of American intrusion.

In the late 1960s, the Ile St. Louis in Paris remained an enclave where a cafe refused to serve my American family, and in the 1970s a French Cultural Minister tried ostrasizing everything American. With a Disney park outside Paris, this no longer is politic. The French, like others, have found that cultures are hardier than generally acknowledged. When you go to France or Italy or Japan or even our geographic neighbor Canada, there is no mistaking that you are there.

French anthropologist-ethnologist Claude Levi-Strauss, for one, repeatedly emphasized this:

> It is dangerous to depict Western or Islamic or Chinese civilization
> as blocks that disintegrate when they come in contact with other civiliza-

tions. If Japan has become Westernized, it has not done so in the image of the West; it has created an original synthesis. China will also attain such a synthesis, as will the Islamic world. Now, when we discuss civilization, we must look for, and we will perceive, hybrids—which will include us.

Another authority, Stuart Hall of the Open University in London, concurs. "The new face of capital, as it reorganizes itself as a cultural force across the globe, has an American signature," he concedes. But national and regional mutations persist, and "the new global culture is never so pleased as when it can represent difference." *Vive la difference!*—if we will trouble to discover it.

The cycles of history also offer hope. While current American popular arts, advertising, and public dialogue frequently embarrass, climates change. If the Schlesinger *(pere et fils)* theory of U.S. political cycles holds, relief may be in prospect—and none too soon.

Worldwide, the darker hues associated with Huxley, Orwell, and other melancholy visionaries may yet prevail. If they do, a conflict over moral and cultural values may be one catalyst. Mexican writer Octavio Paz warns of a "seemingly irreconcilable conflict between our past and our future." It is, he says, "just as serious...[as] the nuclear menace.... [Modernity] must find a way to reconcile itself with...tradition."

*L'affaire* Khomeini-Rushdie, abortion-contraception, and other conflicts affirm this. They cannot be wished away, but must be defused with an empathy for seemingly irreconcilable views. So far this has been lacking.

We "modernists," in our way, have behaved as arrogantly as—albeit less fanatically than—the world's Khomeinis, Gaddafis, and Arafats. Thus we have cloned more and more. We can be more pragmatic in addressing their raisons d'etre, and certainly more empathetic about their grievances, without betraying our fundamental values.

Time is on freedom's side. For it now is clear that freedom has no alternative. Also, that the same technology that can enslave can liberate. This is becoming increasingly apparent in a global village of inherent pluralism, contagious democracy, and multiple checks, balances, anchors, and early-warning alarms.

The will to freedom is irresistible. Affirmations of that, from China, India, Eastern Europe, and the U.S.S.R. to lesser spots, have been exhilirating. Annual surveys by Freedom House in New York City quantify freedom's march. Its 1989 annual report shows the highest percentage (38.8) and number (1.99 billion) of people living in freedom in the organization's seventeen years of comparative surveys. These billions live in sixty countries and nearly forty territories with democratic liberties, including civil and voting rights.

In the end our most intractable challenge may be the oldest: ethics, morality, values. Human values, William Miller of the Stanford Research Institute, has observed, are undergoing "at least as pronounced a shift" as in the Renaissance. The ultimate direction of this shift cannot be foretold. Whatever, swept along by hyperchange, we will be challenged to reinvent personal and national ethical codes.

One should not exclude, either, the brighter possibility that the Global Age—as the last step into the Space Age—may provide the kinds of frontiers that historically have stimulated vision, cooperation, and transcendent achievement. For certain, as the epicenter of globalization, our opportunities and obligations to generate and mediate value changes remain central. For that is where, for the foreseeable future, America will be—at the confluence of the age's crashing and often troubled tides.

So why not optimism?

Norman Macrae, longtime sage of perhaps the world's only indispensable magazine, *The Economist* of London, makes a persuasive case for it.

"When I joined *The Economist* in 1949," he wrote in a retirement valedictory, "it seemed unlikely the world would last....But here we stand, forty memory-sodden years on, and what have we done?...The poorest two-thirds of people are living much longer....During the brief civilian working lives of us returning soldiers from the Second World War, we have added seven times as much to the world's producing power as was added during all the previous millennia of homo sapiens' existence.

"That may help explain why some of us sound and write rather tired. It does not explain why anybody in the next generation...can dare to sound pessimistic."

University of Chicago historian William McNeill concurs. A quarter-century ago, in his award-winning study *The Rise of the West,* he wrote:

> The burden of present uncertainties [oppresses] the minds of many sensitive people. Yet...foresight, cautious resolution, sustained courage never before [have] had such opportunities to shape our lives and those of subsequent generations....We should...count ourselves fortunate to live in one of the great ages of the world.

# *Acknowledgments*

To my longtime friend, mentor, and partner in building *World Press Review,* the late C. Maxwell Stanley, I owe thanks for the incomparable opportunity to see the world through its press, providing much of the perspective that informs this book. To Richard Stanley, now president of *WPR* and the Stanley Foundation, my gratitude for the foundation's assistance in accelerating, through the American Forum for Global Education, the book's production and distribution.

To Andrew Smith of the American Forum, my thanks for his boundless encouragement, ingenuity, and enthusiasm. And to Beverly Goldberg of the Twentieth Century Fund/Priority Press, my admiration and thanks for her steadfast faith and virtuoso expediting of the book's birth through cooperation with the American Forum and Transaction Books.

Among many others owed debts for valued encouragement at opportune times: Isaac Asimov, Alvin Toffler, Richard Tobin, Richard Stolley, Norman Isaacs, Stephen Isaacs, Donald Shanor, Thomas Fleming, Mitchel Levitas, R. Edward Jackson, Robert Lewis Shayon, Michael Janeway, Stewart Richardson, Perry Knowlton, Gerard McCauley, Carl Brandt, Melanie Jackson, and Patrick Bernuth.

For opening doors, including their own, I thank especially Senators Paul Simon and Claiborne Pell, Marvin Stone, Robert Christopher, George Zeidenstein, John Maxwell Hamilton, Rutherford Poats, Selig Harrison, and Donna Demac.

For their generosity in sharing insights verbally or in writing, I thank especially, in the United States, Robert Reich, Theodore Levitt, Daniel Bell, Arthur Schlesinger, Jr., John Kenneth Galbraith, A. W. Clausen, Burns Roper, and Joseph Slater. And elsewhere, among the many foreign journalists who imparted wisdom through writings and interviews: André Fontaine, John Maddox, Michael Kenward, Anatole Kaletsky, Girilal Jain, Bechir Ben Yahmed, and Derek Davies. I commend quality

quality foreign publications such as theirs for Americans who truly want to see the whole world in perspective.*

Innumerable others far exceeded the call of duty in interviews and/or providing material, including William Miller of SRI International, Jan Drum of the Stanley Foundation, John Tessitore of the United Nations Association U.S.A., Deirdre Curley of the National Governors' Association, Judith Katz of the National Association of State Development Agencies, Ellen Herr and Judy Sever of the Commerce Department, George Slover of Congressman John Bryant's staff, Michael Moynihan of the OECD, George Holliday and William Cooper of the Congressional Research Service, John Hein of the Conference Board, Julian Grenfell of the World Bank, and space-law expert Mark Chartrand.

I would be remiss in not thanking Transaction Books' editor, Irving Louis Horowitz, and its senior vice president and chief operating officer, Scott Bramson; designer Ed McEvoy for the cover/dust jacket; and the production overseer par excellence, Glenn Edwards of the Twentieth Century Fund/Priority Press.

Most of all, I thank my wife Phyllis, to whom this book is dedicated, for her love, forebearance, and fortitude in bearing the burdens, financial and otherwise, that became part of this undertaking.

A. B.

---

*To "break in," I especially recommend readily accessible English-language publications with U.S. printers and/or distributors, such as *The Economist* (10 Rockefeller Plaza, New York 10020), *Manchester Guardian Weekly* (with *Le Monde* and the *Washington Post*) (20 E. 53d Street, New York 10022), *Financial Times* (14 E. 60th Street, New York 10022), and *Japan Economic Journal* (OCS America Inc., 5 E. 44th Street, New York 10017). For an overview and samplings of the foreign press, of course, *World Press Review* (200 Madison Avenue, New York 10016). Several have "800" information and all have area code 212 numbers.

# Notes

The introductory quotation from H. G. Wells, written in 1942, was reprinted in "Time to Get Together in Running Our World," by Martin Woollacott, *Manchester Guardian Weekly,* Jan. 15, 1989, p 20.

## Introduction

4    Sources mentioned: *World Press Review* (published by The Stanley Foundation, 200 Madison Avenue, New York, N.Y. 10016); Paul Kennedy, *The Rise and Fall of the Great Powers* (New York: Random House, 1987); Robert Z. Lawrence, *Can America Compete?* (Washington, D.C.: Brookings Institution, 1984); Clyde V. Prestowitz, Jr., *Trading Places: How We Allowed Japan to Take the Lead* (New York: Basic Books, 1988); Daniel Burstein, *Yen! Japan's New Financial Empire and Its Threat to America* (New York: Simon & Schuster, 1988).

2    The investment executive is Robert P. Kennedy, Hammond Kennedy & Co., New York City.

2-3    Sources mentioned: "The U.S.—Decline or Renewal," by Samuel P. Huntington, *Foreign Affairs,* Winter, 1988-89; "World Leadership" series, by Karen Elliott House, *Wall Street Journal,* Jan. 22, 30, Feb. 6, Feb. 13, Feb. 21, 1989; and "The Coming Global Boom," by Charles R. Morris, *Atlantic Monthly,* October, 1989.

## 1. Ascent and Decline: Image and Reality

7    The term "artificially high" is defined in Paul Kennedy *The Rise and Fall of the Great Powers* (New York: Random House, 1987), p 357.

8    Gross national product comparisons are from *The World Almanac* and *Information Please Almanac,* 1988, 1989.

8    The *Financial Times* data are quoted from "The U.S. Disease—Hypochondria," by Samuel Brittan, May 18, 1987, p 23.

8    Samuel P. Huntington is quoted from his article, "The U.S.—Decline or Renewal,"*Foreign Affairs,* Winter, 1988-89, pp 77-96.

9    Pentagon figures are from "The Future Security Environment: Report to the Committee on Integrated Long-Term Strategy," Future Security Environment Working Group, Department of Defense, August, 1988, Chapter 1.

9    Susan Strange is quoted from her article "The Persistent Myth of Lost Hegemony," *International Organization* (World Peace Foundation, Stanford University; published by the MIT Press), Autumn, 1987, pp 551ff.

10    Huntington is quoted from "The U.S.—Decline or Renewal," *Foreign Affairs,* Winter, 1988-89, pp 77-96.

11 Helmut Schmidt is quoted in the *Wall Street Journal* series, "World Leadership," by Karen Elliott House, Jan. 22, 30, Feb. 6, 13, 21, 1989.

11 Hiroshi Takuchi is quoted in "American Power: The View from Japan," by Henry Scott Stokes, *New Perspectives Quarterly,* Summer, 1988, p 20.

11 Fuji Kamiya is quoted from "If Our Economy Is So Weak, Why Is Everyone Investing in It?" *Washington Post National Weekly,* Jan. 25, 1988, p 23.

11 Josef Joffe is quoted from "For All Its Difficulties, U.S. Stands to Retain Its Global Leadership," by Karen Elliott House, *Wall Street Journal,* Jan. 23, 1989, pp A1, A8.

## 2. A New World

13 Arthur Schlesinger, Jr., is quoted from his speech, "The Meaning of the 20th Century" (*Asahi* International Symposium: A Message to the 21st Century, Tokyo, Oct. 23-25, 1984), pp 11-16; elaborated on to the author.

14 Henry Adams is quoted from *The Education of Henry Adams* (Boston: Houghton Mifflin, Sentry Edition, 1961), Chapter 34, "A Law of Acceleration"; and "The Challenge of Change," by Arthur Schlesinger, Jr., *New York Times Magazine,* July 27, 1986.

15 Alvin Toffler's comparison appeared in *Future Shock* (New York: Random House, 1970); among others, William F. Miller of SRI International quoted the ratio of living scientists to history's total in "Technology: Driver of Change in the World Economy," a speech at the PACRIM '86 conference, Perth, Australia, Nov. 19, 1986.

16 Carlo de Benedetti is quoted from "The Era of 'Made in the World,' *Business Week,* Nov. 23, 1987 (Special Advertising Section "Italy 1987"). For more on his views on alliances, see "A High Technology Gap? Europe, America, and Japan" (New York: Council on Foreign Relations, 1987), pp 77-80.

16 William H. McNeill's quotation is from "Progress and Peoples," in "Our Century Our World" (Paris: *International Herald Tribune,* 100th anniversary booklet), September, 1987, p 97.

16 Data on communications are from "International Telecommunications Competition in the Age of Telepower," by Joseph Pelton, *International Journal,* Jan. 30, 1987; "The International Flow of Television Programs," by Tapio Varis, *Journal of Communication,* Winter, 1984; and "Promoting Philanthropy," by David Rockefeller, *The Corporate Board,* January/February, 1987, pp 1-5.

16 Data on TV programming are from "The Poisoned Chalice? International Television and the Idea of Dominance," by Michael Tracey, *Daedalus,* Fall, 1985, pp 17-56; Raymond Snoddy describes the Cannes TV bazaar in "Recouping Costs in Cannes," *Financial Times,* May 5, 1988; Alan Riding describes Brazilian TV in "Brazilian Soap Operas Appeal to Global Tastes," *New York Times,* Oct. 20, 1985; and Richard Reeves reports on CBS' newscasts in Paris in "Why Information Is Now Like Weather," *International Herald Tribune,* Apr. 6, 1988.

17 Data on the English language are from *The Story of English* (PBS series, 1986), reviewed in "The Story of English, Nine-Hour Series on 13," by John Corry, *New York Times,* Sept. 15, 1986; "English: Out to Conquer the World," by Susanna McBee, *U.S. News & World Report,* Feb. 18, 1985, pp 49-52; and "The Coming Universal Language," by George Steiner, *The Listener,* London, adapted in *Atlas World Press Review,* October, 1977, pp 24-26.

17  *Language Monthly* is quoted in "Why English Is Good, But Not Good Enough,"
    by Michael Dixon, *Financial Times,* Feb. 21, 1987.

17  Judd Polk is quoted from his article, "The Rise of World Corporations," *Saturday
    Review,* Nov. 11, 1969, p 32.

17  Theodore Levitt is quoted from his article, "The Globalization of Markets," *Har-
    vard Business Review,* May/June, 1983, pp 92-102; see this and other essays in his
    *The Marketing Imagination* (New York: The Free Press, 1986).

18  Peter F. Drucker is quoted from his article, "The Changed World Economy," *Foreign
    Affairs,* Spring, 1986, pp 768-791; see this and other essays in his *The Frontiers
    of Management* (New York: E.P. Dutton, 1986).

18  Daniel Bell is quoted from "The World and the United States in 2013," *Daedalus,*
    Summer, 1987, p 11; also see "The Third Transition," by Tom Wicker, *New York
    Times,* Sept. 21, 1987, p A19.

18  Multiple sourcing is discussed in Marvin Cetron, *The Future of American Business:
    The U.S. in World Competition* (New York: McGraw-Hill, 1985), pp xxiiiff.

18  Data on foreign assembly are from Joseph Grunwald and Kenneth Flamm, *The
    Global Factory* (Washington, D.C.: Brookings Institution, 1985).

19  Data on and descriptions of superpower arms are from Richard Rosecrance, *The
    Rise of the Trading State* (New York: Basic Books, 1986).

20  Arms costs are from Ruth Leger Sivard, "World Military and Social Expenditures
    1987-88" (Washington, D.C.: World Priorities Inc.). Also see Rosecrance, *The Rise
    of the Trading State,* p 157.

20  Rosecrance is quoted from *The Rise of the Trading State,* page 33.

21  Military expenditures as GNP ratios are discussed in Kennedy, *The Rise and Fall
    of the Great Powers*; Rosecrance, *The Rise of the Trading State*; and Sivard, "World
    Military and Social Expenditures."

21  For trade-growth figures see Rosecrance, Chapter 7, "The Trading
    World"; also, "The Ghost of 1929," by Norman Gall, *Forbes,* July 13, 1987,
    pp 315-324.

21  Jean-Louis Servan-Schreiber was interviewed by the author for "The Post-Political
    Age," *World Press Review,* September, 1980.

21  Francois Mitterrand's speech was quoted in "67 Laureates Consider the Century's
    Legacy," by James Markham, *New York Times,* Jan. 19, 1988.

21  Data on postwar development are from "Development Lessons Learned," by Ruther-
    ford M. Poats, *OECD Observer,* November, 1985, p 39; also see "Saving and
    Economic Growth: Is the United States Really Falling Behind?" by Robert E. Lipsey
    and Irving B. Kravis, Report No. 901, American Council of Life Insurance and
    the Conference Board, New York, 1987, p 8.

22  George Zeidenstein's comment is from "International Assistance in the Popula-
    tion Field: Roads Taken, Paths Ahead" (Occasional Paper, Institute of Nutrition,
    University of North Carolina, Chapel Hill, N.C., Vol. II, Nov. 7, 1981), p 3;
    elaborated on in a personal interview.

22  Data on food output are from "World's Grain Output Surges as Nations Seek Food

Self-Sufficiency," by Wendy L. Wall, *Wall Street Journal*, Apr. 6, 1987; and "A World Awash in Grain," by Barbara Insel, *Foreign Affairs*, Spring, 1985, p 900.

23 Dennis T. Avery is quoted from "Scientific Advances Lead to an Era of Food Surplus Around the World," by Keith Schneider, *New York Times*, Sept. 9, 1986. Also see Schneider's "The Subsidy 'Addiction' on the Farms," *Times*, Sept. 13, 1987; "OECD Study Critical of Farm Program Costs," by Steven Greenhouse, *Times*, May 13, 1987; and "Unnatural Selection," by Giles Merritt, *Financial Times*, Sept. 5, 1987, p I.

23 The "five worlds" formulation is adapted from A. W. Clausen, in "Global Interdependence in the 1980s," speech to Yomiuri International Economic Society International Forum, Tokyo, Jan. 13, 1982, pp 7, 15.

24 Among many sources on South Korea's development, see "A Success Story Which Defies the Textbooks," by Anatole Kaletsky, (July 19, 1985); "The Rise of the Middle Classes," by Ian Roger, "A Modified Japanese Model" and "Confident Industry Aims for Middle Size Slot," by Nick Garnett (May 14, 1987), all in the *Financial Times*; "South Korea: The Next Wave" Dec. 14, 1986 (Magazine), and "Boom Time in South Korea: An Era of Dizzying Changes" (Apr. 7, 1987, p 1) both by Susan Chira in the *New York Times*; and "The International 500," *Fortune*, Aug. 3, 1987, pp 214ff.

24 Among many sources on Taiwan, see "Reheating Asia's 'Little Dragons,'" by Louis Kraar, *Fortune*, May 26, 1986, pp 134-140; "Too Rich to Stay a Lonely Beacon," *The Economist*, Mar. 28, 1987, pp 21 ff; and "Taiwan Rides Japanese Tide of Investment," by Robert King, *Financial Times*, Apr. 15, 1987.

24 Among many sources on Hong Kong, see "China: Hong Kong's Factory," by Nicholas D. Kristof, *New York Times*, Sept. 4, 1987, p D1; and Marvin Cetron, *The Future of American Business* (New York: McGraw-Hill, 1985).

24 Among many sources on Singapore, see "Singapore," *Financial Times*, Nov. 3, 1986 (Survey); "Lee's Legacy," *The Economist*, Nov. 22, 1986 (Survey); "Singapore Is World's Busiest Port, United Press International in the *International Herald Tribune*, June 10, 1985, p 1; and Cetron, *The Future of American Business*.

24 Robert Heilbroner is quoted from "Reflections: Hard Times," *The New Yorker*, Sept. 14, 1987, pp 96ff.

25 W. W. Rostow is quoted from "America Against the World," *Washington Post*, Dec. 23, 1986.

25 Bechir Ben Yahmed was interviewed by the author for "Africa's New Role Models," *World Press Review*, December, 1982, pp 29ff.

26 Peter Drucker's estimates are from "The Changed World Economy," *Foreign Affairs*, Spring, 1986, p 776.

26 For the development profile, see *World Development Report 1987* (Washington, D.C.: World Bank).

27 *The Australian*'s editorial was quoted by George Chaplin, *Honolulu Advertiser*, to a Senior Editors' Seminar, East-West Center, Honolulu, Jan. 8-10, 1986; "Pacific Tilt" information is from "The Pacific Rim," *Financial Times*, Oct. 20, 1986 (Survey, Sec. III); "Boom in Pacific Rim Rocking Our Economy," *Toronto Star*, May 7, 1984, p A14; *Asia-Pacific Report*, East-West Center, Honolulu, 1987.

27 European Community information is from "U.S. Government Relations with the European Community," by George D. Holliday, Congressional Research Service HF 1410E, Washington, D.C., Jan. 30, 1986, p 7.

27 On West Germany, see "The Collected Works of an Eminence Grise" (Review of Drucker's *The Frontiers of Management*), by Michael Skapinker, *Financial Times*, Mar. 4, 1987, p 11; and "Ein Wissenschaftswunder?" *The Economist*, Nov. 11, 1989, pp 103ff.

28 Daniel Bell discusses the "mismatch of scale" in "The World and the United States in 2013," *Daedalus*, Summer, 1987, p 14.

28 For a summary of Europe '92 plans, see "1992 and All That," by Guy de Jonquieres, *Financial Times*, Apr. 18, 1988.

29 Sources on international regulations and laws include "Space Manufacturing and the Proposed Agreement Governing the Activities of States on the Moon and Other Celestial Bodies," by Eilene Galloway, in "Space Manufacturing 4" (Proceedings of Fifth Princeton/AIAA Conference, May 18-21, 1981), American Institute of Aeronautics and Astronautics, New York, 1981, pp 55-60; also, "Judging the World Court," by Thomas M. Franck, Twentieth Century Fund (New York: Priority Press Publications, 1986).

29 On the GCC, see "Unease Around the Gulf," by Eric Rouleau, *World Press Review*, July, 1982, pp 26ff.

### 3. The Globalizing of America

31 Howard M. Wachtel is quoted from *The Money Mandarins* (New York: Pantheon, 1986), pp 9ff.

31 The President's Commission is quoted from "Global Competition: The New Reality" (Washington: U.S. Government Printing Office, 2 vols, 1985), Vol. I, p 9.

32 Among many sources on foreign direct investment in the U.S., *Buying Into America* by Martin and Susan Tolchin (New York: Times Books, 1988), and *Megatrends 2000*, by John Naisbitt amd Patricia Aburdene (New York: Morrow, 1990), are good basic sources to their publication dates. Also see *Fortune, Business Week, Time, Newsweek, U.S. News & World Report, New York Times, Washington Post*, and *Los Angeles Times*.

33 Among many sources on the *maquiladores* program, see "The Rich Pickings in America's Backyard," by David Gardner, *Financial Times*, June 1988, p 1987; "The Magnet of Growth in Mexico's North," by Stephen Baker et al., *Business Week*, June 6, 1988, pp 48-50; and "Bustling Tijuana Lives Down Hooch and Honky Tonk," by Larry Rohter, *New York Times*, Aug. 2, 1989, p 1.

33 One of many reports on foreign-based "back offices" is "Beaming Jobs Overseas," by Bruce Stokes, *National Journal*, July 27, 1985, p 1726-1731; see "Making It Overseas," by Stephen M. Andress, *High Technology Business*, on foreign-industry concessions and profits in Ireland.

33 Russell Baker is quoted from his column "Made Elsewhere," *New York Times Magazine*, Apr. 26, 1987.

34 One of many reports on food imports is "Looking Abroad to Fill Our Bellies," by Keith Schneider, *New York Times*, Aug. 3, 1986, Sec. 3, p 1.

34    Co-production and arms purchases abroad are discussed by Robert Reich in "The
      Rise of Techno-Nationalism," *Atlantic Monthly,* May, 1987, pp 63-67; by Eliot Mar-
      shal in "American Weapons, Alien Parts," *Science,* October, 1986, pp 141ff; and
      by Cetron, *The Future of American Business* (New York: McGraw-Hill, 1985).

34    Robert Reich discusses mixed ownership in "The Rise of Techno-Nationalism,"
      *Atlantic Montly,* May, 1987, elaborated on in an interview with the author; in "Cor-
      poration and Nation," *Atlantic Monthly,* May, 1988, pp 76-81; and in "Who Is Us,"
      *Harvard Business Review,* January/February, 1990, pp 53-64.

35    Among many sources, immigration is discussed in "Flow of 3d World Immigrants
      Alters Weave of U.S. Society," by Robert Reinhold, *New York Times,* Jan. 30, 1986;
      "Fast Times on Avenida Madison," by Pete Engardio, *Business Week,* June 6, 1988,
      p 64; "California's Coming Minority Majority," *Public Opinion,* February/March, 1986, p 50; "The Latinization of America," by
      Robert Held, *Frankfurter Allgemeine,* translated in *World Press Review,* November,
      1980, p 45; and "Among Arabs in U.S., New Dreams," by Isabel Wilkerson, *New
      York Times,* Mar. 13, 1988, p 12.

35    Foreign students are discussed in "Why Asians Are Going to the Head of the Class,"
      by Fox Butterfield, *New York Times,* Aug. 31, 1986, Education Supplement; and
      "Flood of Foreign Students Is Only the Beginning," by Jane N. Dento, *New York
      Times,* Education Supplement, 1982, p 23.

36    Jean-Jacques Servan-Schreiber is quoted from "Wanted: Fresh, Homegrown Talent,"
      by Ezra Bowen, *Time,* Jan. 11, 1988, p 65.

36    June Collier is quoted from "Invasion of the Dixie-Snatchers," by Ken Englade,
      *Southern Magazine,* January, 1987, p 33.

37    Among many sources on the ratios and impact of foreign investment in U.S.
      economic sectors are "Foreign Investment in the United States: Trends and Im-
      pact," by William H. Cooper, Congressional Research Service, Washington, D.C.,
      Sept. 10, 1985; Edward M. Graham, Paul R. Krugman, *Foreign Direct Investment
      in the United States* (Washington, D.C.: Institute for International Economics, 1989);
      "The Selling of America," by Jacyln Fierman, *Fortune,* Dec. 22, 1986, pp 43-56;
      "Entering a New Age of Boundless Competition," by Richard I. Kirkland, Jr.,
      *Fortune,* Mar. 14, 1988, pp 40-48; "The Selling of America (Cont'd)," by Jacyln
      Fierman, *Fortune,* May 23, 1988, p 54ff; and "Foreign Investment May Hit $380
      Billion," by Marlene Givant Star, *Pensions & Investment Age,* July 24, 1989, p 35.

38    Anthony M. Solomon is quoted from his essay, "Checking the Spread of a New
      Xenophobia," *New York Times,* May 31, 1988, op ed page.

38    Controls on investment are discussed by Daniel Yergin, "America, a Wholly Owned
      Subsidiary of...," *New York Times,* Mar. 30, 1988, op ed page.

38    The *Forbes* compilation is from "The 100 Largest Foreign Investments in the U.S.,"
      July 27, 1987, pp 146-150.

38    Details on Britain's U.S. investments are given in "Blindsided by the Brits," by
      John Burgess, *Washington Post National Weekly,* Feb. 6-12, 1989, p 22.

39    The bank assets estimates are by Cooper, "Foreign Investment in the United States:
      Trends and Impact," Congressional Research Service, Washington, D.C., Sept. 10,
      1985.

39    Anatole Kaletsky's comments were to the author, for "Great Damage from a 'Quick Fix,'" *World Press Review,* April, 1988, pp 22ff.

39    Alan Greenspan is quoted from "Verbatim: Toward a World Economy," *New York Times,* Mar. 20, 1988, Week in Review.

39    Alexander Trowbridge is quoted from "We Should Try to Get All the Foreign Money We Can Get," *USA Today,* Mar. 24, 1988, p 11A.

40    The 1987 U.S. investment totals abroad and comparative information a paragraph later are from "America Buys the World," *The Economist,* Sept. 17, 1988, p 71; the 1989 analysis of U.S. investments is reported in "Foreign Investment in U.S. Rises by $61.3 Billion to Record $390.1 Billion," by Peter Riddell, *Financial Times,* Mar. 26, 1990, p 1. For global trends by leading nations, see "International Direct Investment: Global Trends and the U.S. Role" (1984 and the following years) and "Direct Investment Update," by John Rutter, 1986 and the following years (Office of Trade and Investment Analysis, U.S. Department of Commerce). Early postwar corporate moves abroad are described in "The New Multinational Managers," by William Reddig Jr., *Saturday Review,* Nov. 22, 1969, pp 35-41; later ones, in Richard J. Barnet and Ronald E. Muller, *Global Reach* (New York: Simon & Schuster, 1974), pp 26, 258, 303, 360; "Entering a New Age of Boundless Competition," by Richard I. Kirkland, Jr., *Fortune,* Mar. 14, 1988; and "Ford Hoping to Grow in Eastern Europe, Far East," by Paul Eisenstein, *Journal of Commerce,* in the *Indianapolis Star,* Jan. 29, 1989, p K-2.

41    Cyrill Stewart is quoted from "U.S. Businessmen Loosen Link to Mother Country," by Louis Uchitelle, *New York Times,* May 21, 1989, p 1.

### 4. Economic Retreat—or Renewal?

43    Postwar-boom and OPEC-era data are from "An Economic Missile Gap," by Robert J. Samuelson, *Newsweek,* Sept. 19, 1989, p 49.

44    On income and living-standard trends, see "Do We Live as Well as We Used to?" by Sylvia Nasar, *Fortune,* Sept. 14, 1987, pp 32-46; "Are You Better Off Than in 1980?" by Louis S. Richman, *Fortune,* Oct. 10, 1988, pp 38-44; "An Economic Missile Gap," by Robert J. Samuelson, *Newsweek,* Sept. 19, 1989; and "Too Much Ain't Enough," by Jerry Flint, *Forbes,* July 13, 1987, pp 92-102.

45    Among many sources, reindustrialization and productivity are discussed in "The Changed World Economy," by Peter Drucker, *Foreign Affairs,* Spring, 1986; "Jobilism, or, Is the World Really Flat?" by Richard B. McKenzie, *Forbes,* July 13, 1987, pp 68-79; and "America's Competitive Revival," by Sylvia Nasar, *Fortune,* Jan. 4, 1988, p 48. On textile industry productivity, see "U.S. Textile Industry's Turnaround," by Leslie Wayne, *New York Times,* Feb. 15, 1988, p D1; and "Cutting Their Coat," *The Economist,* Feb. 13, 1988, pp 62-63. Among many books, also see *Made in America,* MIT Commission on Industrial Productivity, (Cambridge: MIT Press, 1989); and Bruce R. Scott, George C. Lodge (editors), *U.S. Competitiveness in the World Economy* (Boston: Harvard Business School Press, 1985).

46    The electronics industry's comparative position is discussed by Marvin Cetron, *The Future of American Business* (New York: McGraw-Hill, 1985), p 26ff.

46    Job-creation and industrial reorganization are a theme of "Creative Destruction." by William Baldwin, *Forbes,* July 13, 1987, p 49ff.

46  Job-creation and employment totals are discussed, among many sources, in "Why America Creates the Most Jobs," by Richard I. Kirkland, Jr., *Fortune,* Dec. 21, 1987, 177-178; and "Small Manufacturers Lead Revival," by Robert D. Hershey, Jr., *New York Times,* Feb. 11, 1988, p D1.

47  Semiconductors' economic impact is discussed in "Ma Bell's Christmas Gift to Mankind," by David Fishlock, *Financial Times,* Dec. 23, 1987.

47  Superconductors' potential is discussed in "New Superconductors Offer Chances to Do the Impossible," by James Gleick, *New York Times,* Apr. 9, 1987, p 1.

47  Materials' science progress and potential are described in "Advanced Materials and the Economy," by Joel P. Clark and Merton C. Flemings, *Scientific American,* October, 1986, pp 43ff; and Marvin Cetron, *The Future of American Business* (New York: McGraw-Hill, 1985), p xviiiff.

48  A summary of the baby bust's impact appears in "As Summer Approaches, Employers Compete to Attract Scarce Workers," by Lisa W. Foderaro, *New York Times,* June 12, 1988.

48  Job-quality changes are discussed in "Tomorrow's Jobs: Plentiful, But...," by Louis S. Richman, *Fortune,* Apr. 11, 1988, p 42.

49  Services' jobs are analyzed in "International Competition in Services," Office of Technology Assessment, Washington, D.C., July, 1987; see especially pp 225-254; "Technology and the American Economic Transition," OTA, May, 1988, esp. Chapter 10; and "Technology in Services," by James Brian Quinn, Jordan J. Baruch, and Penny Cushman Paquette, *Scientific American,* December, 1987, pp 50-58; the latter summarizes the NAE report.

50  Bell's four-tier-economy formulation is from "The World and the United States in 2013," *Daedalus,* Summer, 1987, pp 27-28.

51  Productivity data are from the President's Commission, Vol. I; and "America's Place in World Competition," by Brian O'Reilly, *Fortune,* Nov. 6, 1989, pp 83-88. Also see "Can America Make It?" (series), by Guy de Jonquieres and Anatole Kaletsky, *Financial Times,* May 11, 13, 18, 20, 22, 1987; "America Gains an Edge in Competitiveness," *Business Week,* July 6, 1987; and "What Crisis in Productivity?" by Peter Passell, *New York Times,* Nov.1, 1989, p D2, summarizing William Baumol, Sue Anne Batey Blackman, and Edward Wolff, *Productivity and American Leadership* (Cambridge, MIT Press, 1989). The Federal Reserve of Boston's comparisons of U.S., Japanese, and West German productivity are cited in "Is Industry Collapsing All Around Us?" by Bruce Bartlett, *Wall Street Journal,* May 8, 1987, p 21.

52  On the scale and impact of foreign affiliates' sales, see "There's No Trade Deficit, Sam!" by William G. Shepherd and Dexter Hutchins, *Financial World,* Feb. 25, 1988, pp 27-32.; "What the Trade Numbers Hide," by John Hein, *Across the Board,* October, 1987, pp 12-13; and "Spread of U.S. Plants Abroad Is Slowing Exports," by Louis Uchitelle, *New York Times,* Mar. 26, 1989, p 1.

52  On "foreign" exports from the U.S., see "U.S. Exporters Aren't That American," by Rose Brady, *Business Week,* Feb. 29, 1988, pp 70-71.

52  Professor Strange is quoted from "The Persistent Myth of Lost Hegemny," *International Organization,* Autumn, 1987.

53  Chip-industry transitions are summarized in "The U.S. Chipmakers' Shaky Comeback," by Gary Hector, *Fortune*, Jan. 20, 1988, pp 125-126; and "America's New-Wave Chip Firms," by Michael S. Malone, *Wall Street Journal*, May 27, 1987, editorial page.

54  On "imports to ourselves" and oil, see "There's No Trade Deficit, Sam!" by William G. Shepherd and Dexter Hutchins, *Financial World*, Feb. 25, 1988; "What the Trade Numbers Hide," by John Hein, *Across the Board*, October, 1987; "We Should Love the Trade Deficit," by John Rutledge and Deborah Allen, *Fortune*, Feb. 29, 1988, pp 125-126; "Seems Like Old Times" (on oil imports), *Fortune*, May 23, 1988; and "The Trade Gap: Myths and Crocodile Tears," by Robert B. Reich, *New York Times*, Feb. 12, 1988, op ed page.

## 5. Future Has-Beens?

55  For a summary of the "winning hand," see "World Leadership" series by Karen Elliott House, *Wall Street Journal*, Jan. 22, 30, Feb. 6, 13, 21, 1989.

56  Richard Longworth's reminiscenses are from "Lafayette, We Are Here—Good and Hard," *Saturday Review*, Dec. 13, 1975, p 62.

56  Raymond Georis' comment is from an interview with the author.

57  John Maddox was interviewed by the author for "Scientists and Responsibility," *World Press Review*, July, 1983, p 33.

57  Scientific leadership data are from "The Good News About U.S. R & D," by Stuart Gannes, *Fortune*, Feb. 1, 1988, p 48ff.

58  For summaries of campus-business collaboration, see "Corporations on Campus," by Wayne Biddle, *Science*, July 24, 1987; "Strong Park/Campus Links," by Raymond Towse, *Financial Times*, Sept. 24, 1987; "Are U.S. Companies Learning to Share?" by Peter H. Lewis, *New York Times*, Feb. 2, 1988; "Best R & D Is Business-Driven," by Peter Drucker, *Wall Street Journal*, Feb. 10, 1988, editorial page; "Academia Goes Commercial," by Peter Dworkin, *U.S. News & World Report*, May 2, 1988, pp 50-51; "As Science Moves Into Commerce, Openness Is Lost," by William J. Broad, *New York Times*, May 24, 1988, p C1; and "On the Campus: Fat Endowments and Growing Clout," by Leslie Helms, *Business Week*, July 11, 1988, pp 70-72. C. K. Gunsalus spoke to an AAAS panel in New Orleans on Feb. 19, 1990.

59  On techno-globalism and cross-national research collaboration, see Reich's "The Rise of Techno-Nationalism," *Atlantic Monthly*, May, 1987; and "Academia Goes Commercial," by Peter Dworkin, *U.S. News & World Report*, May 2, 1988, p 50.

59  On space cooperation, see "International Cooperation," by Craig Cavault, *Commercial Space*, Winter, 1987, pp 16ff.

59  Michael Kenward was interviewed by the author for "Science's Next Decade," *World Press Review*, November, 1985.

60  For international corporation rankings, see "The World's Largest Industrial Corporations," by Alan Farnham and Carrie Gottlieb, *Fortune*, Aug. 4, 1986, pp 170ff.

60  For comparative offshore assets and new investments, see "The Prizes and Pitfalls of Going Offshore," by Guy de Jonquieres, *Financial Times*, Nov. 24, 1987; and "Overseas Spending by U.S. Companies Set Record Pace," by Louis Uchitelle, *New York Times*, May 20, 1988, p 1.

60  On business in Europe, see "How Business Is Creating Europe, Inc.," by Joyce Heard and Jonathan Kapstein, *Business Week,* Sept. 7, 1987, pp 40-41; and "Coke's Intensified Attack Abroad," by Richard W. Stevenson, *New York Times,* Mar. 14, 1988, p D1.

61  The 1990 services-export forecast was by Marvin Cetron, *The Future of American Business* (New York: McGraw-Hill, 1985); for details on services exports, see "The Bright Future of Services Exports," by Richard I. Kirkland, Jr., *Fortune,* June 8, 1987, pp 31ff.

61  Michigan is among examples discussed in "Guiding Small Factories Into a Future," by William E. Schmidt, *New York Times,* Feb. 17, 1989. See also "Iowa Makes Transition from Corn to Microchips," by Steven P. Rosenfeld, Associated Press, Sept. 18, 1989; and "Development Report Card for the States," Corporation for Enterprise Development, Washington, D.C., 1990.

63  Luce's editorial was quoted in "An American Century Still?" by Stephen S. Rosenfeld, *Washington Post National Weekly,* Aug. 15-21, 1988.

### 6. Japan as Supernation
65  Kennedy's estimate is on page 533, *The Rise and Fall of the Great Powers* (New York: Random House, 1987).

66  For one summary of Japan's "deficiencies" see "World Leadership" (series), by Karen Elliott House, *Wall Street Journal,* Jan. 22, 30, Feb. 6, 13, 21, 1989.

66  For background on Japan's infrastructure, see James Fallows, *More Like Us* (Boston: Houghton-Mifflin, 1989); Bill Emmott, *The Sun Also Sets* (New York: Times Books, 1989); and Clyde V. Prestowitz, Jr., *Trading Places: How We Allowed Japan to Take the Lead* (New York: Basic Books, 1988). Also, "Cheaper Shopping in Japan" (p 15) and "Too Many Shopkeepers" (pp 70-71), *The Economist,* Jan. 28, 1969,

67  Matsubara is quoted in "Japan Faces Big Task in Improving Basic Science," by Marjorie Sun, *Science,* Mar. 10, 1989, pp 1281-1287.

68  MITI's and Japanese companies' errors are discussed in "Great Japanese Mistakes," by Carla Rapoport, *Fortune,* Feb. 13, 1989, pp 108ff; and "Mighty MITI Loses Its Grip," by David E. Sanger, *New York Times,* July 9, 1989, Sec. 3, p 1.

68  On Japan's "amenities gaps," see James Fallows, *More Like Us* (Boston: Houghton Mifflin, 1989) Bill Emmott, *The Sun Also Sets* (New York: Times Books, 1989); and "World Leadership" (series), by Karen Elliott House, *Wall Street Journal,* Jan. 22, 30, Feb. 6, 13, 21, 1989; "Japan's Other Face," by Robert J. Samuelson, *International Herald Tribune,* Feb. 10, 1989; and "Pity Those Poor Japanese," *The Economist,* Dec. 24, 1988, pp 48ff.

69  Avery Fisher was interviewed by the author.

70  Chinese Academy of Social Sciences Vice President Zhao Fusan and West Germany's Schmidt voiced their opinions to Karen Elliott House, "World Leadership" (series), *Wall Street Journal,* Jan. 30, 1989.

71  The *NKS'* English-language *Japan Economic Journal* carried the headlines on Sept. 16 and Dec. 30, 1989; and Feb. 17 and 24, 1990. Publication dates for the non-Japanese reports are, respectively, Mar. 30, 1987 (both *Fortune* articles); Apr. 30, 1987; and Jan. 15, 1987.

71    Emmott's comments are in his essay, "For Japan, Not World Dominance, But Leadership of a Yen Bloc," *Financier*, January, 1989, pp 30-36.

72    The term *nichibei* was introduced by Robert Heilbroner, "Reflection: Hard Time," *The New Yorker*, Sept. 14, 1987; on debt-related interdependence, see also Robert Gilpin, *The Political Economy of International Relations* (Princeton: Princeton University Press, 1987).

72    Australian professor Harry Gelber's views are in his "New Team: America Plus Japan," *International Herald Tribune*, Feb. 16, 1989.

### 7. Living with Bashing

74    On contributions to U.S. military activity, see "Five Ways to Fight Back," John Schwartz, *Newsweek*, Oct. 9, 1989, p 71.

74    For a summary of U.S. corporations' activity in Japan, see Robert C. Christopher, *Second to None: American Companies in Japan* (New York: Crown Publishers, 1986), especially pp 1-6.

75    U.S. ventures in Japan and Schering Plough official John M. Stimson's comment are from "Slowly But Surely, the U.S. Is Buying Into Japan," by Amy Borrus, *Business Week*, Dec. 19, 1988, pp 44-45.

75    The Bechtel official, Michael Farley, is quoted in "Barriers That May Not Be There," *Financial Times*, July 10, 1989.

75    Export Development official Edward Oliver's comment is in "Opportunity Is Knocking for Business in Japan," by Fred Hiatt, *Washington Post National Weekly*, Nov. 7-13, 1988, pp 18-19. Also see "MITI Wants to Be Your Friend," *Business Tokyo*, March, 1990, pp 44-45.

79    Jack Kilby's comment is from "The Chip at 30: Potential Still Vast," by John Markoff, *New York Times*, Sept. 14, 1990, p D1, which also gives a capsule history and forecast.

79    Perspectives on microchip competition are provided in "U.S. Chip Makers Recovering," by David E. Sanger, *New York Times*, May 26, 1987; "The U.S. Is Still the Chipmaking Champ—But Just Barely," *Business Week*, Feb. 13, 1988; "Chip Makers to Seek Joint Ventures," by Clyde H. Farnsworth, *New York Times*, Mar. 3, 1989, p D5; "U.S. Chips Are Quietly Cracking the Japanese Market," by Stephen Kreider Yoder, *Wall Street Journal*, Mar. 22, 1989, p B4; "The Vast Promise of a Laser Chip," by Lawrence M. Fisher, *New York Times*, May 14, 1989, p 1; "Computer Firms Make Bold Pitch to Retake Market Lost to Japan," by G. Christian Hill and Michael W. Miller, *Wall Street Journal*, June 22, 1989, p 1; "IBM, in Surprise, Sees a Vital Edge Over Japan," by David E. Sanger, *New York Times*, June 23, 1989, p 1; and "Silicon Valley's Design Renaissance," by John Markoff, *New York Times*, Aug. 6, 1989, Sec. 3, p 1.

80    The critiques of the Pentagon task force report are in "Japan's Growing Role in Chips Worrying the U.S.," by Andrew Pollack, *New York Times*, Jan. 5, 1987, p 1; and "Pentagon Takes Initiative in War Against Chip Imports," by Louise Kehoe, *Financial Times*, Jan. 27, 1987. *The Economist* is quoted from "Chipmakers Suffer Delusions of Middle Age," July 1, 1989, pp 53-54.

80    On IBM's 16-megabit chip, see "IBM Says It Built 16-Megabit Chip on Existing Line," by Laurence Hooper, *Wall Street Journal*, Feb. 14, 1990.

81 The supercomputer headlines are from, respectively, May 1, 1989, p D1; and May 24, 1989, p 1. Cray, Chen, Control Data, et al., are discussed in the *Times* May 1 and "Cray's Future Without Cray," May 21, 1989, Sec.3, D1 (both by Markoff); and "Washington's Super Worries About Supercomputers," by John Burgess and Evelyn Richards, *Washington Post National Weekly*, May 15-21, 1989, pp 21-22.

82 This proposed nationwide "data superhighway" is discussed in "A Supercomputer in Every Pot," by John Markoff, *New York Times*, Dec. 12, 1988, p D1.

78 Perspectives on HDTV are provided in "The Pentagon Plans to Get Into Television," by Evelyn Richards, *Washington Post National Weekly*, Dec. 26, 1988, p 32; "Will High-Definition TV Be a Turn-Off?" by Bob Davis, *Wall Street Journal*, Jan. 20, 1989, p B1; "IBM-TV?" by George Gilder, *Forbes*, Feb. 20, 1989, pp 72-74; "AT&T and Zenith in TV Deal," by Calvin Sims, *New York Times*, Mar. 1, 1989, p D1; "Japanese Test Illustrates Big Lead in TV of Future," by David E. Sanger, *New York Times*, Mar. 21, 1989, p 1; "A High-Definition Dilemma," by Hobart Rowen, *Washington Post National Weekly*, Apr. 3-9, 1989, p 5; "America's Billion-Dollar Boob Tube Battle," *The Economist*, May 27, 1989, pp 67-68; "Is HDTV Actually Behind the Curve?" by Evelyn Richards, *Washington Post National Weekly*, May 29, 1989, pp 23-24; "A Rosy, Rectangular View of the Future," by Robert Goldberg, *Wall Street Journal*, June 5, 1989, p A12; "Members Only," by Robert Reich, *The New Republic*, June 26, 1989, pp 14ff; and "Format Emerging for Advanced TV," by Andrew Pollack, *New York Times*, Mar. 23, 1990, p D1. M. S. Forbes, Jr.'s comment is from "In the Name of Improving American Competitiveness," *Forbes*, Mar. 6, 1989.

83 The CBO report is summarized in "Study: High Definition TV Not the Biggest Break in High Tech," by Jay Arnold, Associated Press, in *The Reporter-Dispatch*, White Plains, N.Y., Aug. 8, 1989.

84 The HDTV conference report is summarized in "HDTV's Rough Road Ahead," by Ronald K. Jurgen, *The Institute* (Institute of Electrical and Electronics Engineers, New York), Apr., 1990, p 1.

84 *The Economist*'s comment is from "America's Billion-Dollar Boob Tube Battle," May 27, 1989.

85 Iverson and McCloskey are quoted in "Friendly Adversaries Help U.S. Companies," by Ronald K. Jurgen, *IEEE Spectrum*, May, 1990.

## 8. Foreign Corporate Bodies—Ours and Theirs

87 For IBM's philosophy and deployment profile, see "What It Takes to Compete in the World," by John F. Akers, *Financier*, July, 1989, pp 21-24. Also see "Reinventing IBM," by Joel Dreyfuss, *Fortune*, Aug. 14, 1989, pp 30ff.

88 For a summary of the A&P's revival, see "How a German Supergrocer Gobbled Up a Winner," by Andrea Rothman, *Business Week*, Apr. 10, 1989, p 91.

88 On Tennessee and the Japanese, see "Foreign Money Changing U.S. Social-Cultural Life," by Andrew H. Malcolm," *New York Times*, Dec. 31, 1985, p 1; "Will Sake and Sour Mash Go Together?" by William J. Holstein, *Business Week*, July 14, 1987, pp 53-55; "We Learned That Them May Be Us," by Jerry Buckley, and "A New Land of the Rising Sun," *U.S. News & World Report*, May 9, 1988, pp 44ff; and "Rising Sun Over Sweetwater," by Suksan Tifft, *Time*, May 22, 1989, p 92.

89 The Tokyo pole of the multi-state war for foreign investments is described by Terence

Murphy in *Tokyo Business Today,* Apr., 1987, pp 24-29. The U.S. pole, among many sources, in "Japan's Third Wave," by Richard Corrigan, *National Journal,* Apr. 20, 1985, pp 840, 847; "In Contest for Industry, Indiana Scores," by Isabel Wilkerson, *New York Times*; and "18 Million in Incentives for Inland Mill," by Matt O'Connor, *Chicago Tribune,* Mar. 25, 1987.

89    Eagerness for jobs and social adaptations related to Japanese firms are covered in "Job Seekers Await Japanese Auto Plant in Indiana" (Jan. 3, 1987, p 5) and "Influx of Japanese Changing Style of Midwest" (Feb. 15, 1987, p 1), both by Isabel Wilkerson in *New York Times.* The "sushi" quotation is from Jan. 3; the Japanese altar, anthem, and video-store examples from Feb. 15.

89    The Detroit mistaken-identity murder of Vincent Chin is mentioned in Wilkerson (above), Dec. 15, 1987; the Tonawanda flag-burning is reported in "Japanese Flag Burned at Tire Plant Protest," by the Associated Press, in *The Reporter-Dispatch,* White Plains, N.Y. Dec. 18, 1988.

90    Japan's auto manufacturing complex is described in "Shaking up Detroit," by James B. Treece, *Business Week,* Aug. 14, 1989. Also see "The Japanese Infiltration," *Science,* July 18, 1986, p 275.

90    NUUMI's operations are described in "New Toyota-GM Plant Is U.S. Model for Japanese Management," by Constance Holden, *Science,* July, 1986, pp 273-77; "Hands Across the Workplace," by Marguerite Michaels, *Time,* Dec. 26, 1988; and "No Utopia, but to Workers It's a Job," by John Holusha, *New York Times,* Jan. 29, 1989, Sec. 3, p 1.

92    The *Business Month* report is "A Matter of Control," by Leah Nathans, September, 1988, pp 46-52. Also see "Bought by the Japanese," by Richard Bruns, *Business Tokyo,* March, 1990, pp 19-26.

93    Toshiba's campaign is discussed in "Toshiba Warns on Jobs in U.S.," by Andrew Pollack, *New York Times,* July 2, 1987; and "Look Who's Got the Loudest Lobbyists Now," by Stuart Auerbach, *Washington Post National Weekly,* Sept. 21, 1987, pp 23-24. On Japan's lobbying representatives, see "The Shadow Warriors," by Edward Klein, *Manhattan Inc.,* May, 1989, pp 86-94. On counterpart U.S. representatives in Europe, see "Ford Goes European," by Jon Pepper, Gannett News Service, in *The Reporter-Dispatch,* White Plains, N.Y., July 5, 1989.

95    For Senator Sasser's comment and an overview of foreign owners' U.S. influence, see "Foreigners' Political Roles in U.S. Grow by Investing" (series), by Martin Tolchin, *New York Times,* Dec. 30, 1985, p 1.

### 9. Global Village—or Media Oligopoly?

95    For information on the top ten global media conglomerates, see "The Lords of the Global Village," by Ben H. Bagdikian, *The Nation,* June 12, 1989, pp 805-820; "Media's 'Big Bang,'" by Patrick Reilly, *Advertising Age,* March 20, 1989. Also see "A Worldwide Media Mania," *Newsweek,* June 26, 1989, p 54; "The Media Barons Battle to Dominate Europe," by John Rossant and Richard A. Melcher, *Business Week,* May 25, 1987, pp 158-162; "The Empire Builders," by Peter Ainslie, *Channels*, Apr., 1987, pp 36ff; "A Media Empire Marches East" (Silvio Berlusconi), by Steven Solomon, *New York Times,* May 29, 1988, Business, p 1; "The Press Barons Duke It Out Across Europe," Richard A. Melcher and Frank Comes, *Business Week,* Oct. 3, 1988, pp 48-49; "A Passion for America" (Daniel Filipacchi), by Carolyn Pfaff and Jennet Conant, *Manhattan Inc.,* October, 1988,

pp 77-83; "Larger Than Life" (Robert Maxwell), by Martha Smilgis, *Time,* Nov. 28, 1988; and "The Power of Concentration" (Europe), *Eurobusiness,* January, 1989.

98 For information on Ted Turner not in the sources above, see "Captain Comeback," by Scott Ticer, *Business Week,* July 17, 1989, pp 98-106; on international newspaper publication, "The Global Newspaper Game," by Richard Z. Chesnoff, *U.S. News & World Report,* May 25, 1987, p 53; and on the *International Herald Tribune,* "Tribune Fete: An American in Paris at 100," by James M. Markham, *New York Times,* Oct. 4, 1987, p 4; and "Daily Newspapers Are Going Truly International at Last," by Lee W. Huebner, *IPI Report* (International Press Institute, London), November, 1988, and January, 1989.

95 On Hollywood's status and ownership, see "Hollywood Takes to the Global Stage," by Richard W. Stevenson, *New York Times,* Apr. 16, 1989, Sec. 3, p 1; "Next Stop, Tinseltown," by Joshua Hammer, *Newsweek,* Mar. 20, 1989, pp 48-49; and "Invasion of the Studio Snatchers," by Ronald Grover, *Business Week,* Oct. 16, 1989, pp 52-54.

99 On international advertising, in addition to Bagdikian cited above, see "Brits Buy Up the Ad Business," by Randall Rothenberg, *New York Times Magazine,* July 2, 1989, pp 14ff. For top agency rankings, see "Global Ad Volume Soars for Top 500," *Advertising Age,* Mar. 29, 1989, pp 1ff.

100 On books, in addition to sources cited for global media conglomerates, see "Cash Flow for Goethe," by Raymond Sokolov, *Wall Street Journal,* Jan. 26, 1987; and "The Diseconomies of Scale," *The Economist,* Apr. 7, 1990, pp. 25-28.

100 For Bagdikian's comments, see "Lords of the Global Village," *The Nation,* June 12, 1989, especially, pp 819-820. His book *The Media Monopoly* was published by Beacon (Boston, 1983).

### 10. Lost in a Witchy Thicket?

103 For John Maddox' comments, see the interview source previously cited; for Girilal Jain, interview with the author, "India's Upward Struggle," *World Press Review,* January, 1982, pp 32-35.

104 *India Today*'s observations are from its "Rise of the Middle Class," Dec. 11, 1985, pp 109-112; see also, pp 73-74; and "India's Harvest: Giving It Away," *The Economist,* May 11, 1985; "Planet Computer," by Marc Beauchamp, *Forbes,* Feb. 24, 1986; "India Locks in on a High-Tech Economy," by Cheryl Debes, *Business Week,* Aug. 24, 1987, pp 80Dff; and "A Thriving Middle Class Is Changing the Face of India," by Anthony Spaeth, *Wall Street Journal,* May 19, 1988, p 30. Also see "Cut a Regional Deal," by Selig S. Harrison, *Foreign Policy,* Spring, 1986, pp 126ff.

104 On Brazil, see "Tomorrow's Italy" (Jan. 17, 1987, pp 19-22) and "Brazil, Unstoppable" (Apr. 25, 1987, Survey), both in *The Economist;* "Brazil's Tomorrow Is Finally in Sight," by Jeremy Main, *Fortune,* Sept. 15, 1986, pp 73-83; and "The Four Horsemen Ride Again," by Norman Gall, *Forbes,* July 28, 1986, especially p 99. Also, Marvin Cetron, *The Future of American Business* (New York: McGraw-Hill, 1985) and "Brazil," *Wall Street Journal,* Jan. 27, 1983 (Special Advertising Section).

104 On the Soviet Union, among many sources, see "Dawn of the Enterprise Culture" (May 1, 1987), and "Soviet Plan to Boost Joint Ventures (Sept. 25, 1986)," both by Patrick Cockburn, *Financial Times,* and *Fortune, Business Week,* and *The Economist* (current issues).

105  On China, among many sources, see "Beyond Japan," by John S. McClenahen, *Industry Week,* July 7, 1986, especially pp 34-35; "China: Hong Kong's Factory," by Nicholas D. Kristof, *New York Times,* Sept. 4, 1987, p D1; "State of the World 1987," by Lester Brown, Worldwatch Institute, Washington, D.C.; and Marvin Cetron, *The Future of American Business* (New York: McGraw-Hill, 1985) pp 185 ff. On Taiwan, Malaysia, and Indonesia, these same sources.

106  On trade blocs, see "Trading Blocs and the Evolving World Economy," by Jeffrey E. Garten, *Current History,* January, 1989, pp 15-16.

107  For a summary of protectionism's costs and quotas' failures, see "A Hidden Tax on All Our Houses," by Robert J. Shapiro, *U.S. News & World Report,* Mar. 21, 1988, pp 51-52.

107  On pessimism and economic prospects, see "The Buying Binge in Business Books," by Christopher Knowlton, and "When Will a Recession Hit?" by Louis S. Richman, both in *Fortune,* Feb. 13, 1989.

109  Levitt was interviewed by the author.

109  On the Marshall Plan, see "Why Was the Marshall Plan Successful?" by Charles Maier, and "Third World Debt Costs Jobs," by Sen. Bill Bradley, *Transatlantic Perspectives* (German Marshall Fund of the U.S., Washington, D.C.), Winter, 1988. On developing nations' markets and potential in general, see "If Only...," by Stephen Kindel and Robert Teitelman, *Forbes,* Aug. 29, 1983, pp 126ff; and "U.S. Trade Relations with the Newly Industrializing Countries," by William H. Cooper, Congressional Research Service, Washington, D.C., Oct. 3, 1984.

110  On Japanese redevelopment aid, see "Japan, Under Pressure, Is Raising Foreign Aid," by Clyde Haberman, *New York Times,* June 15, 1988.

## 11. Needed: A New Periscope

111  The French editor is Jacqueline Beytout of *Les Echos,* in "Finding a New Crusade," *World Press Review,* May, 1982.

111  Edward Hoagland's comments are from his op ed essay, "Americans Exclude the Globe," *New York Times,* Jan. 11, 1986, p 23.

111  On top American and foreign newspapers, see the author's "Editor's Corner" columns, *World Press Review,* May, 1980, and Apr., 1982, for discussion of three key sources: John C. Merrill and Harold A. Fisher, *The World's Great Dailies* (New York: Hastings House); Merrill, *The Elite Press* (New York: Pitman) and George Kurian, *World Press Encyclopedia* (New York: Facts on File, 1982). On U.S. press foreign bureaus, see "No News May Not Be Good News," by James Cornell, *Technology Review,* October, 1986, pp 20ff.

112  Reston's comments are from his "History's Revenge," *New York Times,* June 23, 1985, op ed page.

112  Under secretary general Sevigny was interviewed by the author for "'Feeling of Renaissance,'" *World Press Review,* July, 1988, pp 45-46.

114  Hamilton's comments are in *Main Street America and the Third World* (Cabin John, Md.: Seven Locks Press, 1986).

114  On our foreign-language illiteracy, see "Strength Through Wisdom," President's Commission Report, quoted in the descriptive brochure of the National Council on Foreign Language and International Studies, New York.

178  THE MYTH OF AMERICAN ECLIPSE

115 The Southern Governors' study is reported in "Southern Leaders Cast Eyes Abroad," by George Volsky, *New York Times,* Sept. 8, 1985; Kerr's comments are in "The United States Prepares for Its Future," Report of the Study Commission on Global Education (Global Perspectives in Education, New York).

115 For foreign-phrase malapropisms, see the brochure of the National Council on Foreign Language and International Studies, New York.

115 Hamilton's project description and findings are from *Main Street America and the Third World* (Cabin John Md.: Seven Locks Press, 1986).

### 12. Our True Decline Problem

117 For a summary of infrastructure failings, see "Listen to the Bridges," by George Will, *Newsweek,* Apr. 25, 1988, p 70; and "Our Crumbling Infrastructure," by Joan C. Szabo, *Nation's Business,* August, 1989, pp 16-24.

119 For details on defense budget priorities, see "Two Trillion Dollars in Seven Years," *The Defense Monitor* (Center for Defense Information, Washington, D.C.), Vol. XVI, No. 7, 1987; on reserve readiness, "Reserves' Readiness Questioned," by Madeleine Carroll, *Military Logistics Forum,* May 22, 1988, p 13.

119 General Rogers and McNamara are quoted in "The New Guns and Butter Battle," by Leonard Silk, *New York Times,* May 22, 1988, p 1.

120 The president's panel comments are from "Diversify America's Weapons Arsenal, Panel Tells Reagan," by George C. Wilson, *Washington Post National Weekly,* Jan. 25, 1988, p 18; and "Study Fuels Strategic Shift to Advanced Conventional Weapons," by Paul Mann, *Aviation Week & Space Technology,* Jan. 25, 1988, p 135.

120 For summaries on waste, see "Billions Down the Pentagon Drain," by Robert S. Dudney, *U.S. News & World Report,* Apr. 27, 1981, pp 25-28; and "U.S. Found to Be Losing Billions Through Poor Accounting Systems" (Associated Press, Dec. 31, 1987); "Lacking Parts, Armed Forces Cannibalize Costly Warplanes" (by Richard Halloran, July 16, 1987); and "Missile Security of Army Criticized" (by Associated Press, Oct. 23, 1987); all in the *New York Times.*

120 John Keegan is quoted from his essay, "Break Up the Baronies," *U.S. News & World Report,* April 18, 1988, p 42.

120 President Eisenhower's speech is quoted in "Profit, Patriotism Product a Ubiquitous Alliance," by Michael Weiskopf, *Washington Post,* Jan. 17, 1986, p A8; and "Ike's Nightmare Is Upon Us," by Hugh Sidey, *Time,* Sept. 14, 1987. His letter to the Alsops is from "Ike on 'Man Against War,'" by David S. Broder, *Washington Post,* Sept. 7, 1983, p A17.

121 On budgetsmanship and "gaposis," see Tom Gervasi, *The Myth of Soviet Military Supremacy* (New York: Harper & Row, 1986); and Sivard's "World Military and Social Expenditures," previously cited.

122 On research talent diversion and declining commercial "fallout" from the Pentagon, see "Profitable Technology from Uncle Sam," by Ron Schneiderman, *High Technology Business,* February, 1989, pp 25ff; and "Arms and America's Fortunes," by Fred Hiatt and Rick Atkinson, *Washington Post,* Dec. 1, 1985, p 1. Also see "Military R&D Depletes Economic Might," by Frank R. Lichtenberg, *Wall Street Journal,* Aug. 21, 1986, editorial page.

123 The Council on Economic Priorities' study, "Military Expansion, Economic Decline" (Washington, D.C., 1983) was written by Robert W. DeGrasse, Jr., whose "The Military: Shortchanging the Economy," *Bulletin of the Atomic Scientists,* May, 1984, discusses the alternative costs noted.

123 On closing military bases, see Richard Armey's essay, "It Pays to Close Old Military Bases," *Christian Science Monitor,* June 8, 1988; and, on commercial uses of former bases, "All Defence Is Local, Too," *The Economist,* May 21, 1986, pp 27-28.

124 On entitlements abuses and reforms, see "The Morning After," by Peter G. Peterson, *Atlantic Monthly,* October 1987, pp 43ff. Also Peter G. Peterson, *On Borrowed Time* (Washington, D.C.: ICS Press, 1988).

### 13. The Education Imperative

127 Data on schools' failings are from "Investing in Our Children," Research and Policy Committee, Committee for Economic Development, New York (1985), p 2; and "A Nation at Risk" and "What Do Our 17-Year-Olds Know?"

128 Dr. Hill is quoted in "Report Says Math Teaching in U.S. Needs an Overhaul," by Warren E. Leary, *New York Times,* Jan. 27, 1989, p A16.

129 Chemical Bank's and other employers' problems are discussed in "Needed: Human Capital," *Business Week,* Sept. 19, 1988, Special Report.

129 Maurice Strong is quoted in an interview, "Maurice F. Strong: Adaptations of the Blocs," by Willard C. Rappleye, Jr., *Financier,* Apr., 1989, p 18.

130 Germany's "dual system" is described in "West Germany's Competitive Advantage," *Fortune,* June 19, 1989, p 136, and "Training People for Real Jobs," by Paul Osterman, *Transatlantic Perspectives,* Spring, 1989, pp 6-8. His article is from his *Employment Futures* (New York: Oxford, 1989). On Germany and other EC countries, see also "Schoolworks," by William Northdurft, German Marshall Fund of the United States, Washington, D.C., 1989.

131 For details on Japan's schools, see Merry White, *The Japanese Educational Challenge* (New York: Free Press, 1987). Also, "The Brain Battle," *U.S. News & World Report,* Jan. 19, 1987, in which she is interviewed.

132 The CED's statement is from "Investing in Our Children" (1985).

132 *Business Week*'s comment is from "Human Capital," Sept. 19, 1988, p 140.

132 Alternatives to arms purchases are from "Education: Getting What You Pay For," by Jack E. White, *Time,* Sept. 12, 1988, p 32.

132 Outlets for the NAB supplement included *Time,* May 29, 1989.

132 On teacher recruitment and certification, see "Wanted: 50,000 Good Teachers," by Pat Ordovensky, *USA Today,* May 25, 1989, p 1; "How to Smarten Up the Schools," by Myron Magnet, *Fortune,* Feb. 1, 1988, pp 86ff; and "Alternative Certificates, New Paths to Teaching," by William J. Warren, *New York Times,* Sept. 28, 1988, p B15; Warren's story includes Nancy Adelman's comment.

133 On foreign languages, see "Why Foreign Languages Are Relevant Again," by Larry Rohter, *New York Times,* Jan. 4, 1987, Education, p 33.

133 On global studies, see "What's Happening in Global Education," by Andrew F. Smith, *Curriculum Review,* November/December, 1985, p 15; and "World Affairs

Can Be Child's Play," by Ari L. Goldman, *New York Times*, "As the World Learns" supplement, Apr. 9, 1989.

133 Year-round schools are discussed in "Los Angeles Votes Year-Round School Schedule," by Seth Mydans, *New York Times*, Feb. 7, 1990.

133 Business' involvement in school enrichment is discussed in "Investing In Our Children," Committee for Economic Development, New York, 1985; "School Reform: Business Moves In," by Steven A. Holmes, *New York Times*, Feb. 1, 1990, p D1; "Employers Pay the Tab as U.S. Workers Head Back to School," by Larry Green and Wendy Leopold, *Los Angeles Times*, in *The Reporter-Dispatch*, White Plains, N.Y., Feb. 15, 1987; and in several *Fortune* and *Business Week* special reports.

134 On vocational education, see especially "The New, Improved Vocational School," by Nancy J. Perry (June 19, 1989, pp 127ff); "Saving the Schools: How Business Can Help" (Nov. 7, 1988, pp 42Dff); and "Helping Workers Work Smarter" (June 8, 1987, pp 86ff), all in *Fortune*; "Trained to Order," by Steve Weiner and Charles Siler, *Forbes*, June 26, 1989, pp 73ff; and "A Push to Improve Vocational Education," by Dan Sperling, *USA Today*, June 27, 1989, p 6D.

134 On student choice, see "Wave of Future: A Choice of Schools," by Edward B. Fiske (June 4, 1989, p 32) and "About Education," by Fred M. Hechinger (March 29, 1989), both in the *New York Times*.

135 On adult illiteracy programs, see "National Policy Urged to Combat Adult Illiteracy," by Edward B. Fiske, *New York Times*, Sept. 9, 1988. Senator Simon is quoted, and data on illiteracy's costs summarized, in "Sen. Simon Offering Proposal to End Adult Illiteracy in the U.S.," *Rock Island Argus* (Rock Island, Ill.), July 14, 1989.

## 14. Rx for Renewal

137 *The Reckoning* was published by Morrow (New York: 1986).

137 Cuomo is quoted in "Will Industrial Policy Be Dr. Cuomo's Rx for the Economy?" (especially the box, "What Mario Wants: Supply Side for Workers'"), *Business Week*, Apr. 11, 1968, pp 78-79. His ideas are elaborated on in *The Cuomo Commission Report* (New York: Simon & Schuster, 1988), Introduction.

138 Lynn Williams is quoted in "Corporate Reshaping: Labor, Management in Partnership," by John V. Hickey, *World of Work Report* (Scarsdale, N.Y.: Work in America Institute), June, 1986, pp 2-3.

138 Shop-floor organization is discussed in "A New Spirit at U.S. Auto Plants," by John Holusha, *New York Times*, Dec. 29, 1987, p D1; and "Borrowing Techniques from the Japanese—and Beating Them," by Frank Swoboda, *Washington Post National Weekly*, Jan. 4, 1988, p 20.

138 Job security is discussed in "Auto Job Guarantees Sought," by John Holusha, *New York Times*, July 7, 1987, p D1; retraining, in "Successful Worker Training Programs Help Ease Impact of Technology," by Steven Deutsch, *Monthly Labor Review*, November, 1987, pp 14ff; and "Out-of Work Michiganders No Longer Out of Luck," by William E. Schmidt, *New York Times*, Mar. 31, 1988. Comments by the president's commission are from its report, "Global Competition: The New Reality," p 41.

139 On adjustment of displaced workers abroad, see Ira C. Magaziner, Robert B. Reich, *Minding America's Business* (New York: Harcourt Brace Jovanovich, 1982).

139  On plant closings, adjustment aid, early notification, and so on, see The Business Week Team, *The Reindustrialization of America* (New York: McGraw-Hill, 1982), which is also a useful source on broader reindustrialization questions; "Plant-Closings Quarrel Distorts a Modest Idea," by Walter S. Mossberg, *Wall Street Journal,* Apr. 25, 1988, p 1; "Deciding Whose Business It Is When Plants Close," *New York Times,* May 8, 1988, p E5; "Plant Closings: Why It Pays to Notify Workers in Advance," *Business Week,* May 30, 1988, p 22.

139  The estimate of export-related job creation is by the GAO, from the commission report, p 41. For examples of small firms successfully exporting, see "The Little Guys Are Making It Big Overseas," by William J. Holstein, *Business Week,* Feb. 27, 1989, pp 94ff.; "Export Expertise," by Steven Golob, *Nation's Business,* January, 1988, pp 26ff.

140  On Pentagon emulation of MITI (DARPA), see "America's Answer to Japan's MITI," by Andrew Pollack, *New York Times,* Mar. 5, 1989, Sec. 3, p 1.

141  On deficits, see "How Reagan Changed America," by George F. Will, *Newsweek,* Jan. 9, 1989, p 16; also, "Proposed 1991 Federal Budget Dollar," Knight-Ridder News Service, Jan. 30, 1990.

141  President's Commission references are to "Global Competition: The New Reality," Vol. I.

142  On U.S. trade barriers, see "Gephardt's Genie of Ignorance," by Anthony Harris, *Financial Times,* Mar. 7, 1988, p 6; and "Uncle Sam as Unfair Trader," by Clemens P. Work, *U.S. News & World Report,* June 12, 1989, pp 42-44.

143  For examples of states' activities, see the Governors' Association report *Jobs, Growth & Competitiveness,* (Washington, D.C., 1987), and "It Works, But Don't Call It Industrial Policy," by Noel Epstein, *Washington Post National Weekly,* Jan. 12, 1987, p 25.

143  Governor Baliles is quoted in "Governors Assert Key to Prosperity Is a Global View," by William Stevens, *New York Times,* July 26, 1987, p 1.

143  On the national service corps, state variations, and kibbutzim, see "The Push for National Service," by Jeffrey L. Sheler and David Whitman, *U.S. News & World Report,* Feb. 13, 1989, pp 21-25; and Charles C. Moskos, *A Call to Civic Service* (New York: The Free Press, 1988). On a national WPA-type jobs program sponsored by Senator Paul Simon, see "Ever Fewer Workers, Brock Says, Have Skills for the Jobs Available," by Maureen Dowd, *New York Times,* Jan. 14, 1987. On summer jobs, "For the Young, Summer Is 20,000 Jobs," by William E. Schmidt, *New York Times,* June 20, 1989.

### 15. Optimism or Pessimism?

145  On political cycles, see Arthur M. Schlesinger, Jr., *The Cycles of American History* (Boston: Houghton Mifflin, 1986).

147  For Friendly's views on commercial TV, see his *Due to Circumstances Beyond Our Control...* (New York: Random House, 1967).

147  On free TV time as part of campaign reform, see "A Swamp of Political Abuses Spurs Constituents of Change," by Mitchell Oreskes, *New York Times,* Mar. 21, 1990, p 1.

148  Liebling is anthologized in *The Press* (New York: Ballantine Books, 1961).

148  The Hutchins Commissions's agenda was published in *A Free and Responsible Press,*
Report of the Commission on Freedom of the Press (Chicago: University of Chicago
Press, 1947).

150  *The Closing of the American Mind* was published by Simon & Schuster (New York,
1987).

## 16. Afterword

151  Malraux's comment is from an interview, "Musings," *World Press Review,* May,
1984, p 50.

151  Monnet's comments are in "The Crippled Genius," by James Reston, *New York
Times,* Aug. 25, 1987, p A21.

152  Galbraith's comments are in his essay, "Economic Development: Engine of
Democracy," *New York Times,* Aug. 25, 1987, p A21; elaborated on to the author.

153  On arms proliferation, see Ruth Leger Sivard, "World Military and Social Expenditures 1987-88" (Washington, D.C.: World Priorities), pp 5, 10; also, "The Bombs
in the Basement," by Rod Nordland, *Newsweek,* July 11, 1988, pp 42ff.

154  For Keynes' and Rees Mogg's comments, see Rees Mogg's "Why the New Middle
Classes Will Inherit the Earth," *The Independent* (London), Oct. 14, 1986,

154  Food production data are from "Scientific Advances Lead to Era of Food Surplus
Around the World," by Keith Schneider, *New York Times,* Sept. 9, 1986, p C1;
and "Spearhead of a Second Green Revolution," by Stephanie Yanchinski, *Financial Times,* Sept. 17, 1988, p 28.

154  Drucker is quoted from "The Changing World Economy," *Foreign Affairs,* Spring,
1986, p 772.

155  On Ghana, see "Ghana, Once 'Hopeless,' Gets at Least the Look of Success," by
James Brooke, *New York Times,* Jan. 3, 1989, p 1; on Africa as a Whole, "Don't
Be Misled by Africa," by Max Singer, *Wall Street Journal,* Jan. 28, 1988; also
Max Singer, *Passage to a Human World: The Dynamics of Creating Global Wealth*
(Indianapolis: Hudson Institute, 1988)

155  Clausen is quoted from a speech to the Overseas Press Club, New York City, Apr.
24, 1985, elaborated on to the author.

155  Demeny's comments are from his article "World Population Trends," *Current
History,* January, 1989, p 64.

155  On children as "Social Security," see "Yes, But the Poor Want Children," by Peter
Adamson, *Atlas World Press Review,* August, 1974, p 20.

155  On the RU 486 pill, see "A Fierce Battle," by Steven Greenhouse, *New York Times
Magazine,* Feb. 12, 1989, pp 23-26; see also, "Foundations Expand Family Planning Aid Abroad," by Kathleen Telsch, *New York Times,* Sept. 5, 1988, p 1.

155  Zeidenstein was interviewed by the author; data on coming increases are from
Zeidenstein, Occasional Paper, Institute of Nutrition, University of North Carolina,
Chapel Hill, N.C., Vol. II, Nov. 7, 1981.

156  On the greenhouse effect, see "Major 'Greenhouse' Impact Is Unavoidable, Experts Say," by Philip Shabecoff, *New York Times,* July 19, 1988, p C1; also, "Skeptics Are Challenging Dire 'Greenhouse' Views," by William K. Stevens, *New York*

*Times,* Dec. 13, 1989, p 1. On revival of the U.S. project, see "Washington Embraces Global Earth Sciences," *Science,* Sept. 5, 1986, pp 1040ff.

157  'Barbara Ward was interviewed by Peter C. Newman, *Maclean's,* reprinted in *Atlas World Press Review,* August, 1976, pp 18ff.

158  Treglown was interviewed by the author, for "Books in a Video Age," *World Press Review,* December, 1985, pp 33ff.

159  Levi-Strauss was interviewed for "The Rebirth of Ideology," *World Press Review* (from *L'Espresso*), August, 1979, pp 28-29.

159  Hall's comments are from "Hall Analyzes Media Politics and Global Culture," *Murphy Reporter* (University of Minnesota School of Journalism, Minneapolis, Minn.), Spring, 1987, p 7.

159  For a French editor's view of moralistic arrogance, particularly American, see "Beyond Wilson and Rambo," by Andre Fontaine, *Foreign Policy,* Winter, 1986-87, pp 33ff.

159  For the Survey of Freedom, see *Freedom at Issue* (Freedom House, New York), January, 1989.

160  Miller wrote his comment on values to the author.

160  Macrae's comments are in his "Next Ages of Man," *The Economist,* Dec.24, 1988, Survey, p 20.

160  McNeill is quoted from his *The Rise of the West* (Chicago: University of Chicago Press, 1963), p 807.

# Index

# The Author

Alfred Balk is the founding editor of the foreign press digest *World Press Review,* former editor of the *Columbia Journalism Review,* and feature editor and editor-at-large of *Saturday Review.* A graduate of Northwestern University (M.S., journalism), he has taught at Columbia University, traveled widely abroad, lived in Japan, and is acquainted with leading editors around the world.

Before becoming an editor he was one of America's leading magazine reporters, writing more than 100 articles for national periodicals. Among them were *Harper's,* the *New York Times Magazine, Saturday Review,* and the *Saturday Evening Post.*

He has served as a consultant to Ford and other foundations, as a visiting fellow at the Russell Sage Foundation, as a President's Fellow of the Aspen Institute, and as an officer and member of several journalism organizations, including the American Society of Magazine Editors, the Overseas Press Club, and the International Press Institute. His other books include: *A Free and Responsive Press, Our Troubled Press* (co-editor), and *The Free List: Property Without Taxes.* After completing this book he became Managing Editor of the award-winning international technology monthly *IEEE Spectrum,* published by the Institute of Electrical and Electronics Engineers in Manhattan.